D1611527

RATIONALIZING GENIUS

Rationalizing Genius

IDEOLOGICAL STRATEGIES
IN THE CLASSIC
AMERICAN SCIENCE FICTION
SHORT STORY

John Huntington

 RUTGERS UNIVERSITY PRESS   New Brunswick and London

To Virginia

Copyright © 1989 by Rutgers, The State University
All Rights Reserved
Manufactured in the United States of America

Library of Congress Cataloging-in-Publication Data

Huntington, John.
   Rationalizing genius : ideological strategies in the
classic American science fiction short story / John
Huntington.
      p.   cm.
   Bibliography: p.
   Includes index.
   ISBN 0-8135-1429-0 (cloth)   ISBN 0-8135-1430-4 (pbk.)
   1. Science fiction, American—History and
criticism.   2. Short stories, American—History and
criticism.   3. Social values in literature.
4. Technocracy in literature.   I. Title.
PS374.S35H86   1989
813'.0876'09—dc19   88-36991
                                               CIP

British Cataloging-in-Publication information available

CONTENTS

ACKNOWLEDGMENTS

Parts of this book have appeared in somewhat different form in collections of essays from the Eaton Conference on SF and Fantasy. Portions of chapter 4 first appeared as "Hard Core Science Fiction and the Illusion of Science," in *Hard Science Fiction*, ed. George Slusser and Eric Rabkin (Carbondale; Southern Illinois University Press, 1986), pp. 45–57. Portions of chapter 6 first appeared as "Discriminating Among Friends: The Social Dynamics of the Friendly Alien," in *Aliens: The Anthropology of Science Fiction*, ed. George Slusser and Eric Rabkin (Carbondale: Southern Illinois University Press, 1987), pp. 69–77. Portions of chapter 7 are taken from "Orwell and the Uses of the Future," in *Storm Warnings: Science Fiction Confronts the Future*, ed. George Slusser, Colin Greenland, and Eric Rabkin (Carbondale: Southern Illinois University Press, 1987), pp. 135–145. Other portions of chapter 6 first appeared as "Impossible Love in Science Fiction," *Raritan*, 4:2 (1984), 85–99.

I thank the Humanities Institute of the University of Illinois at Chicago for a year-long fellowship in 1986–87 that gave me time finally to compose this book. My colleagues in the English Department at UIC have contributed to my understanding of problems of the canon, of ideology, and of interpretation. Judy Gardiner and Chris Messenger have read this work in early forms and given valuable advice. I owe much to the students in my SF courses over the last decade-and-a-half at Rutgers, the University of Rhode Island, and UIC for their enthusiasm, their knowledge of SF, and their patience as I tried out on them the prototypes of these ideas. And at all stages Virginia Wright Wexman has helped me see where I was going.

INTRODUCTION

MY TITLE PLAYS ON CENTRAL ASPECTS OF THE TECHNOCRATIC
ideology that inspired "Golden Age" science fiction (SF) in America. The
phrase "Rationalizing Genius" can be read in four ways. First, this literature
attempts to make genius a clear rational category, at its simplest a number on
an IQ scale. Second, the literature attempts to justify genius, to make up
reasons for it. The third meaning is that this literature is the product of a
"genius" for rationalizing, in the sense of making excuses. And the fourth
meaning completes the circle by saying that the genius of this literature is its
insistence on what it sees as rational behavior and explanation.

The book's main argument, which is implicit throughout, is that we can
learn from the most literarily conventional popular literature if we question
it closely. In this project I am following the lead of such recent critics as
Tania Modleski, Janice Radway, Stephen Knight, Ariel Dorfman, and Martin
Jordin, who have studied the ideological implications of the *practice* of certain genres of popular literature.[1] Such an argument runs against the common critical wisdom which assumes that because much popular literature,
especially pulp, has been hastily written with the expectation that it will be
read casually, it will not bear close examination. In chapter two I make the
explicit case for paying detailed attention to noncanonical works, but I see
the real justification of the practice as the body of the book itself.

We might usefully envision the time period during which these stories
appear not as a block of time with precise borders but as a cluster, centered
roughly around 1946, and thinning outward, both backward and forward.
The boundary dates of 1934 and 1963 have a somewhat arbitrary quality;
they mark not points of sudden beginning or end but roughly a temporal area
outside of which the genre is less coherent, either because it is in formation
or because it is in the process of transformation into a new phase. The phases
of the genre are not clearly marked by original and terminal texts; thus, the
boundary dates are not to be understood as exclusionary. I will look with
some care at works that much precede the period of study (e.g., Gernsback's

Ralph 124C 41+ [1911]) and that post-date it (e.g., Le Guin's "Nine Lives" [1971]).

Just before the period I focus on lies what we might call simply the beginnings of popular SF in America. Though the evidence for this moment—the publication of magazines and stories—is clear, the reasons for its occurring and its implications are not. And at the end of the period lies the transformation of classic SF into "new wave SF." As William Sims Bainbridge's study confirms, this shift is generally acknowledged by the SF community itself, and now, a quarter-century later, it has come to define one of the two essential and quite different modes of the genre.[2]

By the sixties SF had crossed a boundary and ceased to be the literature of only an intensely devoted minority. The broad popularity in the late sixties of *Stranger in a Strange Land* and *Dune* is a phenomenon quite unlike the comparatively select popularity of, say, "The Green Hills of Earth" or *City*. The growth of new wave SF in the sixties can be seen as a rendering of attitudes implicit in the SF of the middle and later fifties. It is not accidental that the flourishing of the new wave in SF coincides with a decade of political activism and of skepticism about technological solutions to social and environmental problems. It is not my purpose to explicate this phase of the genre's growth, but it is important to see that the symptoms of ennui and disillusionment that we find in fifties SF are not a dead end but part of a process of development that will continue beyond the scope of this study.

ROBERT HEINLEIN'S BOAST IN 1957 THAT SF'S GREATEST accomplishment has been to prepare the nation for space-flight is typical of the importance those who participate in SF attribute to it.[3] The genre's insistence on its own "rationality" and its claim to combine "science" and "fiction" are aspects of this self-promoted image. In part it is this claim for high thematic importance that separates SF from other popular genres. While enthusiasts of the detective story or romance story may claim to find moral wisdom in their favorite literature, they rarely if ever attribute a significant social effect to it.[4] For purposes of this study, SF's sense of its own importance and thoughtfulness is itself an intrinsic part of the SF phenomenon and is a feature to be studied, not a value to be defended. To read SF seriously in the way I am proposing requires first of all that one get outside of SF, to see what it means by "serious," and to analyze it not in the context of its own concerns and values but in a broader system.

Science Fiction also stands apart from the other popular genres because it is consciously identified with a specific subculture and its ideology.[5] While the detective story, the western, or even the historical romance might be read by a fairly wide-ranging clientele, especially during the period I studied, SF was by and large read by a closely knit group of people who read little else.[6] The sense SF has of prophetic mission has been encouraged by the close collaboration between readers and authors that characterizes the genre. The frequent conventions are gatherings of both, and at them fans are honored as well as writers. In the thirties and forties most of the young writers were avid fans, and many writers later became editors of magazines or of anthologies—just a partial list of these writer-editors would include Brian Aldiss, Isaac Asimov, Ben Bova, John W. Campbell, Samuel Delaney, Lester del Rey, Harlan Ellison, Hugo Gernsback, James Gunn, Damon Knight, Judith Merril, Michael Moorcock, Fredrick Pohl, Pamela Sargent, Robert Sheckley, Robert Silverberg, and Norman Spinrad. This sort of incestuous relation among fans, writers, and editors is unique among the popular genres. One effect of such familial closeness is that the genre has a high degree of self-awareness which leads not to criticism from within but to a rather effective control whereby, for certain periods at least, the genre is unusually coherent and consistent ideologically; and at a level which may well be subconscious, it excludes works which might explicitly challenge the genre and its values. The subculture takes SF completely seriously as a literature of ideas with social and historical consequences. Even if analysis reveals that other popular genres also have ideological agenda, none conceives of itself as explicitly ideological in quite this way.

During the era I study, United States society gradually shifted from a capitalism based on a strong and blatant ideology of individual freedom and opportunity but dominated by traditional class values and prejudices, toward a capitalism based on a technocratic ideology which claimed to have supplanted political tensions and to have put in motion a genuine meritocracy. This important historical shift has been noted by various commentators of a variety of political positions.[7] Daniel Bell's declaration of the triumph of technique and the end of ideology comes near the end of the process; it acknowledges and, with some irony, even defines a set of values and ideas that have been developing for a number of decades. But the shift of values was advocated and prepared for, and many of its difficulties were worked out not by totalizing theorists but piecemeal by elements of the culture itself. An important part of that cultural thinking process was SF itself.

Science fiction fantasized an ideal of technocracy that, though depicted in extravagant, wish-fulfilling imagery, was not politically outlandish or impossible. In its beginnings the ideal had a revolutionary element in that it challenged prevailing class values and proposed that "natural intelligence," what was often labeled "genius," and its ability to quickly create new, socially transforming technology, were crucial to the definition and the success of

American culture. The almost mythic figures of Edison and Ford loomed large in this conception.

Since World War II such a vision of a triumphant technocratic capitalism has become more or less commonplace in social thought. The conception of technocracy imagined by Daniel Bell in 1973, which is close to a description of the actual state of affairs in various sections of American corporate and governmental organization, is easily compatible with the idea which inspired early SF. To be sure, Bell sees drawbacks in a pure technocracy and modifies it by insisting that it must also be a meritocracy.[8] The SF imagination, more optimistic than Bell, trusts that a technocracy will inevitably be also a meritocracy. The genius, SF's version of the technocratic hero, does not have to *earn* status. The achievements of the genius, like the "works" of the Calvinist elect, merely confirm the correctness of the technocratic selection.

In order to understand the way SF speaks to the issues of technocracy, we need to define the field of historical inquiry at the beginning. Grand generalities about SF will blind us to subtle but significant shifts that have taken place in the genre's form and in its own social presence. The crucial historical event for the form was the end of the Second World War. At this point the economic crisis of the thirties seems over and the exercise of the war itself, especially the efficient mobilization of labor and industry and the rapid development of technology (the atomic bomb in particular) would seem to have put a technocratic system firmly in place. But even before the end of the war there were signs in SF of distrust of such a triumph of technocratic will. On the other hand, while the specific historical moment of the end of the war changed certain emphases, it did not abruptly terminate a genre or a theme. Near the end of this study I will focus on the gradual, almost unconscious, way the genre itself became aware of the contradictions within its ideals as they were, even distortedly, realized in the society of the post-war period.

The development of popular SF in the late twenties and its achievement of generic coherence and stability by the latter part of the thirties is a familiar story.[9] Reading backward from the social concerns that dominate the genre somewhat later, we may speculate that this new genre is one expression of class aspirations similar to those we see also encouraged and expressed in the social movement of technocracy. Themes of a utopian technology—the values of science and engineering, of rationality and organization, of intelligence, all advanced as nonpolitical and in the service of a nationalist ideal—are certainly in the air, and SF may develop as a way of linking them. Though I have come across little evidence of a direct connection between the technocracy movement itself and early SF, they seem clearly to represent parallel expressions of a single social development.[10] Both movements focus on machinery and on the technician-manager as the agent for social progress and stability. Unlike

SF, technocracy has a base of sorts in the academic world: for a short while it was sponsored by a core group under Walter Rautenstrauch at Columbia, and it owes some of its early attraction to the authority of Thorstein Veblen.[11] But, like SF, it also speaks with remarkable intensity to a scattered group of avid followers outside the academy, often in lower-level management or engineering positions, or even outside of the general productive system altogether.[12] Both movements share a utopian ideal that speaks strongly to people unattached to the conventional political parties or to the more familiar forms of radical activism.[13] The two movements, while reacting strongly to the social crisis—not only the Depression, but to the giddy and unstable prosperity that preceded it—sought a social solution outside of politics per se.

Such a conscious rejection of "politics" distinguishes these movements from other literary trends of the thirties, much honored in the following decades, which spoke to explicit political concerns. One thinks of Steinbeck's *The Grapes of Wrath* or, somewhat later, Agee's *Let Us Now Praise Famous Men* as texts that, along with the "realism" of such writers as Erskine Caldwell and William Faulkner, make a point of paying (not always sympathetic) attention to suffering and its social causes. By contrast one must be struck by the almost total absence of such concerns in the SF of the same period. And yet, at the same time, the genre is deeply concerned with social issues. Even a cursory reading of the pulp SF of the thirties shows an almost obsessive concern for fantasizing economic success and for condemning an outdated and false class system whose agents are villainous bankers and lawyers who arrange monopolies, defraud inventors, and generally manipulate the otherwise admirable rules in corrupt ways. The angle of social vision, however, is upward; there is envy of the rich, but not much sympathy for the poor.

The ideology of technocracy that early SF promotes and that later SF will have to rationalize seems a rather simple creed, but within its plain set of values lie deep ambiguities. It idealizes rationality and sees it as socially benign so long as it is not contaminated by self-interest. Power is not recognized as a problem, and irresolvable conflicts of interest are denied. The creed espouses strongly democratic ideals of economic distribution, but at the same time it sees intellect as a distinctive quality deserving special recognition. Its elevation of reason and intellect lead it to repress emotionality and to deny subconscious or irrational motives; as a result, strong feelings, especially those of hatred and envy, are denied, and the actions they motivate are explained as simply reasonable responses to the situation.

The revelation supplied by the SF genre is important because technocracy itself, insofar as it puts the values of efficiency and technique before self-consciousness, inhibits reflection.[14] Much of the criticism and even some of the praise of technocracy will appear to the technocrat—and I will assert that most of us are to some extent technocrats, whether we like it or not—as irrelevant. The genre of high technocratic discourse does not allow the language or the logic that would find fault with the genre. It is at this point, when conscious thought has closed itself off, that popular literature offers us analytical access to understandings that would be otherwise smoothed over. Popular SF, both in individual works and in its conversation with itself as a genre, is a thinking through, in a way impossible to the technocrats themselves, of the implications of the on-coming paradigm. By that I do not mean to say that the fiction itself is especially conscious or intelligent, only that, in ways I will develop, it expresses complex and often contradictory sets of values, and it uses narrative to make sense of that complexity. In these narratives of heroic technicians we can also observe a recognition of contradictions within the technocratic scheme that must be resolved in some way if the new gospel is to succeed.

The development of the genre is itself a process of the genre's reading of itself. And we can find confirmation of our readings of earlier works in the emphases of later works. The history of the genre is an unravelment of certain animating issues. When the genre "solves" an issue, the issue ceases to interest the genre. But of course there is no such thing as a solution to the kinds of dilemmas the genre engages; such endings are really historically-contingent terminals, moments when the genre simply cannot think of anything new. The year 1955, or thereabouts, marked such a moment; a kind of horse-latitudes of thought in the U.S. when the unhappy conclusions of the utopian idea of technocracy seem to have been drawn, when the monster that had been set in motion with the best of intentions was unable to be challenged. Daniel Bell and Jacques Ellul bear witness to this sense of doldrum finality.

FOR THE INTERPRETATION OF THIS DEVELOPMENT I have chosen to focus primarily on the short story because during this period the discourse of the SF subculture consists almost entirely of this form. The great English and continental SF novels of the thirties and forties—by Stapledon, Capek, Lewis, Orwell, and others—speak to a somewhat different readership than those who avidly read pulp stories every month. The novel did not become significant for the popular SF subculture in America until the early fifties. Yet, while the short story has long been recognized as the central imaginative vehicle for early SF, it has not received much detailed examination. Most of the popular readers' guides to SF focus on classic novels. There has been an economics of the intellect at work here: in the study of the short story, the profits have not appeared to justify the inquiry. For the critic, better to invest in, at the least, a novel; better yet to invest in a writer. Such a critical value system has meant that the virtues of the individual short story—its ability to build a daring and provocative structure without concerning itself with a tangled and elaborate reasonableness that distracts from the core fantasy—have tended to be disregarded. The present study attempts, quite apart from its historical-critical thesis, to renew our sense that the individual SF short story is, in its very compression, deserving of intense critical scrutiny. It goes without saying that the full complexity of such an interpretive project cannot be encompassed in a single book. I hope that my rudimentary work here will inspire other students of SF to explore this same comparatively small body of material even more deeply.

While the fantasies I study have an individual, authorial dimension, I am interested not in the work of any particular author, but in the growth of the collective generic fantasy. I treat the stories the way Lévi-Strauss treats myths: the stories themselves can be said to "think." Thought here is a largely unconscious process by which, like Samuel Butler's potato root, the narrative avoids obstacles and seeks the light.[15] These fantasies about technology, the future, and genius are working out rather complex and deeply conflicted social issues. An analysis of these works, with some attention to the sociology of their production and to their relation to history, can reveal to those of us who have a more academic approach insights into our history and our ideas that more polished and sophisticated thought may repress.

This book is composed of two sections: the first considers some preliminary problems that confront any project that attempts to interpret the social meaning of a popular genre. The second focuses on the actual interpretation of American SF from the thirties through the fifties and draws its examples from *Science Fiction Hall of Fame*, Volume 1, an anthology first published in 1971. My hope is that this second aspect of the study, which constitutes the main part of the book, can speak to interpretive problems specific to SF and at the same time suggest an approach applicable to other genres of non-canonic literature.

The first two chapters deal with choosing the sample and problems of interpretation and may not be of interest to all readers. Indeed for some it may seem perfectly reasonable to reorder the book to begin with chapter three and to return to the more technical methodological issues at the end. However the first two chapters clear a space for an intensive analysis of a restricted number of SF stories.

The six chapters that follow isolate four major imaginative motives of SF. Chapter three, "The Myth of Genius," addresses an aspect of SF that is commonly observed by people outside the SF subculture: that much of this fantasy is built on rather simple identifications with powerful heroes. "An

Economy of Reason," "Reason and Love," and "Feeling the Unthinkable" treat SF's own claim to be scientific and explicate some of the repressions such a claim entails. "History, Politics, and the Future" relates SF itself to another twentieth century genre, the technological forecast, and interprets SF's recurrent claim to have insight into the future. Finally, "Under the Shadow of Literature" studies SF's self-consciousness as a literary form. Almost all the defining characteristics of SF fit into one or another of these categories.

I have attempted to add to the generally accepted picture of the genre's history an attention to the way the genre *rhetorically* manipulates a few leading social ideas such as the authority of science, the association of technology and progress, the superiority of reason over emotion, and the necessity of genius, in order to support unconscious social fantasies. By introducing the unconscious and by reaching toward political implications, I have, I hope, given a depth to the reading of this popular literature that has been unavailable to its boosters and denied by its debunkers.

Though this study analyzes an undeniably rich imaginative vein, its purpose is not to "appreciate" or promote what it studies. I therefore anticipate that some admirers of SF will think that its aim is to denounce SF. Such a reaction is understandable, but it misconstrues my commentary. Whatever the embarrassments the struggle of analysis may uncover, and whatever strain the works themselves may have to undergo in the process, the significance of the issues engaged by SF and the complexity of SF's imaginative process revealed by my analysis are beyond dispute. However lightly it has been treated by the mainstream literary community, SF is an important cultural phenomenon which has, in its way, thought deeply about matters that define modern America.

Classic Popularity: Isolating a Noncanonic Canon

1

THE PROJECT I AM EMBARKING ON
will interpret a thirty-year period of SF by careful and prolonged analysis of a few important texts. Therefore, before I can begin I must establish the important texts whose interpretation can be said to account for the genre as a whole. I have isolated a corpus which is 1) small enough to be covered by the methods of analysis I am using, 2) representative, and 3) undeniably popular. Straightforward as these requirements are, there may not be any single list of texts that can fulfill all three. The problem is that at some level each of the requirements works against the others and entails a different perception of the argument implicit in the selection itself. It is easy enough to see how limiting the size of the selection puts in jeopardy its representativeness. A more complicated issue arises in the relation of a work's representativeness to its "popularity"—an ambiguous term that I will explore more closely in a moment. To pose the most simply problematic relations: a very popular work might be quite untypical and therefore unrepresentative, and a generally ignored work might, nevertheless, be typical.

Conventional literary criticism has not usually concerned itself with the problem of the sample. When some version of the traditional canon is taken for granted as the core needing study, even criticism with a strong social-historical interest has tended to move quickly and easily past issues of why the specific texts have been chosen. A previous agreement on what texts matter, which the canon represents, allows critics to put aside issues of aesthetic and socio-historic values and to focus their debate on interpretive issues. Thus, when Raymond Williams, in *The English Novel*, traces how in the 1840s "the novel" raises issues of "community" and works them out in the following century, he does not treat *all* novels of the period.[1] He works with a relatively short list of English novels which at the middle of the twentieth century are considered canonical. Such a use of the canon raises its own problems, of course. We might argue that Williams has shaped his evidence by treating the current canon without consideration of what the later nineteenth century considered the important works. For instance, Meredith, who seventy-five years ago would have loomed as a major presence in any survey that claimed to generalize about the novel, here gets only two brief mentions. But whatever the origins and basis of Williams's canon, it offers him a starting point, and even critics of his thesis will often accept such a canon as a common ground on which useful discussion can begin.

In high literature when there is debate about the canon it usually takes place in terms of a debate about aesthetics. But in the field we are studying, it would contradict the very meaning of the term "popular" to invoke aesthetic criteria. If we do not have a canon, and if we will not consider aesthetics, on what can we even begin to construct a list of what we agree are the "important" works, to privilege them over the "minor" works? Without some sort of canon, the critic has no starting place for historical generalization. He or she can only examine individual works and link them in what will then be seen as arbitrary sequences. Unless we can agree on the works that "matter," any assertion of order or thesis is vulnerable to challenge by any counter-example.

Part of the problem derives from an ambiguity that lurks at the heart of the term popular itself. In aesthetic debates the term, derived from *populus*, will be opposed to "high" art and will denote the class that consumes this nonhigh art. In its strictly economic and sociological aspects the popular denotes specific commercial markets which came into existence in the eighteenth century with the proliferation of a reading bourgeoisie and a technology that allowed for relatively cheap printing.[2] The distinction implicit in the term is not as clear as it used to be. In this century, what Pierre Bourdieu would call the dominated segment of the dominant class has repeatedly, in the name of "art," transgressed the borders between high and popular culture.[3] We have even had the anomaly of a high artistic mode which calls itself "pop art." Clearly this last, while it is arguably more intellectually accessible than such a modernist trend as abstract expressionism, is not economically popular in a sense a sociologist would recognize. In order to avoid such confusion, some critics use the term "mass culture" to refer to cheap, mechanical production that can be distinguished from expensive "artistic" or "elite" culture.[4]

A more recent sense of the term emphasizes not the class basis, but by argument from the class's size, the aspect of being well and broadly liked (e.g. "a popular person"). While one can easily understand how this second meaning could have developed from the first, it nevertheless poses a very different criterion for selection. If popular in the original sense of populus defines a literature directed toward a certain class, popular in the second sense of being liked defines a literature that is spontaneously enjoyed and thus perceived as in opposition to a more difficult literature that supposedly entails an unpleasant exercise which is, somehow, "good for you." Shakespeare, Dickens, and Twain are frequently invoked as instances of the popular in both meanings of the term: although they may be considered high and serious, they are appreciated by a wide variety of people. Such moments in which both definitions of popular are fulfilled are important, but, as the continuing debates about popular and high literature show, such moments are exceptional. One cannot help but suspect that in these cases the ambiguity of the term popular is rendered almost invisible because of the indubitable sanction the canon gives these authors.

When as critics we focus on noncanonic works, we find that not only are the first two definitions of the term popular quite incongruous, but that the second—well liked—can be taken in two quite different senses. One can, to be sure, determine what is popular at this moment by looking at production and consumption figures, and a best-seller list of one sort or another can be constructed for any period. The works on such a list usually have their moment of glory and a long eclipse. One concept of the history of popular culture sees its task to recount the activity of such ephemerae.[5] But in any genre there are also works that become popular in a third sense in that their popularity is not limited to a single historical moment. There grows up something like a canon, a list of "classic popular texts." This list of popular works is quite different from the list of specific works of popular art "approved" by the aestheticians of high art, which is really just a subsection of the traditional canon itself. The works that constitute the list of classic popular texts are acknowledged as classic without ever becoming canonic. *Gone With the Wind*, both as novel and as film, is paradigmatic of this phenomenon. And within the various generic fields there are inevitably special groups of texts which are seen as important and as generically paradigmatic quite apart from their aesthetic value. Sometimes, as with *Gone With the Wind*, this third form of popularity is at least in part a result of the work's popularity in the second sense. One imagines *Star Wars* will be popular in the third sense just because its initial popularity was such a remarkable historical phenomenon itself. But more commonly this third kind of popularity grows and changes in time. The popular "classics" of the detective genre, apart of course from the work of Conan Doyle, are for the most part texts that were not particularly remarked on when they first appeared.

"Classic popularity" is in large part the creation of a university-based critical movement that has been active for the last half-century and whose culminating and summarizing text is John Cawelti's *Adventure, Mystery, and Romance*.[6] In the traditional aesthetic defense of individual works, the critic defends his or her selection of a popular work on the ground that it is art. When a whole genre is being studied, the isolation of a particular text becomes problematic. When the individual work that is studied is put forth as an "example" of the genre, the term example, while it disavows rigor can subtlely turn into a paradigm.[7] Cawelti derives the structural rules for the form from such "examples" and then defines the whole form in terms of these high paradigmatic instances. Since he has, even if not explicitly so, something like a canon in mind, the circularity of his paradigmatic examples is not a problem for him. What he is interested in proving is that in these works the popular genre through its formulas achieves "art." The actual popularity, in senses one or two, of the works he studies does not matter. Poe's "The Purloined Letter" is catalogued as popular by a very loose standard: famous as it is in the academy, it is honored as "popular" only by the genealogical accident that the popular detective story can be said to trace itself back to it. Therefore "The Purloined Letter" is a bona fide member of the popular form, whatever its actual popularity was. The popular form and the canonic story work together, each contributing to the aesthetic argument what the other lacks. Cawelti defines a field which resides at the intersection of canonicity and popularities one and two.

When we approach works and forms whose primary interest for us is not their artistic value, but their popularity, such hermeneutic circles become a difficulty. The selection of the works for study may claim to be aesthetically value free, yet, just because it is a selection, aesthetic value is implied. In the last decade we have seen a number of attempts to deal with the problem the sample presents. One solution is for the critic to choose texts for study by an aesthetically neutral process. At the pole opposite to Cawelti's *Adventure, Mystery, and Romance*, which selects its exemplary texts by aesthetic intuition, is a study like David Bordwell, Kristin Thompson, and Janet Staiger's *The Classical Hollywood Cinema*, which in an effort to avoid any aesthetic bias sets up a rigorously random method of text selection by which to define the field.[8] Starting with a list published in 1961 of the almost 30,000 feature films released in the U.S. between 1915 and 1960 the authors deleted all films not made by American studios, and then, using a random number table, they made a short list of 841 films. They then "located" 100 of these (many have been destroyed or just simply lost) which they call their "unbiased sample": "Our selection procedures represent the closest a researcher can come to random sampling when dealing with historical artifacts. The point remains that our choices were not biased by personal preferences or conceptions of influential or masterful films" (p. 388).

It is important that we understand what Bordwell, Thompson, and Staiger have accomplished by this elaborate method. They are seeking to define what they call "the concept of *group* style." Such a concept, while it encompasses various specific subgenres as defined by theme, imagery, plot, et cetera, is a generic concept analogous to a style of art. In order to interpret what Bazin calls "the genius of the system" of production itself, they assume that "Hollywood films constitute a fairly coherent aesthetic tradition which sustains individual creation" (p. 4), and they establish a set of stylistic "historical norms" which characterize and define the "classical Hollywood film." The project aspires to a structuralism which, while it is repeatedly forced to acknowledge the historical evolution of the form, seeks ultimately to discover a set of universal principles which will define the deep structure of the style even as it points to the various "functional equivalents" (p. 5) by which different eras adapt the core. Cawelti always defines the form in terms of its paradigmatic instances, but Bordwell, Thompson, and Staiger argue that "No Hollywood film is the classical system, each is an 'unstable equilibrium' of classical norms" (p. 5).

The elaborately neutral process by which the authors of *The Classical Hollywood Cinema* have selected their texts is a necessary defense against the charge, which would cripple their structural generalization, that by their selection the critics have pre-determined the character of the genre they are attempting to define. Their sample is intentionally ahistorical, and their goal is to define the structural unity of a style that characterizes the whole period from 1917 to 1960. Even when, in addition to their unbiased sample, they discuss almost 200 other films chosen for their "quality or historical influence" (p. 10), they do so not to develop historical lines of change, causality, and influence, but to "test the conclusions" derived from the unbiased sample.

The problem raised by this mode of selection is that while the process frees the choices from the bias of the critics, it also frees them from what we might call the bias of popularity, in senses two and three. Even more than the high arts, the commercial media and genres are influenced by individual works. The influence may be due as much to crass economic envy as to artistic anxiety, but it is nevertheless powerful. Some films have been more popular than others. Bordwell, Thompson, and Staiger's structuralist rigor, by ignoring the element of popularity and its influence, blinds itself to the dynamics and meaning of the history of the form.

The complexity of the term popular means that to correct this blindness we cannot simply claim to select texts on the basis of popularity, because whatever aspect of popularity we satisfy entails disregarding another. We can see the difficulty if we turn to a study that attempts to use popularity itself, however ambiguous the term, as the criterion for selection. Will Wright's *Sixguns and Society: A Structural Study of the Western* selects its texts by the simple device of limiting the study to westerns that have grossed at least $4 million in rental receipts.[9] The advantage of such an economic rule is that it defines a field entirely on a numerical register of popularity and frees the critic from any claim of asserting his own *aesthetic* standards in place of popular appeal.

Though the procedure by which Wright selects his films looks unambiguous in its mechanicalness, that simplicity is deceptive. The very number, $4 million, means different things in different periods. As a scale against which to judge the cost of a film, $4 million is high in the thirties and fairly low in the sixties. The comparatively large number of "professional plot" westerns Wright discovers in the sixties must certainly be at least in part a result of inflation. And it is thanks to this distortion that Wright's field looks symmetrical, with roughly equal numbers of the two main plots. The point of bringing up such a difficulty is not to disqualify Wright's process, but to show that even a mechanically economic definition of a popular field, though it may appear admirably unprejudiced by ideological and aesthetic presuppositions, is still deeply ambiguous and in need of further interpretation.

The categories generated by Wright's method of selection do not in themselves explain the element that makes these films popular. The difficulty becomes evident when, in an unguarded moment, Wright violates his method and rejects *Charge at Feather River* because it is an "awful western" whose "success was solely due to its big release as a three-dimensional film at a time when this gimmick was new and exciting" (p. 30). What is revealing here is not Wright's deviation from his economic mode of selection, but his denunciation of it at this point. Wright's problem is that he is trying to be loyal to two different conceptions of popularity. What I have called popularity of the second type, contemporary commercial success, would require him to include *Charge at Feather River* in his list, but popularity of the third type, "classic popularity," requires him to reject the film. In the case of *Charge at Feather River*, Wright feels secure in his understanding that nonstructural issues made the film commercially popular. But we may also suspect that there are numerous westerns whose contemporary popularity is not at all due to their narratives, but which nevertheless remain on his list. Most obviously, many westerns are popular because of the stars who appear in them. Whatever the plot, a film with Gary Cooper or James Stewart is likely to be more successful than one with, say, Buster Crabb. Moreover, though this may change between the thirties and the sixties, directors like John Ford and Howard Hawks may be in themselves good box office. The process by which a film or a work of literature becomes popular may be in some way functionally related to the theme and structure of the work itself, but that relation is at best oblique in a world of extraordinary promotion. We can argue that elaborate promotion does not justify excluding the film, both because such promotion characterizes many films, and because it is not at all certain that a film so promoted is not still, perhaps even especially, revealing about the expectations and desires of the audience.

A third problem arises not so much from Wright's method itself but from the fact that its simplicity seems to blind him to other interpretative issues. It must strike us that Wright, for all his economic rigor, finds his generic category unambiguous. He seems to accept the industry's marketing categories. He disregards such western oddities as *Son of Paleface*, and such generic neighbors of the western as *Young Mr. Lincoln*. And he ignores the generic issues his own categories of "classical," "vengeance," "transition," and "professional" plot might raise. A mechanical register of contemporary popularity can block reflection on what a slightly different approach would consider important generic distinctions. For Wright the western is as pure, as isolated from the larger literary system, as a biological genus is from the whole of nature. He disregards the extent to which any genre mingles with others and breaks from itself.[10]

The problem is to find a way to discuss classic popularity while retaining a mode of selection unbiased by aesthetic presumptions. There may be no simple method by which to solve this dilemma. A purely economic selection, at least given the kind available to Wright, fails to indicate the basis of popularity or to begin to interpret the field. Other modes of selection, while perhaps more sensitive to ideological issues, are either biased or insensitive to popularity.

AS A START, THE SOLUTION TO THE PROBLEM OF BIAS IN the selection may be not to create a sample at all, but to find one. One of the first things a developing science seeks to find is the illuminating anomaly. In many sciences such anomalies are created in the conditions of the laboratory; from the unique and controlled experiment, broad hypothetical generalizations can be made which can then be confirmed elsewhere. And in sciences in which the objects of study are unable to be examined in the laboratory, such as astronomy or evolutionary biology, the illuminating anomaly must be discovered in the field. Such exceptional situations as binary stars, eclipses, or the La brea tar pits offer the scientist the chance to understand the principle of the science in a way that a simple survey of nature would never permit.

In the study of cultural history, and especially the popular genres, we are in much the same situation as these last scientists. We have no laboratory in which to set up controlled experiments. Simply to describe the situation leaves us stuck at the surface of the phenomenon. We need to collect data, but we also need to find special situations which display the principles that will never be evident in the ordinary operations of the form. Such situations will be rare, and after we have interpreted them we will need to turn around and question how much the anomalous situation may be a distortion of the common state of things. But we cannot do without such anomalies. We do better to begin with them and then ask what have we learned.

For the specific case of science fiction, we can envision how a small, representative selection of popular works might look and how it should be handled. The basic selection should be as undetermined as possible by the critic's own aesthetic or historical principles. At a late stage in the study the critic may be in a position to reinterpret the original field of study and redefine it on what are now seen as intrinsic principles, but such authority is earned by the process of analysis. Such principles cannot be the basis of initial definitions of the field. And, as a corollary of this rule, we must insist that what appears as an anomaly in the unbiased sample must not be rejected as eccentric. On the contrary, it is a validation of the interpretation that it can account for what on the first view looks to be anomalous. And finally, the laying out of the field, while it is the first part of the analytic exercise, can never be final. It is intrinsic to the analytical process that it work dialectically so that at each stage of its achievement it uses the insight it has achieved to question the assumptions that originally determined the field of study.

We need to begin by finding an extraordinary situation which will yield information about common events that one could never get by simply studying the common phenomena. The book, *Science Fiction Hall of Fame*, is just such a lucky eccentricity. It is an anthology, first published in 1970 and still in print, of pulp science fiction originally printed between 1934 and 1963 and chosen as the "best" SF by a vote of the members of the Science Fiction Writers of America. The process of selecting the stories is free from the kinds of distortion, both aesthetic and economic, we have just observed.[11] First, it is not critics or scholars, but working writers who voted on the selection, and while their motives for selection are obscure—whether "best" means money-making, optimistic, beautiful, ingenious, or most profound is not at all clear—that very ambiguity prevents the selection from promoting one kind of story, one version of the genre at the expense of others. The editor, Robert Silverberg, has exercised some minor discretionary power, so that the selection is not simply a record of votes, but his hand would not seem to have seriously violated the neutrality of the selection process. The decision to give no single writer more than one story can be seen as a flattening device that slightly obscures the exceptional popularity of some writers. By focusing on individual popular stories rather than the popularity of specific *oeuvres*, such as those of Bradbury or Clarke, the selection process distorts one aspect of what makes works popular. And yet, by preventing the domination by a few widely recognized authors, such flattening insures a representation of a wider range of work than might a selection more in awe of a few major lights. Since all the stories are reprints, their choice is in some way a response to a tried popularity, not the expression of some booster's splurge. Here is a found version of classic popularity, chosen by "market forces" rather than by any single analyst with a bias, and relatively free from the defining preferences of a single magazine or a single editor. And finally, though one presumes the twenty-six authors may derive some profit from the reprinting of their stories, one can claim that the selection is not particularly subject to significant economic distortion. Thus *Science Fiction Hall of Fame* offers a field of stories free from the most immediate personal and economic biases that are common in the selection of popular literature.

Science Fiction Hall of Fame contains these stories:

1. Stanley Weinbaum, "A Martian Odyssey" (1934)
2. John W. Campbell, "Twilight" (1934)
3. Lester del Rey, "Helen O'Loy" (1938)
4. Robert A. Heinlein, "The Roads Must Roll" (1940)
5. Theodore Sturgeon, "Microcosmic God" (1941)
6. Isaac Asimov, "Nightfall" (1941)
7. A. E. van Vogt, "The Weapon Shop" (1942)
8. Lewis Padgett, "Mimsy Were the Borogoves" (1943)
9. Clifford Simak, "Huddling Place" (1944)
10. Fredric Brown, "Arena" (1944)
11. Murray Leinster, "First Contact" (1945)
12. Judith Merril, "That Only a Mother" (1948)
13. Cordwainer Smith, "Scanners Live in Vain" (1948)
14. Ray Bradbury, "Mars is Heaven!" (1948)
15. C. M. Kornbluth, "The Little Black Bag" (1950)
16. Richard Matheson, "Born of Man and Woman" (1950)
17. Fritz Leiber, "Coming Attraction" (1950)
18. Anthony Boucher, "The Quest for Saint Aquin" (1951)
19. James Blish, "Surface Tension" (1952)
20. Arthur C. Clarke, "The Nine Billion Names of God" (1953)
21. Jerome Bixby, "It's a *Good* Life" (1953)
22. Tom Godwin, "The Cold Equations" (1954)
23. Alfred Bester, "Fondly Fahrenheit" (1954)
24. Damon Knight, "The Country of the Kind" (1955)
25. Daniel Keyes, "Flowers for Algernon" (1959)
26. Roger Zelazny, "A Rose for Ecclesiastes" (1963)

This is a reasonably short selection of certifiably popular stories that in some way satisfies both the demands of contemporary and classic popularity.

The question one has, then, is how *representative* is this collection? Since no selection limited to twenty-six works can help but omit some important stories, the main question is, how can we determine how eccentric is the present selection? To give some statistical sense of how well the anthology represents the whole field during this period, I have compiled two lists (see Appendices 1 and 2): the first shows the popularity of the individual stories in relation to other stories by these authors written during the same period; the second shows what significant stories of the period the anthology has omitted. The first chart lists for each of the authors who appear in *Science Fiction Hall of Fame* all of the stories that have been anthologized four or more times (*Science Fiction Hall of Fame* is included as one of the anthologies). I have chosen four as a number large enough to weed out the odd story that a single, prolific editor might eccentrically reprint a number of times, and yet not so large that it will exclude important but for some reason seldom reprinted stories. Using statistical information derived from William Contento's *Index to SF Anthologies and Collections*, I arrive at a list of 319 stories.[12] Of the particular stories in *Science Fiction Hall of Fame*, only Van Vogt's "The Weapon Shop" does not make the list.[13] Thus, the evidence in Appendix 1 argues for the representativeness of Silverberg's selections.

Using a similar method, we can begin to ask what has *Science Fiction Hall of Fame* neglected? The second chart (Appendix 2) lists two categories of authors not appearing in *Science Fiction Hall of Fame*. The authors in the first category have four or more stories first published after 1930 and before 1963 (the date of the last story included in *Science Fiction Hall of Fame*) that have been anthologized four or more times (thereby making them what we can call "significant authors"). The other authors have one story that has been anthologized seven or more times (thereby making them "significant stories"). This chart includes five significant authors not included in *Science Fiction Hall of Fame*, Volume 1. Two, Aldiss and Ballard, are English. It says something for the selection process of the Hall of Fame series that the other three are included in *Science Fiction Hall of Fame*, Volume 2.[14] While there are significant stories on this second list, there are plausible reasons why they may not have made the original *Science Fiction Hall of Fame*. Some aspire to mainstream status ("The Portable Phonograph," "Harrison Bergeron"). Some have become especially popular only after 1963 ("Impostor," "Mother"). Some can be said to veer too near pure fantasy ("The Golem"). "A Canticle For Liebowitz" was selected for Volume 2 but was "unavailable." One could argue for the importance of a number of these stories for a thorough history of SF, but I do not think anyone would claim that to omit any of these popular stories is to distort the field in an important way.

Given the length of the first list—and I should emphasize what a simplification of the field it already represents—one appreciates how difficult it is to derive any reasonably short list of works that would adequately register classic popularity. On the other hand, there is no story in *Science Fiction Hall of Fame* whose presence cannot be justified quite easily. The most problematic story is Van Vogt's "The Weapon Shop," an occasionally reprinted story by an author with a number of much reprinted stories.

As I choose the stories in *Science Fiction Hall of Fame* as my sample, I am aware that I still have many further choices to make and that these will be open to the accusation of bias. Twenty-six stories may be an enormous reduction from the approximately eight thousand stories listed in the Contento *Index*, but it is still too large a number to analyze in depth without creating an unwieldy and unfocused study. Even twenty-six stories can lure one toward the encyclopedist fallacy of believing that the larger the number of references, the more acute the analysis. On the contrary, according to structuralist principles, three stories—representing the early, middle, and late periods—might show all the issues, techniques, and developments one can find in twenty-six. What such a formally elegant demonstration would lack, of course, is the very convincing power that comes from a proper sample. No three stories could ever be accepted as accurately representative.

The dilemma of the representative sample cannot be solved: twenty-six stories are, at the same time, too few and too many. Insofar as they are too few, I have compensated by making free reference to certifiably popular works outside *Science Fiction Hall of Fame*. Insofar as they are too many, I have made interpretative choices of focus. I have, however, tried to diminish arbitrary bias by enforcing the rule that all the stories in the anthology will be treated in some layer of the analysis. I thus, finally, will be treating *Science Fiction Hall of Fame* not simply as a sample but as a book itself, composed in 1970, depicting a vision of earlier SF's history and interests. As in the conventional literary interpretation of, say, a novel, in which the analysis is the more persuasive the more of the novel it accounts for, I have found most useful an analysis which explains the presence of elements that would otherwise seem out of place or irrelevant. Such a principle of value has operated both in the analysis of the individual stories and in the final analysis of the whole anthology. Since *Science Fiction Hall of Fame* is itself an interpretation, the final interpretative act of this study has been to look at the book against the background of 1971, the year it was published. *Science Fiction Hall of Fame* is not just a reconstruction in brief of "the golden age"; it is an argument, made at an identifiable moment in American history, about the form, place, and value of SF.

Reading
Popular Genres

2

HAVING SELECTED OUR SAMPLE, WE
need to choose our method for analysis. What is categorized as popular
literature, because it is not considered "literary," is often subjected to methods of analysis different from those we accord "high" literature. Presumptions about the art shape the approach, and the approach usually reinforces
the presumptions. Escaping such interpretive circles is difficult. I begin by
examining the assumptions behind some recent sociological approaches to
popular literature.

Empirical Sociology and Popular Literature

For a number of decades there has been a tradition in America that honors
popular art. It owes much to thirties interest in proletarian art, to critics like
Robert Warshow, Tom Wolfe, and Susan Sontag, and to the American Studies movement. The modern text that seemed most definitively to valorize
popular art and to certify the whole movement was Herbert Gans's *Popular
Culture and High Culture* (1975).

Gans's thesis is simple and tolerant: any "taste public" is entitled to its
own "taste culture," and since many taste publics are incapable of appreciating high culture, they should be allowed to enjoy the culture they do appreciate. Gans goes so far as to argue that the public is obligated to provide
them with their culture. This egalitarian spirit does not mean that Gans finds
all "taste cultures" equal. He envisions a clear hierarchy of cultures, and he
unambiguously asserts that "the higher cultures are better or at least more
comprehensive and more informative than the lower ones. . . . because
they may be able to provide greater and more lasting aesthetic gratifications."[1] By the phrase "more comprehensive" he means they "cover more
spheres of life and encompass more ideas." The gesture toward some vaguely
quantitative scheme—more spheres of life, more ideas—cannot conceal the
aesthetic basis ("more lasting aesthetic gratifications") of the categories.

We thus end up with a double standard whose contradiction is held to-gether by ambiguity about the idea of value. Having admitted aesthetic value, Gans then argues for a second idea of value which we can understand only by taking the background and needs of any "taste public" (often a class, sometimes a racial group or an age group) into account. Insofar as "all taste cultures reflect the standards of their publics, they are of equal value" (p. 128). Gans maintains this democratic tolerance in a world of absolute aes-thetics by a play on words: "I do not believe that all taste cultures are of equal worth, but that they are of equal worth when considered in relation to their taste publics" (p. 128). The first time "worth" appears in this sentence it refers to an essentially aesthetic value ("more ideas"), but the second time it appears it refers to a concept of social relations—the fit between user and product.

The second concept of worth implies that social values are relative and to be judged by the felt needs of the various "taste publics." But elsewhere Gans reveals a more absolute sense of social values, liberal and tolerant to be sure, but also deeply ideological. "Popular culture," he says, "has played a useful role in the process of enabling ordinary people to become individu-als, develop their identities, and find ways of achieving creativity and self-expression" (p. 57). The mass media, he reminds us, "have always been stalwart defenders of individualism and personal freedom," (pp. 57–58) as witness the heroes of pre-television era films. These same films, he asserts, "which dealt with or idealized the life-styles of the middle and upper classes provided role-models which helped the immigrants to become Americanized and middle class, and they gave poor people, as they still do, a picture of what life was like without poverty" (p. 58). Soap operas "have supplied housewives with information about how to solve their problems (p. 58)." Gans does not seem entirely comfortable with this educational value: "the issues are rarely presented as they appear in ordinary life, and problems are solved much too easily, but still, they offer ideas to the audience which it can apply to its own situation (p. 58)." The thought that such popular drama might be more realistically educational or that homemaking suggestions more practical leads Gans to the open-ended musing that "perhaps their users want some fantasy" (p. 59). What is clear in this attempt to find a use for popular culture is that Gans's claim of sociological neutrality is in the ser-vice of a very specific set of political presumptions about class value and be-havior that he seems unable to question or doubt.

Ostensibly committed to a simple relation of taste culture to taste public, he gets drawn into arguments about the political influence of art and is forced into declarations which reduce politics to advertising. "Until one can determine *to what extent* popular culture causes or encourages public support of war, poverty, racism, chauvinism, and so forth, and whether people would be more *willing to do away with* these evils if popular culture were abolished or altered, it is impossible to consider popular culture as a counter-revolutionary tool even if one were to accept Marcuse's goals" (p. 49, emphasis added). The conception of political issues implicit in the casual list of wrongs ("war, poverty, racism, chauvinism, and so forth") and the innocent presupposition that "people" could simply choose "to do away with" them denies the complexity of political argument and action. The assumption here is that empirical study, the determination of "to what extent" the art affects its public, can precede the interpretation of the art's political implications. Thus, Gans is, in his way, a technocrat: he denies the significance of political and explicitly ideological arguments, and he presumes that the solution to the world's problems—war, poverty, and so forth—can be achieved purely by education and proper management.

There is a large body of work by advertisers and political pollsters exploring people's responsiveness to the attractiveness of various products, styles, and political positions at various times, but such studies are quite a different thing from an in-depth understanding of how a popular culture rhetorically affects its audience. In the last decade, with the increased scholarly attention to noncanonic literature, we have the opportunity for such study. But for reasons which may be more intrinsic to the nature of literature than most American sociology seems able to understand, such study remains rare. One important attempt at just such an understanding, Janice Radway's *Reading the Romance*, points to the difficulty of the dilemma.[2] Invoking the authority of reader response criticism, Radway uses interviews and a questionnaire in order to interpret the nature of the genre's appeal to a group of active romance readers, and she bases her sense of the structural essentials that define the genre on these empirical findings.

What is mainly revealed by the readers' answers is not the real source of pleasure that these books offer, but the readership's ideas about what pleasure should be. Their ideas are clearly related as much to class, education, sex, family background, all of what Pierre Bourdieu would call "habitus," as they are to what a critic might consider the distinguishing aspects of the romance genre.[3] Often, the answers that Radway takes as revealing truths about the genre may simply be the repetitions of advertising cliches. Thus, she can take the fact that many women say "escape" is a value they look for as an insight into their motive for reading and then go on to argue that the advertisers have "discovered the escape function of romance fiction" (p. 89). But is it not just as likely that "escape" is a term the advertisers have taught the readers to invoke to make the reading activity respectable?[4] Elsewhere

Radway takes at face value her respondents' claim that they like the romance because it is "educational." At one point Radway can begin to see that such a claim may be motivated by something other than a response to a book: "I think it likely that the 'reading for instruction' explanation is a secondary justification for repetitive romance consumption that has been articulated by the women to convince skeptical husbands, friends, and interviewers that the novels are not merely frothy, purposeless entertainment but possess a certain intrinsic value that can be transferred to the reader" (p. 107). But then, a few pages later, instead of following out the social implications of such a strategy, Radway converts this defensive social move back into an explanation of the genre's appeal: women read romances, she says, "because they believe the books expand their horizons and add to their knowledge of the world" (p. 111).

Radway presumes that what people say about their preferences is adequate and true. She can be adamant in her defense of "the worth of the readers' understanding of their own experience" (p. 187): "they know perfectly well why they like to read" (p. 86). "Despite their evident ability to tolerate certain kinds of sexual description, I think the readers' assertion that such detail ought to be subordinated, in the words of one woman, 'to tenderness and the expression of emotional love,' should be accepted as given"[5] (p. 105). Such an approach was attempted by Norman Holland when, in *Five Readers Reading*, he correlated responses to a poem with personality type. As Jonathan Culler has argued, the comments of the readers "revealed above all the cliches of the various subcultures and cultural discourses that work to constitute the consciousness of American college students."[6] Such a procedure of asking readers about the source of their pleasure, at least at our present stage of sophistication, can tell us little about the nature of the texts read or about the actual psychology of the reading process. As we move into the realm of popular texts and readers relatively uncoerced by formal education, the problems of such a survey do not diminish.

Insofar as the production of ideology is the object of inquiry—at times Radway will claim such a purpose, at other times she wants to see the romance as a defense against prevailing ideology—the method of direct questionnaire is particularly blind, for the respondents are incapable of seeing what is happening to them in their pleasure. All Radway's questionnaires could ever reveal is a reinforcement of basic ideological structures to which the romances themselves contribute. The situation is analogous to the problem Freud posed about self-analysis: the individual's defenses, whose compromised success has brought the patient to psychoanalysis in the first place, will work to prevent the analysand from perceiving the actual difficulty. In just the same way, the plain reader, far from seeing through the pleasure to the real operations of the text, will be, of all people, the least capable of such understanding.

As in psychoanalysis, in which it takes a second person, the analyst, to see what may be clear but what the structure of defense prevents the analysand from seeing, in the study of literary response it takes a critic, not an addict of the genre, to interpret the sources of pleasure that the healthy defenses of the reader would obscure. Radway might have pursued this tack, but early in the study she committed herself to a partnership with her readers that prevented any move toward analytic insight. In psychoanalysis the analyst is also a loyal partner, but not in Radway's sense. Instead of helping them see themselves in a new way, she collaborates with the romance readers in what Eagleton calls, invoking a different context, a "conspiracy of eloquence." Very early in the process she finds herself in such a position that any intellectual move, any analysis of their responses, will be seen as betrayal. It is a delicate social situation, and we can acknowledge the feelings of loyalty it creates, but nevertheless it is situation in which neither party can break free from the self-justifying rationalizations of the readership.

By taking as truth and revelation the very statements that as a sociologist she would want to categorize, by dignifying her informants' own theories, Radway has deprived herself of her own tools as a critic. Her snide jabs at "English professors" represent more than just attacks on rival academics; they are denunciations of the very act of analytical criticism itself in favor of a populist ideal of the value of her informants' self-understanding. Thus, in the name of solidarity, Radway has placed herself in a middle ground where she can be neither critic nor sociologist.[7]

Any sociological study of a particular genre or set of texts will eventually confront the problem of the relation of interpretation and empirical research. The example of Radway may remind us that over forty years ago Leo Lowenthal cautioned us against expecting an easy empirical solution to interpretive problems. In his classic essay on magazine biographies, Lowenthal observes that there is ample evidence that "there must be a social need seeking gratification for [biographical information]," but he also warns against one of the common modes of trying to prove such a hypothesis: "One way to find out would be to study the readers' reactions, to explore by means of various interviewing techniques what they are looking for, what they think about the biographical jungle. But it seems to be rather premature to collect and to evaluate such solicited response until more is known about the content structure itself."[8] We can think of Gans at this point and his desire to establish "empirical evidence" of a point of literary-psychological interpretation. There is a temptation to expect quite casually that, whatever inadequacies there might be, it could not hurt to take a survey. On the contrary, however, a survey taken prematurely, without a literary interpretation of the body of work under study, will not merely obscure the nature of the field, but, by embedding unexamined presuppositions at the core of the inquiry, in all likelihood severely distort the investigator's perception of the meaning and significance of the data and thereby lead to a false understanding of the phenomenon itself.

If we recall Harold Lasswell's celebrated paradigm of the communications system, we can point directly to the problem area. The elegant aphorism, "*Who* says *what* to *whom* in *which channel* with *what effect?*"[9] has its uses. But as advertisers will quickly point out, it is also deceptively complex: the formula it adumbrates will consist of five variables with complex functional relations to each other. The *who*, the *whom*, and the *channel* can be identified with some precision. The *effect*, in gross terms, can sometimes be measured empirically. But *says what* is inherently problematic: unless we are simply to repeat the text's own words, an act of interpretation will be required before we can agree on *what is said*.

The Critique of Ideology

Radway's urge to ground analysis in some kind of empirical data may be, in part, a reaction to a strong sociological tradition in Great Britain and Europe, which analyzes social dynamics not by inquiry into the understandings of actual people but by interpreting the texts they read. For this approach literature, in the words of Terry Eagleton, is "a crucial mechanism by which the language and ideology of an imperialist class establishes its hegemony, or by which a subordinated state, class or region preserves or perpetuates at the ideological level an historical identity shattered or eroded at the political. It is also a zone in which such struggles achieve stabilization."[10] "Ideology" here is to be understood not as false consciousness, but rather as the inevitable rationalizations by which any social structure tries to justify itself. Eagleton sees literary texts as active agents, used by both dominating and subordinated classes, in the production of such ideology. He conceives the purpose of literary analysis to be, not to appreciate or honor the text, but, by interrupting the ideological harmony of the text, to use the text to expose the nature of the ideology that produced it.

One way a text can give pleasure is to use a seemingly neutral narrative which claims to be "realistic" to reinforce ideological presumptions. We who inhabit the same ideology and are naturalized to its presumptions about the world and human behavior, feel comfortable in such a text's world. And while such pleasure may reinforce the ideology, at the same time this very quality of naturalization is also the opening that will eventually allow us to become aware of the operation of ideology. "An ideology exists because there are certain things which must not be spoken of. In so putting ideology to work, the text begins to illuminate the absences which are the foundation of its articulate discourse" (p. 90). By "illuminating" absences, the text "begins to 'make speak' the silences of that ideology" (p. 89). This voice of the text comes from the inevitable dissonance within any text which arises, as Pierre Macherey says, because "the work in order to say one thing, has at the same time to say another thing which is not necessarily of the same nature."[11] The text's very ambitions to achieve aesthetic satisfaction lead it into contradiction. Adorno argues that this process is endemic to culture itself: "Just because culture affirms the validity of the principle of harmony within an antagonistic society, albeit in order to glorify that society, it cannot avoid confronting society with its own notion of harmony and thereby stumbling on discord."[12] As Eagleton puts it, "In such a text the relative coherence of ideological categories is revealed under the form of a concealment— revealed by the very *incoherence* of the text, by the significant disarray into which it is thrown in its efforts to operate its materials in the interests of a 'solution'" (p. 86). What makes such ideology particularly difficult to analyze is that it is invisible to anyone within the ideology. It becomes apparent only at moments when the inhabited ideology clashes with another ideology. Recent examples of such revelation can be found in analyses of popular art in which racist or sexist presumptions meet their come-uppance. At such moments—and these moments are crucial to the attainment of any kind of self-consciousness—the contradictions within an ideology's logic of the "real" may begin to appear. Though such criticism is at times discomforting, it is necessary. As the German sociologist, H. Plessner puts it, "without estrangement, no understanding."[13]

Critics undertaking such ideological analysis do not involve themselves in aesthetic evaluation, nor do they explicate in order to appreciate. Whereas the typical strategy of appreciative criticism is to begin by declaring aesthetic values and then to reveal them in the work, ideological study, since it is interested in social diagnosis and not in the defense of particular works, is free from such circularity. In this approach the text is neither elevated beyond historical and social issues into the mystical realm of "art" nor reduced to a mere commodity that can be ascribed to a system of social production, a simple expression of class identity and preference, but understood as a rhetorical device by which the ideology of the culture that produces it is expressed and defended. Each text needs to be interpreted. Eagleton argues,

The task of criticism is not to insulate itself within the same space as the text, allowing it to speak or completing what it necessarily leaves unsaid. On the contrary, its function is to install itself in the very incompleteness of the work in order to *theorise* it—to explain the ideological necessity of those '*not-saids*' which constitute the very principle of its identity. Its object is the *unconscious* of the work—that of which it is not, and cannot be, aware (p. 89).

There are obvious and significant parallels between this vision of the fictional text as an expression of repressed social awareness that cannot be acknowledged and the basic Freudian paradigm of the unconscious and the way it achieves expression in dreams and in psychopathological behavior. A criticism attempting to understand this level of expression must learn to see past the manifest statement of the work, which is to some serious extent a defense against the awareness that lies at the work's deepest level, and to uncover the latent need that has motivated the narrative.

Under such conditions of understanding, we can learn about a culture, not only by analyzing specific texts, but by observing which texts it has valued and which it has disregarded. If the canon itself is an instrument of social wishes and repressions, the relegation of other texts to noncanonic status is also a deeply revealing social gesture. For Eagleton, "the history of the life, death and resurrection of literary texts (i.e. the historical discriminations between high and low literature) is a part of the history of ideologies" (p. 178). He rejects appeals to an aesthetic that would praise a work for transcending its own time: "Literary works 'transcend' their contemporary history . . . by virtue of their concrete relations to it" (p. 178). "Valuable art comes into being not *despite* its historical limitations but *by virtue of* them" (p. 179). If historical limitation is to be considered a virtue in the understanding of canonic works, we might ask whether it does not follow that, in this respect at least, popular art is exceptionally expressive? Both the meaning and the devaluation of popular art reveals much about historical values and ideological structures.

Eagleton's approach to literary texts should be valuable for our thinking about popular literature because it sanctions treating low literature, which is to a great extent defined by its historical limitations, in exactly the same way we would treat high literature. However, in practice such an egalitarian program can often find itself sustaining the canon and disdaining low literature. At least one of the motives for Radway's empirical emphasis seems to be her frustration with the implicit collaboration with specific class values that this sociological tradition of literary analysis can foster. It is not that this tradition is not acute in its analysis—Radway herself in the latter parts of her book engages in exactly such work—but that it tends to be dismissive of its subject. By exposing ideology, Eagletonian critics put themselves in the position of condescending to the readership that, by enjoying the popular text, has shown that it has accepted its ideology. Radway takes offense at the analytical insights of critics of the romance like Tania Modleski and Ann Douglas because she sees such insights as expressions of intellectual condescension to the class of women who read romances. Sociological empiricism represents for Radway an intellectual refuge because it will not judge the material it studies. And one has to agree with her that much work that uses techniques of intrinsic literary analysis to study noncanonic literature often has at its core a cultural-aesthetic evaluation. The older traditions of *Scrutiny* or of the Frankfurt School tended to debunk noncanonic art. On the other side, a more recent style, exemplified in much of the work to come out of the early years of the *Journal of Popular Culture*, has sought to promote popular arts in terms of conventional high aesthetic values. In both modes the popular competes in an arena in which rules are set by high aesthetic theory. In the last ten or fifteen years the European mode of social analysis, by exploring how ideology operates in texts, would seem to have put us in a position to avoid such aesthetic judgments. But Radway seems to be aware that this modern enterprise often—though neither invariably nor necessarily—continues to maintain what we might call a Frankfurt School bias, which at some level cannot help but treat the popular text as debased in relation to the idealized canon.

Even analysis which is critical of the canon can by isolating that canon for study imply a bias against popular literature. Despite the potential for escaping canonic aesthetic judgments implicit in his program, Eagleton's own work is remarkable for its almost exclusive attention to work within the accepted, conventional canon. His books on *Clarissa* and Shakespeare, while examining works of immense popularity and while undertaking to understand their forms of ideological production, still do not venture outside the narrowest ranges of the high canon.[14] In *Walter Benjamin* he explores what makes a culture call a work "literary," but he does not explore the essential corollary question of what are the bases by which an elite culture rejects a work.[15] To be sure, older texts seem to raise this problem less obviously than do more modern texts. *The Second Shepherd's Play* or *The Malcontent*, works originating out of folk and commercial sources before the advent of modern commercial literature, have in this century been studied with the enthusiasm and attention usually reserved for high literature and without any embarrassed acknowledgment of their origins. The issue of the canon and its exclusions is crucial for the study of more modern genres like

the Gothic novel or adventure melodrama. And yet the most politically conscious critics can treat the politics of generic material without raising the
issue of canon. Pierre Macherey's long essay on Jules Verne ignores the difficulty, perhaps felt more strongly by Anglo-American readers and critics than
by French, of the literary "rank" of Verne's work.[16] By analyzing works that
have been accepted as classics and treating them as such, socially aware criticism reaffirms the canon.

Of course this focus on the canon makes considerable sense: the works
that the hegemonic culture honors are most likely to be the works that express most strongly, and often complexly, the dominant and dominating ideology for that culture. Insofar as the purpose of the literary analysis is to
understand the rationalizations and contradictions of that dominant ideology,
it should examine the culture's most honored works. But if all literature operates as ideological expression, then noncanonic work should be of interest
as the production of the ideology of "subordinated" groups. It is at this point
that the rules change, however. Popular literature, even before it is analyzed, is treated as expressive in a way very different from high literature.[17]
The Frankfurt School's attitude toward "The Culture Industry,"[18] with its
acute sense of the ways this industry has manipulated its audience with sen-
sational rhetorical tricks has so influenced the field that even critics like Ian
Ang, who are most eager to analyze the pleasure in the popular work, cannot
escape an analysis that is to some extent an exposé.[19] The most sociological
analysis tends to lapse back into aesthetic evaluation. Eagleton himself is
certainly not free from aesthetic postures. In the last chapter of *Criticism
and Ideology*, the distinction he makes between Jonson and Landor is an exercise in aesthetic taste, an attempt to justify aesthetic responses on a Marxist basis. Eagleton's language is full of contempt: *banal* is a favorite word, and
anaemic, naive, and *vulgar,* also serve (pp. 186–187). One can understand
why he would want to denigrate Landor as a representative of privilege, but
such judgment is double-edged, for it is not merely aristocratic art which will
be dismissed as banal, naive, and vulgar. Eagleton's analysis here can easily
become the excuse for even a socially concerned criticism to ignore popular
literature and to treat it as unworthy of analysis.

The Importance of Interpretation

For Leo Lowenthal literature embraces "two powerful cultural complexes:
art on the one hand, and a market-oriented commodity on the other." The
latter dimension, which developed in the course of the eighteenth century,
"can make no claim to insight and truth." We study it simply as a symptom of

culture.[20] This is a useful dichotomy that we can apply to the study of all literature, but it also easily slides into the casual assumption that canonic literature is art, but popular literature is only a commodity.

If we accept Lowenthal's conception of literature as composed of artistic and commercial aspects, we should not be thereby misled into thinking that the latter, because they are not artistic, are without meaning. A powerful semiotic element exists in even the most purely commercially motivated product. Even a book whose popularity depends on an expensive, aggressive advertising campaign, or one that is propaganda in its narrowest sense, has a rhetorical presence that has to be interpreted. Propaganda needs to be studied closely both to discover its distortions and to understand the emotional and cognitive significations that make it work. In fact, popular literature presents a most revealing subject for analysis just because it is, from an artistic point of view, so "contaminated." It marks the meeting of the propagandist desire of the producers and the imaginative pleasures of the readers. The admired work of art tells us little about either; it may over the years generate converts, but it may always remain in tension with a large part of its culture.[21] It is the complex "fit" of the popular work that gives it value and attracts our attention here.

In the distinction between art and commodity can lie a second questionable assumption: that art is somehow conscious of the ideological difficulties it treats and therefore adversarial to the hegemonic ideology, while commodity is the unconscious vehicle of that ideology. This distinction is one of the cruces of Frankfurt School aesthetics, and it continues to control the analysis of recent Marxist criticism. Adorno could argue, "A successful work of art is not one which resolves contradictions in a spurious harmony, but one which expresses the idea of harmony negatively by embodying the contradictions, pure and uncompromised, in its innermost structure."[22] Such an abstract statement of aesthetic value becomes extremely problematic the moment one tries to distinguish a specific work which promotes a "spurious harmony" from one which "embodies contradiction." In music harmony is a technical term which identifies the physical resonance existing among a set of tones. But in aesthetics, harmony is more relative; it refers to a sense of resolution or satisfactory closure experienced by the audience.[23] The oxymoronic "spurious harmony," whatever effect it may have on the general readership—and, as I have argued, this effect remains unclear to present day theorists—can appear to the alert critic as itself an ironic revelation of the presence of a contradiction. The very spuriousness of a harmony, while at one level it may be considered a mark of failure, at another level becomes an important source of understanding. Once we perceive contradiction in a text, whether we classify it as art or as commodity, the question of its relation to ideology again becomes open.

A classic instance of the difficulty of interpreting such a relation between a text and ideology is presented by the question of racism in *Heart of Darkness*. I invoke an example from what is nowadays considered high literature because it is only in such art that the issue is permitted to be alive: were I to quote a similar passage from a piece of 1899 journalism there would probably be no issue—we would all simply agree that the passage was racist. In *Heart of Darkness*, however, it will be generally acknowledged that the issue is complicated. When in the following passage Marlow describes his fireman, how much of Marlow's attitude toward Africans is conscious irony on the part of a morally sophisticated European narrator mocking the imperialist attitudes of his own class; how much the author, Conrad's, bitter irony at his character's expense; and how much simply Conrad's own voicing of turn-of-the-century European attitudes? And how are the answers to such a question to be determined?

> He was an improved specimen; he could fire up a vertical boiler. He was there below me, and, upon my word, to look at him was as edifying as seeing a dog in a parody of breeches and a feather hat, walking on his hind-legs. A few months of training had done for that really fine chap. He squinted at the steam-gauge and at the water-gauge with an evident effort of intrepidity—and he had filed teeth, too, the poor devil, and the wool of his pate shaved into queer patterns, and three ornamental scars on each of his cheeks. He ought to have been clapping his hands and stamping his feet on the bank, instead of which he was hard at work, a thrall to strange witchcraft, full of improving knowledge.[24]

We may find it more flattering to Conrad and to Marlow to see Marlow's own attitude as ironic, but that is a defensive interpretation which seeks to preserve the illusion of Conrad as an entirely conscious artist. It cannot be derived from an analysis of the text.[25] However, whatever the level of irony, at some level most critics see the passage as an instance of the language of racism. After having established this agreed upon meaning, some critics praise the work as ironic art while others, without disagreeing with the first group about the passage's meaning, attack it as racially demeaning. The pleasure of irony, as Freud describes it, comes from our relief that we do not have to perform the labor of rebuttal because the speaker, who seemed at first to be against us, is on our side.[26] That pleasure is aesthetic, and while it may be central to evaluation, it involves only the final and cognitively least important stage of interpretation.

If, as in the case of this Conrad passage, we cannot determine the degree of consciousness, are we then stymied aesthetically? For E. D. Hirsch the authorial consciousness in such a passage is essential to interpreting the meaning (as opposed to the significance) of the work.[27] Conceivably, Hirsch could argue that insofar as there is no way of determining the authorial consciousness, the meaning of the work is undeterminable and therefore the work is an artistic failure. On the other hand, as much recent deconstructive criticism has been arguing, most writing—perhaps all writing—is indeterminate in exactly this way.[28] The Conrad passage is not exceptional in its ambiguity; it is typical and its ambiguity is inevitable. The issue of the consciousness of contradiction is so frequently unresolvable that one has to see it, finally, as a value invoked, not to analyze or to understand social meaning, but in order to establish a basis for aesthetic judgment.

Just as the U.S. legal system allows some people to be considered innocent until proven guilty, the conventions of critical interpretation allow a canonic text to be considered conscious until proven unconscious. By this convention, Conrad's text is often allowed to speak to a late twentieth century consciousness of racism and, therefore, to show as thoroughly ironic. Similarly, when we find Jameson seeing Wuthering Heights as entailing "something like a dialectical self-consciousness of romance itself," we must remember that he does not attribute the self-consciousness or the critique to Bronte, but to the text as it is studied by the self-conscious critic.[29] If we look back at the film of Wuthering Heights we may wonder where this self-consciousness resides, for here is a "reading" of the novel as the epitome of romance. It is, therefore, the canonization of such a text that allows it to grow as criticism grows and that can turn one generation's enthusiasm into another's confusion, and this confusion can, in its turn, become critique. But this privileged tolerance, which has generated increasingly self-conscious readings of canonic literature over the last fifty years, does not easily stretch to popular literature. If a work is seen as pulp, it is generally assumed that its harmony is spurious and contradictions unself-reflective. The interpretive circle is a tight one: if Heart of Darkness were not self-conscious, we would not have canonized it, and its canonization proves its consciousness. And the circle can work the other way: if pulp were read as self-conscious, it would not be pulp. There is, of course, the argument that pulp, by its simplicities, proves it is not self-conscious; but as much of this book will show, that argument does not follow. Simplicity can be as rhetorically complex as the most ornate style. Works can have more or less complex meanings in Hirsch's sense of that term, but how they are read is a social phenomenon. It is the reading of the work, not the work itself, that determines whether the harmony is "spurious" or authentically negative, exposing contradiction.[30]

The Question of "How to Read"

In the case of popular fiction there is a temptation to avoid the massive interpretive difficulties such a rhetorical situation generates and to follow Radway and Bainbridge into empirical study of the readership. The question in such a case is not how does the text work rhetorically, but how did its readers respond to it? At first this seems like a fruitful and conclusive critical technique, but it has serious limitations. First, is the interpretion of the story by a common reader a function of the specific text, of the insensitive, blunt expectations of genre, or of the broader sociological forces that at a specific historical moment enforce certain responses? Second, as we shall see in the case of SF, even a cursory look at the readings of the interpretative community, as evidenced by occasional published explications and summaries, shows that the difficulties we find in the texts themselves recur almost exactly in the commentary on them. We shall have occasion to look at stories whose very precisely ambiguous texts do not generate equivalently ambiguous readings. In such cases, an empirical appeal to the interpretive community, far from giving us clues to the interpretation of the story, reveals a discrepancy between the text and its reception, a discrepancy which, given our current understanding of the reading process, will always present difficulties to a purely empirical interpretation.

Our recourse at this moment is not to empirical sociology. The text remains for us, as it does for Stanley Fish and Hans Robert Jauss, the most dependable source of understanding.[31] For the purposes of our present inquiry we need not challenge Jameson's interpretation of a canonic text, but we need to understand the presumptions that generate it, and we need to look to the consequences of such presumptions as they apply to our understanding of noncanonic art. Appreciation, whether in terms of conventional aesthetic unities or in terms of self-conscious negativity, depends upon participation in a civilized order and therefore always entails cooperation of some sort with a set of cultural values. In Jameson's case the value is self-critique. We can share these values and still acknowledge that they strongly condition how we see.

An aesthetic that praises consciousness and claims it for canonic art will not be entirely at a loss when it looks for value in noncanonic art. Cawelti, for instance, will find value in the self-critical play of formula in popular fiction. This defense tells us to look at such fiction in a special way, to renounce expectations that it will not satisfy, to find pleasure in a specific and limited repertory of formulae and modes of variation.[32] The appreciative reader finds such play subtle and delicate. A more recent critic has codified this approach even more carefully. Peter Rabinowitz argues that popular literature should be interpreted as a genre in itself with its own generic conventions. Rabinowitz sets up four "rules" by which our attention is focused: rules of notice, signification, configuration, and coherence.[33] The generic preconditions that these rules define for understanding a text are part of a social convention; they are not rules that the text itself enforces. Rabinowitz's rules account for what Culler calls "literary competence."[34] Such rules prevent us from making the mistake of the woman in Thurber's "The Macbeth Murder Case" who is sure that it is wrong to think that Macbeth killed Duncan because such a reading is too obvious. The rules teach us to "read a text in such a way that it becomes the 'best text possible'"(Rabinowitz, pp. 422–423).

Such an enterprise in appreciation is antithetical to the social mission for criticism proposed by Eagleton, who wants to see through the manifest meaning of the text to the latent, ideological issues that it is managing. "Criticism," he argues, "is not a passage from text to reader: its task is not to redouble the text's self-understanding, to collude with its object in a conspiracy of eloquence. Its task is to show the text as it cannot know itself, to manifest those conditions of its making (inscribed in its very letter) about which it is necessarily silent. It is not just that the text knows some things and not others; it is rather that its very self-knowledge is the construction of a self-oblivion" (Eagleton, p. 43). From this critical perspective, the generically conditioned rules that Rabinowitz poses show up as part of the "conspiracy of eloquence" by which the text operates. They help to naturalize the text by preventing the disruptive questions which would make us aware of what the text is hiding.

Something like Rabinowitz's rules for reading, because they have neatly shaped and pre-understood popular literature, have to a significant degree prevented detailed analysis of popular literature. Because it is presumed from the start that the problems of intention and consciousness, whose solutions demand attention to rhetorical detail, dignify only high literature, the critics of popular fiction have tended to discourage intensive textual analysis of the sort that has been typical of high literature for the last few decades. As Rabinowitz demonstrates, there is a kind of generic prejudgment that says that if you ask of pulp writing the kind of hard questions you normally address to high literature you will undermine the text; it will not stand up under such analysis. And because of this assumption, material that has received the label of popular literature is not usually subjected to the kinds of close analysis reserved for high literature. Instead, it is studied for its formulas, for its mythic structures, and for the way it broadly reflects culture. And behind these attitudes lies the general presumption that the experience of such literature is one of broad recognitions, not of textuality and detail, that it never "says" anything, that it simply manipulates generic expectations.

There are, of course, good reasons for some of these presumptions. They are a defense against a kind of criticism that laboriously summarizes a piece of hack work and claims that it consciously teaches us profound truths, that a writer of popular horror stories is a philosopher of "the nature of evil," or that a popular SF film has captured "the mystery of identity." Given such strainings at value, it is no wonder that many defenders of popular art resort to broader and more humble claims, such as Wolfe's praise of "prole vitality," Sontag's "openness," or Gans's practical usefulness.[35] But in fact, both the attackers and the defenders are subscribing to the same presumption about popular literature: that it is too hasty, awkward, and simple to bear up under close analysis.

The argument that popular writing will not bear close analysis is encouraged by the assumption that because much pulp writing is hasty, it is coarsegrained in the same way that pulp graphics are. Newspaper photographs and television pictures are capable of only a limited resolution, and therefore cannot be studied in close detail. The more the analyst focuses on such visual material, the more ambiguous it becomes. In Antonioni's film *Blow Up* the protagonist finds that the more carefully he examines his photographs, the more the grain of the negative itself becomes a factor and the less can he be sure of what he is seeing. As psychological studies have shown, if the subject of the composition is familiar enough (the face of Lincoln, for example) an extraordinarily small number of light and dark sections is capable of rendering a recognizable portrait.[36] In the cases of such coarse renderings, seeing is almost entirely a matter of recognizing. Only as the grain gets finer do the possibilities for genuinely original images emerge.

Such an analogy has an intuitive rightness to it and accounts for the easy and supposedly thoughtless way most popular literature is written and read. It neatly conforms to current appreciative attitudes toward formula.[37] In addition to helping us define the limits of expression and the limits beyond which analysis is futile, the analogy would justify our disregarding detail and our treating the work as a rough allusion to ideas and attitudes that exist outside of the work itself. Given the analogy, we would expect the critic to see past detail and contradiction in order to recognize the total picture, which is the only thing the composition is after. But just as a piece of fiction can give pleasure because it reinforces ideological presumptions, this critical analogy may satisfy us not because it fits our actual reading experience in any way but because it justifies the presuppositions we already hold about the inferiority of popular literature. We are again caught in what is by now a familiar hermeneutic circle: our illustrative analogy, which is in part intended to shed light on the reading process and thereby to set conditions on our method, is in large measure the construction of an aesthetic prejudice that causes us to look in such a way that we find what we want to see.

A little thought shows us that the analogy with pulp graphics is profoundly misleading. It may be true, as Rabinowitz argues, that "the flat unresonant prose of most paperback romances discourages us from the kind of attentive reading we usually apply to high art" (p. 426), but such surface dullness does not mean that the text is unexpressive. The linguistic detail of both high art and pulp is grammatical English. There are, we presume, differences in conscious control and complexity, but at the linguistic surface the pulp work is just as detailed as the serious novel. If I should quote a short sentence in isolation, no one can assure me that it is pulp or high art. Even "bad English" may show up in high art.[38] It may be truer to the actual nature of popular literature to invert the analogy to the visual picture: it is at the level of the linguistic detail that the text is precise; however clumsily used, the words are governed by the rules and requirements of English. They cannot be abridged and coarsened the way a newsprint picture can be. It is at the broadest level—plot, setting, character, theme, style—that popular literature will depend most on recognition of preexisting shapes, and therefore it is at this macro level that such literature is least able to break from ideological presumptions. Characters will be conventional, settings and plots formulaic, themes trite. But whether or not the writer is in artistic control, the linguistic details, however banal, are precise. Therefore, despite our instincts and prejudices, it is at this level, not at the higher levels, that we should begin any analysis of how such literature really works.

In the case of popular SF, a literature deeply conventional in its language, to devalue what I am calling the large elements—character, setting, plot, theme, style—would seem to be simply a way of robbing analysis of the few areas in which it has so far been at all successful. But as we look closely at how specific examples of this literature have been understood, we may have occasion to question the nature of this supposed success. Has the analysis of the large elements done anything more than recognize the presumptions of the investigator? Has it not simply assumed that the individual work fits into its generic form? As we go on we shall find in the field of SF and its criticism a strange paradox: there is almost no explicit argument among critics about how individual works are to be understood, and yet we can find cases in which various critics read specific texts in diametrically opposite ways. As an examination of these works will show, the feeling of general agreement that pervades the field cannot be caused by texts which say exactly what they mean, for the texts themselves are deeply ambiguous. The broad agreement we find among SF critics, so thorough that they often do not even recognize that they disagree, must come from *a way of reading*. The texts are seen as unambiguous and uncontradictory, not because they are precise and clear, but because the reading community has already settled on a certain ideology and certain kinds of attention, so that even when the details of a specific text are read in quite incompatible ways, no conflict is recognized. Like Rabinowitz and his rules, the SF community, as it will often tell outsiders, knows how to read SF. It has mastered the art of discovering what it considers "the best text possible."

The next question is, then, what happens if we violate the community's agreement and read the text in some other possible ways? An illuminating situation is then set up. Once we show that the text, which the readers and critics seem to find unproblematic, is susceptible to other meanings, then we have in part defined the community's ideology by showing the meanings that it has not allowed. And because the meaning that has not been allowed is inherent in the text, it is, at some level, experienced. It has been repressed. Popular literature now begins to look something like a dream. And on this by now familiar analogy, we might reverse the common attitude about popular literature's expressiveness and argue that just because popular literature is awkwardly written, it bears close analysis. Popular literature can serve a function more important and intricate than simply reinforcing assumptions and expectations. Like a dream, this naive and hasty literature can acknowledge confusions and mediate dilemmas. The very awkwardnesses that obviate close analysis according to the usual argument, carry the real message according to the argument I am here proposing. To be sure, there is what the high aesthetic tradition will identify as hackneyed, uninspired writing, but such "bad" writing, if looked at from the proper angle, can show up, in its evasions and assumptions, as deeply expressive.

Readers probably understand more than they can say. Popular literature is usually translated into fairly simple formulas by those who try to explain their enjoyment. But we should not thereby be misled into believing that the meaning of the work is merely limited to the reader's explanations of enjoyment. By taking these texts seriously and considering the readership's understanding of them in relation to the possibilities for meaning that we can point to in the text, we come to an understanding of larger meanings implicit in the genre itself, thereby gaining insight into the culture that values or condemns it.

SF, Genre, and Displacement

Such a process of interpreting the genre by interpreting the individual texts is, to be sure, a reversal of the usual understanding of the priority of the genre itself. No text exists before or outside of some sort of generic expectation. On the other hand, no text is entirely interpretable by reference to its genre. Conventionally, one way of treating interpretive difficulties presented by a text is to appeal to the genre as the agreed "horizon of expectation" that makes sense of any individual work.[39] Thus, if we are confused about how to respond to a thirties detective who casually slaps a woman, genre conventions will tell us that such behavior is generally understood as manly, not sadistic. When Mike Hammer slaps a woman, we seem to be so deep in accepted generic behavior that there are no questions asked. Of course, there is always the possibility that in the particular case the story may want us to rethink the basic generic conventions. Thus in Polanski's *Chinatown*, in what seems a clear case of generic self-reflection, when the hero, Gittes, knocks the heroine, Evelyn, around the house and then learns that he has completely misconstrued her situation, we can reevaluate his manliness.[40] But in many formulaic situations it is unclear whether such self-consciousness is in effect. The generic context can never be a conclusive determinant of meaning. E. D. Hirsch poses the concept of the "intrinsic genre" to which each work belongs and which, unlike the extrinsic genre which is only heuristic, determines the text's meaning.[41] Our problem with this concept is that it merely pushes the questions of interpretation back to the point at which each work defines its genre and we are saddled with the same interpretative dilemma with which we began.

The already complex relation of text to genre is made even more difficult in the case of SF. SF raises a special problem for generic interpretation because while, like other popular forms, it depends heavily on generic formulas, at the same time, unlike other popular forms, it usually poses itself as critical at some level of mere convention. One thing that makes SF special among the popular forms is that, on its surface at least, it subscribes to an ideology that sees value in the violation of genre. While other forms blatantly and happily anticipate the repetitions implicit in highly formulaic art, SF often explicitly advocates a new way of seeing. We should not be misled into thinking that simply by this claim SF escapes formula. On the contrary, by averting its eyes the way it does, it often falls more innocently into formula than might a more generically alert form like the detective story. But the formula is always rendered problematic in SF; there is always a question of how deeply or sophisticatedly one should read. One can never, as one sometimes can in the case of a detective story, readily define the particular story's relation to generic convention.

The striking conceptual displacement that identifies SF is largely abjured by most other popular genres, which lay a claim to refer to a world that is, or, if historical, that was.[42] Even the most realistic SF, at some point poses a reality different from what we imagine is or was. In that gesture the story sets up a discrepancy which is at its base ironic. It is this displacement and its consequent irony that Darko Suvin points to when he defines SF as the literature of cognitive estrangement.[43] And it is this estrangement, even if not put to cognitive purposes, that has been pointed to by numerous other critics in the now commonplace analysis of an opening line that throws the reader abruptly into a world which is strange but is nevertheless treated as familiar.[44] In its defensiveness most criticism of SF, even as it has promoted the idea that in significant ways the form of SF addresses the "New," the "future," the "unknown," the "alien,"—in sum what Suvin, drawing on Ernst Bloch, calls the *novum*—has shied away from recognizing the full rhetorical implications of this stance.[45] Displacement thwarts ordinary rhetorical expectations and leads ultimately to an inevitable interpretative ambiguity, which, I suggest, is important to the form's aesthetic.

Most discussions of this quality of displacement have been content to point to it without pursuing the interpretative problems created by the rhetorical figure. Like its master trope irony, displacement establishes a system involving a double consciousness that puts the reader in a position wherein a reading takes place with a sharp awareness of an alternate possibility. In pure irony the question usually is, how are we to evaluate what is being said? Are we to subscribe to the economics of eating children? or are we to see the practice as an outrage and to treat the whole system whose logic can lead to such "rational" conclusions as an atrocity? In the case of Swift's "A Modest Proposal" there is general agreement on how it is to be read: we know Swift's political and national sympathies, we know the broad conventions of eighteenth century culture, and we know the popularity of irony and satire in the period. But in SF we are explicitly denied these interpretive securities. The world that displaces the familiar one calls into question the values that we might take for granted otherwise. This interpretative dilemma is a particularly modern one, but it has its roots deep in the utopian tradition. Even in a work as didactically satirical as Thomas More's *Utopia* there are recurrent interpretive puzzles. How, for instance, are we to take Utopian foreign policy? Is it simply a continuation of the benign rationalism that has characterized the internal economics of the kingdom? a perversion of rationalism? a xenophobic imperialism disguised as humane self interest?[46]

In SF the interpretive problem can become acute. We can epitomize it by raising the problem of how to read the end of James Blish's "Surface Tension." In this story, one of a sequence of tales Blish wrote about "seeded" worlds, humanity has been miniaturized and given gills to enable it to survive under water. We watch scientific and religious controversies work themselves out in this underwater society. The little inhabitants finally invent a machine which will take them, safe in a dollop of water, over a patch of dry land to the next puddle where, on arriving, they rescue a maiden fleeing monstrous rotifers. The story ends with the humans and their allies, the paramecia, praising human brains and cooperation. In its dying words a paramecium declares, "Man has taught us this. There is nothing that knowledge . . . cannot do. With it, men . . . have crossed . . . have crossed space . . ." (Ellipses in original) At one level this passage simply explicates the allegorical significance of the story. There is nothing in this language itself that would cue us to suspect irony. But the image of tiny creatures struggling from one puddle to another might well lead us to raise some serious questions about the meaningfulness of spaceflight. The SF situation certainly has the potential for deflating the essentially positive language. And, once the question is raised, we may query whether the pulp formulas of killing the monster and falling in love with the rescued maiden should not, perhaps, be read ironically.

Even though the SF community might agree on the way "Surface Tension" should be read, we would still have to acknowledge that the text presents the reader with an interpretative choice. To read the story as an allegory of the glory of scientific development means disregarding the significance of the miniaturization. We might hold up in contrast to "Surface Tension" the example of Book I of *Gulliver's Travels* in which smallness of this very sort is used as a powerful satiric device. On the other hand, to read "Surface Tension" as a satire on human grandiosity means to disregard the seemingly uncritical praise of invention and exploration that is expressed throughout the story. If Swift can depend on our sense of scale to develop a satiric perspective, Blish—and any SF writer for that matter—relies on a genre in which such displacement is entirely capable of being used without satiric moral signification.

This rhetorical neutrality is, I would suggest, in part a significant historical development. The rhetorical security we may feel in eighteenth century satire is a function of ideology. What SF—and we might argue, the twentieth century—has done is challenge these ideological securities. As late as H. G. Wells's *The Food of the Gods* physical size almost invariably correlates with moral stature. But even in Wells's slightly earlier *The First Men in the Moon*, in Cavor's descriptions of the Selenites, we find passages, such as those describing Selenite education and the treatment of the unemployed, which, if viewed in the Swiftian tradition are clearly satiric, but if treated as SF offer radical, if tentative, reevaluations of human social institutions.[47] We cannot determine from the text what ideology is being supported and what criticized. The conventional rhetorical postures are tossed into limbo. Once the exotic otherworlds of SF become conventional, to make moral-physical equations of a Swiftian sort may be simply to fall back on a blind and narrow chauvinism. But, to follow the problem a step further, to abstain from such judgment is in itself to take a position with strong moral and ideological implications.

The difficulty that faces us in interpreting displacement is made particularly clear if we look to the interpretation of a critic who is intensely aware of the way genre operates. Mark Rose argues that it is the very violation of realistic genre conventions that begins to define SF and fantasy as a genre. He can show convincingly how stories are generically meaningful in relation to other stories. Rose himself reads "Surface Tension" "as an exercise in generic criticism." In contrast to the readings I have proposed, he sees it as "a comment on the giganticism of stories that pretend to significance because they are concerned with entire galaxies and other 'large' matters."[48] This certainly seems plausible, but, as my earlier discussion shows, this meaningfulness within one generic system does not answer questions about others. In the case of "Surface Tension" it becomes a question of which genres come into play. In relation to E. E. Smith, the Blish story dignifies smallness; in relation to Jonathan Swift, it mocks it.

We cannot settle the dilemma by appealing to Blish's own moral and literary position: he was both an enthusiastic promoter of serious SF and an ardent admirer of canonic literature. The story itself points to the difficulty we will have in interpretation: a paramecium, after posing the possibility that there may be other universes, declares that it lacks imagination and Lavon, the leader of the expedition, wonders whether it is being ironic and decides he cannot tell (p. 485). At the beginning of the story's prologue, a criticism of scientific initiative is posed when La Ventura declares "It takes arrogant pride to think that you can scatter men." Doctor Chatvieux's rebuttal that the accident to the seeding crew is probably not divine retribution since they are only one of a number of such crews, does not disqualify the charge of pride, only the possibility that the accident is divinely motivated. Blish himself seems to have been undecided about what note he wanted for the story's conclusion. As David Ketterer has pointed out, there are two versions of the end, both of which call into question a simple, heroic allegory.[49] The *Galaxy* magazine version questions Lavon's reiteration of Para's words ("We have crossed space") by having Shar express a doubt, "but have we?" This is an ambiguous remark which may suggest his sense of the larger dimensions of the universe and thereby deflate their accomplishment. Lavon's counter-response, "As far as I'm concerned, yes," is completely problematic, for it may express a blunt and egoistic ignorance or a heroic sense of perspective. In the version of the story in Blish's novel *The Seedling Stars* Lavon's asser-tive declaration is replaced by an even more enigmatic reaction: "Lavon was looking at the girl. He had no answer for Shar's question. It did not seem to be important." After spending all its energy on imagining a version of social progress based on a myth of heroic technology, the story here raises the pos-sibility that the project itself may be a secondary concern for human exis-tence. Even if we are able to determine what genre is relevant, there still remains the complex rhetorical issue of the particular story's relation to the particular genre—is it conforming to genre expectations or playing against them? Generic systems can open up interpretative possibilities, but they can never establish interpretive closure.

The SF readership has, so far as we can tell, not found the displacement in these stories problematic or contradictory. Far from causing us to doubt our sense of the interpretive problem, however, such easy acceptance confirms our sense that we are raising a significant issue. Genre identifies a quality in the interpretive community as much as in the text. We may consider genre in such formulaic work to be a set of agreed upon rationalizations by which a community limits the questions it will ask, thereby allowing itself to lay claim to understanding.[50] The strength of this ideological power of genre be-comes most apparent when we are able to see precisely the difficulties that are not experienced by the members of the interpretive community. In order to analyze this ideological quality, however, we do best to stay with a close examination of the text itself. The response of the readership, while fascinating, is extraordinarily imprecise and hard to document. Of course, it is only from the vantage of another ideology that we can perceive this blind-ness. Ultimately any critique of the ideology of the genre will reveal as much about the ideology of the critic as it does about that of the SF readership and authorship.

There is good reason to believe that the difficulties we find in the Blish text are part of a conscious rhetorical scheme to raise meaningful questions while still subscribing to a generally positive belief in technocratic develop-ment. As we shall see, however, though Blish himself may be an excep-tionally careful and thoughtful writer in the genre, the difficulties his text raises are typical of the genre. The rhetorical difficulties that complicate the micro level persist at the macro level, and at the thematic level a major crisis of meaning arises: the narratives themselves, though they often repeatedly insist on their meanings, work to distract conscious attention from more intrinsic latent fantasies that shape the text. As we move deeper into the genre we discover that rationality and science, while they draw attention to themselves and dominate the narratives, also serve to disguise the essential fantasies at work. Perhaps all narrative stretches a concealing net of rational interpretation over the latent interests of the unconscious, but SF, both because it is so insistently public, rational, and scientific on its surface, and because it is so naive about the complexities of narrative rhetoric, exposes the disjunction which more sophisticated and more psychologically acute genres, even if they too partake of the problem, are able to disguise.

The Myth of Genius:
The Fantasy of
Unpolitical Power

3

AT THE CORE OF MUCH SF FANTASY IS
an identification with power. We see it rendered in recent SF by an exalta-
tion in sheer size: empires war with ships the size of planets. A student once
explained to me that SF was interesting and important because the weapons
it imagined were capable of destroying a planet, even a universe. How trivial
the cowboy's six-shooter was by comparison. Such an observation is not entirely naive. In this chapter I explore how the genre indulges just such fantasies of giganticism. What I will primarily deal with, however, is not the
terms of the fantasy of power itself, but the way the fantasy manages the inevitable conflict between the powerful figure and the social world. The genius, who in classic American SF is almost always male, is an immensely rich
object of identification, but the more a story tries to make the fantasy seem
plausible, the more it has to engage in rationalizations. The process in turn
involves distortions and repressions that together constitute what I am calling the thought process of the genre. The genre may not solve social problems, but in the process of holding the problems it discovers at bay so as to
preserve a space in which the fantasy can play, the genre explores its ideology. Crucial stories in the history of SF, such as Cyril Kornbluth's "The
Little Black Bag" and "The Marching Morons" rise to acute insights which,
given the imperatives of the genre, they cannot make explicit. In such
stories we see the genre repressing the understanding it is enacting.

Ideas of Genius

At the start of Theodore Sturgeon's "Microcosmic God," (1941) the story
about a benign genius and an evil banker, the narrator announces: "Here is a
story about a man who had too much power, and a man who took too much,
but don't worry; I'm not going political on you." This last hasty assurance
seems to be intended to disclaim any criticism of the American social structure while the uses of power are discussed. It is this contradiction—an eager

THE MYTH OF GENIUS / 45

fantasy of power and a disclaimer of politics—that characterizes the technocratic vision, and it would not be too much to say that the resolution of this
contradiction, the achievement of nonpolitical power, is in some sense the
goal of all the mechanisms of SF. The fantasy about the genius focuses the
dilemma.

The figure of the heroic and irreplaceable genius is recurrent in American
SF.[1] In contrast to the "mad scientist" figure common to the horror story, the
genius of SF is usually seen as a benign figure. The figure is distinctive for
the way it tries to solve a deep problem in the ideology of capitalist democracy. The genius is promoted as an egalitarian ideal free of issues of class and
social background. At the same time it represents a fantasy of being transcen-
dentally superior to its world. Much of the earliest SF finds a simple fantasy
of the genius' success satisfying in itself. As later SF concentrates on imagining a technocratic utopia in more realistic detail, it takes pleasure in positing
a meritocracy in which the genius will earn the highest place.[2] However,
such fantasies about the genius lead inevitably back to political issues. Even
as they imagine a new social structure the stories are reluctant to admit the
political aspect; they repeatedly try to treat the difficulties the fantasy gives
rise to technocratically. As these stories try to enrich the original fantasy, the
contradiction inherent in the idea of the genius between a dream of egalitarian classlessness and one of brilliant, unique superiority begins to make itself
felt. By the fifties we find stories that by exploring the utopian fantasy discover a nightmare in which the qualities that should make the genius admirable have become the source of deep envy and lead to a confused and
vicious revenge against "ordinary" people. What is most curious about this
SF development is that neither the authors nor the audience seem aware of
the real nature of the dilemma they have discovered.

Let us from the start make it clear that the belief that, as Emerson put it,
"When Nature has work to be done, she creates a genius to do it," is not just
a naive fantasy limited to childish SF. The distinguished sociologist Robert
Nisbet can close a recent essay on genius with the aphorism, "One can somehow live with the evils [of the family, which, Nisbet argues, is necessary for
the development of individual geniuses], but civilization could hardly exist
without the nurturing ground of its geniuses."[3] It is telling for our understanding of the issue of genius that even this sentence, as it aspires to de-
clarative finality, perhaps unintentionally begins to raise questions. One has
to ask about the value of this thing called "civilization" which requires that
"one somehow live with evils" in order to sustain it. Why do we make this
sacrifice?

Science Fiction tends to agree with Emerson and Nisbet and to subscribe
enthusiastically and uncritically to the broad thesis that genius is crucial to

civilization. A typical formulation is the following from Clifford Simak's "Huddling Place" (1944). The "concept" being developed by a Martian genius is irreplaceable. As one character argues, it is "a concept . . . that we cannot do without. A concept that will remake the solar system, that will put mankind ahead a hundred thousand years in the space of two generations. A new direction of purpose that will aim toward a goal we heretofore had not suspected, had not even known existed. A brand new truth, you see. One that never before had occurred to anyone." Here, just as in the case of Nisbet's aphorism, the attempt to render a simple positive valuation of the genius involves itself in a set of antithetical questions. If the genius's idea is so essential, how did we do without it this long? If we do not know what it is, how do we know we cannot do without it? How can we know how far it will advance us without understanding it already?[4]

It is appropriate that such emphatic assertions of the social necessity of the genius should give rise to doubts and questions. After all, the promoters of the social need for genius are rarely disinterested thinkers. At the heart of their arguments is often a fantasy of self-congratulation: the thesis that civilization depends on its geniuses is a version of the assertion that the world needs *me*. At some point, however, this private, psychological aspect of the fantasy must come into conflict with the social issues by which the fantasy is publicly justified. In the case of pulp SF, the idea of genius, though superficially it seems compatible with the genre's vision of a utopian technocracy, will finally lead to difficult questions about the purpose of technology itself.

While the image of genius as socially useful has had strong currency in western culture for the last three centuries, it has not always been valued for the same reason.[5] For the Enlightenment it could be closely linked to the figure of the rational scientist: God said, "*Let Newton be*! and all was light." But fairly early in the Promethean mythology of the Romantics this essentially positive social idea was given an individual and tragic cast: the genius was a lonely, driven figure, alienated from social pleasures and the consolations available to more common humans. Such a line of thought can lead to a contempt for society and a celebration of the individuality of the genius. From this isolation can also develop the negative idea of the genius as an inquirer into forbidden knowledge and, therefore, society's plague. Shelley's *Frankenstein* remains the *locus classicus* of this negative vision. And other writers, such as Carlyle, can continue to promote the picture of the genius as a social hero, though from a moral and aesthetic perspective instead of the Enlightenment's rational one.

In the second half of the nineteenth century the debate about the social value of the genius is given a major new orientation by being associated with evolution. Francis Galton's *Hereditary Genius* (1869) begins a project, which continues to this day, to establish a purely biological meaning for the idea of genius. By the early part of this century this biological idea has been widely accepted as scientific and inspires a literature of the superhuman who is seen as a forerunner of the race to come. In the 1920s the work of Lewis Terman and his associates at Stanford gives the idea of biological genius more refined articulation by identifying it with a number, a score on an IQ test. Catherine Cox's *The Early Mental Traits of Three Hundred Geniuses* (1926) becomes the central text for this myth. If in recent years the close correlation of IQ and genius has been questioned and the idea of genius itself been criticized and replaced by such terms as "gifted person" or "eminence," nevertheless Cox's study remains a much honored model for the field.[6] In the popular mind the equation of IQ and genius became, and to a great extent remains, a commonplace.

I will not go into the complex issues of the IQ test and its potential mis-applications but simply observe that whatever simplifications and distortions of the nature of intellect this myth of IQ generates, it represents a significant gesture toward the democratization of human value. If, as was frequently assumed throughout the period we will be studying, IQ is mainly a genetic measure, any person can now find that he or she has inherited worth. In a world which still honors people for their ancestors' social rank and which grants wildly unequal opportunities to developing youth, the possibility that the genetic lottery will make one a genius, as proven by one's IQ, is liberating, even revolutionary. But if the genius transcends and disrupts conventional social categories, it also exists outside ordinary social values. Once genius is equated with IQ the term genius can be bestowed not for actual accomplishment and not for postures of martyred perseverance and dedication, as in Romantic Prometheanism, but for the mere promise contained in the potential of pure "intelligence."[7] Genius now denotes a person who is valued for genes without reference to anything he or she may have done, and without any reference to social goals.

In this situation, the "unrecognized genius" is not a paradox but a plausible adolescent situation. Many of the texts of popular SF at some level refer back to this aspect of the idea of genius, to a fantasy SF fans may well have about themselves. Reading SF is, for them, not simply a flexing of the mind; it is a participation in an elite society. In this way it may be an aesthetic experience of the sort that Pierre Bourdieu analizes in *Distinction*, whereby "taste" is a way people negotiate their "cultural capital" and mark out a secure place for themselves in a society that according to purely economic criteria would ignore them.[8] The essence of this self-declared elite subculture and its conception of itself is clearly defined in the speech given by E. E. Smith, Ph.D., the author of the very popular *Skylark* and *Lensman* series, in 1940 at the world SF conference, "Chicon":

> The casual reader does not understand science fiction, does not have sufficient imagination or depth and breadth of vision to grasp it, and hence does not like it. What brings us together and underlies this convention is a fundamental unity of mind. We are imaginative, with a tempered, analytical imaginativeness which fairy tales will not satisfy. We are critical. We are fastidious. We have a mental grasp and scope which do not find sufficient substance in stereotypes, in the cut and dried. Science fiction fans form a group unparalleled in history, in our close-knit although informal organization, in our strong likes and dislikes, in our partisanships and our loyalties. The necessity of possessing what I may call the science-fantasy mind does now and probably always will limit our number to a very small fraction of the total population. In these personal meetings, there is a depth of satisfaction, a height of fellowship which no one who has never experienced it can even partially understand.[9]

We should note here the qualities of abstract exclusion that mark for its practitioners this special imagination. Like other coterie aesthetics, the sign of superior taste is not any knowledge or accomplishment but simply the claim to find pleasure in what merely confuses and annoys ordinary people.

Ayn Rand

The SF subculture's sense of itself as exceptional and separate from ordinary people is essentially utopian and needs to be distinguished from the embittered and more purely exclusive version of genius, common enough in much neo-romantic art, and epitomized in the work of Ayn Rand.[10] For Rand only the individual genius has value, and genius proves itself only by upholding its possessor's radical and uncompromised individuality. Rand's society is inevitably and essentially debased; it is incapable of appreciating genius, and it oppresses that which it cannot understand. In *Anthem* (1938), the hero invents the electric light completely on his own, but his world, far from applauding his achievement, condemns him for heterodoxy.[11] In the end he escapes to the wilderness to build a world elsewhere. By failing to admire the genius' accomplishment, this society proves its unworthiness. For Rand genius is its own intrinsic justification.

In *The Fountainhead* (1943), Rand makes her hero an architect, rather than an inventor or even a scientist.[12] By doing so, she renders his relation to society particularly paradoxical. The scientists and inventors who populate SF can usually find justification in the actual working of the formulas or machines which they produce. In a sense, an inventor does not need an audience; the accomplishment speaks for itself. Architects, on the other hand, depend on patrons and on fashions. But in Rand's world architecture builds on absolute formal values. Rand is particularly contemptuous of anyone who attempts an art based on historical allusion. In rendering absolute that most social and historical of arts, Rand creates an impenetrable paradox at the heart of her idea of genius. The genius, whose creations are valuable to society but are also incomprehensible to it, must hate society and be attacked by it in turn.

Rand's genius' antagonistic relation to society is reflected at the level of personal relationships. *The Fountainhead* is extraordinary for its attempt to imagine an absolute individualism so pure that even the couple is a compromise. The hero, Roark, and his lover, Dominique, find that the only way they can prove each other worthy is by continually trying to destroy each other. Only the man who can withstand Dominique's most intense attacks is heroic enough, genius enough, to earn her love. And since Roark can only love a woman who is strong enough to destroy him, if he withstands her attack, he proves her inferior. With appalling consistency the lovers succeed in destroying each other's careers and rendering each other unhappy as proof of their mutual worthiness.

Ralph 124C 41+

Rand's monomaniacal heroes will not satisfy the utopian aspirations that animate early SF. If we go back to what is often considered the founding work of American SF, Hugo Gernsback's *Ralph 124C 41+* (1911), we can see in all its innocent clarity the fantasy of the genius as the key to a utopian vision of the technological future. At the core of the reverie about being a special genius is a very simple, insistent fantasy of power, which is evident in the opening words of the novel:

> As the vibrations died down in the laboratory the big man arose from the glass chair and viewed the complicated apparatus on the table. It was complete to the last detail. He glanced at the calendar. It was September 1st in the year 2660. Tomorrow was to be a big and busy day for him, for it was to witness the final phase of the three-year experiment.

He yawned and stretched himself to his full height, revealing a physique much larger than that of the average man of his times and approaching that of the huge Martians.

His physical superiority, however, was as nothing compared to his gigantic mind. He was *Ralph 124C 41+*, one of the greatest living scientists and *one of the ten men on the whole planet earth permitted to use the Plus sign after his name.* (emphases in original)[13]

The simplicity of the ideas behind this narrative is such that none of the terms here seems to present any problems: complication, completion, time, bigness, superior intelligence—they are all unquestioned and clearly positive. In the novel Ralph goes from triumph to triumph inventing various machines that make life easier and safer and that render him more beloved by a grateful planet.

The almost pastoral simplicity of this vision is reinforced at a number of levels. There is no trace of the problem of recognition that so torments Rand. This is a world in which all people get the respect owed them. Many of the inventions that constitute the marvels of the world of 2660 are Ralph's own. Those which are not are given careful attribution. For instance, we are told that the *Bacillatorium*, in which the human body is purged of harmful bacteria, was "invented in 2509 by the Swede 1A 299" (p. 59). Ralph, as we are told in the opening paragraphs, is allowed to use the plus sign; he is acknowledged as a genius by all. When he wants recognition, all he has to do is go to "the transmission room" where his televised image is sent out to the world, and where he can see and hear his adoring audience. Before the development of modern narrative cinema and the star system, Gernsback understands what it means to be the star of your own film. The only hint of internal conflict comes when the governor of the planet forbids Ralph to rescue his beloved because the adventure is dangerous and the planet cannot risk Ralph's genius. With little hesitation, Ralph disobeys, but he is also careful to send a message of apology to the governor.

In Gernsback's fantasy all inventions conspire to aid their inventor. When Fernand, rejected by Ralph's beloved, Alice, abducts her and flees, Ralph is able to follow him: since he invented the rocket, he knows exactly its capabilities. When Ralph catches up with Fernand, he discovers Alice has been rekidnapped by Llysanorh', a Martian who, prevented by law from marrying a human, has decided that if he cannot have her, no one will. Though Llysanorh' kills Alice, the novel ends happily because there exist techniques, which Ralph himself developed, for restoring the dead to life.

Envy and desire, which in the conventional gothic novel are sources of disruption, are carefully kept separate from the idea of genius and lodged in the two amorous villains, Fernand and Llysanorh'. And even these figures are softened in their villainy. Fernand takes time in his flight with Alice to help a crippled flying ship (it turns out that Llysanorh' is in the ship). And the Martian, in killing Alice as he himself dies, is performing an act that in some traditions is considered highly honorable.[14] Such a love-death may not please Alice, but it is still probably to be read as a sign of love, however obsessive and misguided. There is no real villainy in this future world. Alice's beauty, which cannot be shared and which causes men, both human and Martian, to be competitive, is the only source of genuine conflict.

Ralph 124C 41+ is a truly extraordinary work for its success at fulfilling the fantasy of an utterly benign rational intellect. It must pay for that success by a pervasive childishness, the main sign of which is the governor's parental protectiveness of Ralph, the treasured and irreplaceable child. Ralph's disobedience, while a gesture toward adult independence, never leads to any sort of fallen knowledge. We can imagine a future for Ralph and Alice in which he continues to impress her with his toys. Gernsback's strange little novel is a promising beginning for a hopeful genre that will attempt to deepen the picture of the benign genius and render it more plausible while still retaining the overwhelmingly positive and utopian values that Gernsback has managed to attach to it. In the abstract, such a development sounds simple, but in fact it is impossible. With an almost uncanny sense of limits, Gernsback has gone to the exact edge of the happy myth without showing the complications that will arise as one thinks further. Only in the few moments of unlikely plot motivation does one sense Gernsback's awareness of problems which he would rather not undertake. At the very beginning Ralph meets Alice because of a mistake by a telephone operator. There seems to be no other way that Gernsback can introduce eroticism into the almost totally mechanical world that Ralph controls. And Llysanorh' can be kept honorable only by elaborate contortion: "He had been hopelessly, pitifully in love with Alice. It was easy to see that, having, *probably quite by accident*, intercepted Fernand's letter to Paul telling of his plans, he had in a moment of desperation, born of despair, determined to carry her off himself" (p. 112, emphasis added). How one accidentally intercepts a letter from someone one hardly knows to someone one doesn't know at all is a mystery that will not bear examination. Again, as in the meeting between Ralph and Alice, motive must be erased and the sequence of events must be attributed to elaborate chance.

Oedipal Issues: "Huddling Place"

As I have suggested, part of the original value of the myth of genius' for the SF community lay in its revision of conventional social hierarchies. If you are a genius, it does not matter what class you were born in, or how rich you are, or what education you have had. But while the biological idea of genius challenges these more traditional classifications of human worth, it is still at its core a myth of privilege. And the reintroduction of hierarchy in the valuing of IQ raises problems. While one can be proud of being a genius, there is now the worry that, since one has inherited genius, there is no reason to feel proud of one's own accomplishment; as in other forms of social prestige, one's claim to genius is to a certain extent dependent on one's ability to prove the quality of one's parentage. And yet, at the same time, while IQ is often seen as an absolute value, the narrative demands that the genius somehow enact his or her superiority. The trick is to be both an aristocrat and self-made.

This double motive is succinctly rendered in a passage in John W. Campbell's "Twilight" in which Sen Kenlin, the man from three thousand years into the future, who like Ralph has been the inventor of a technology that has totally shaped the future, tells who he is. Paradoxically, the genius here is both heir and patriarch: [15]

> "I was an experimenter," [Sen Kenlin] went on. "Science, as I have said. My father was a scientist, too, but in human genetics. I myself am an experiment. He proved his point, and all the world followed suit. I was the first of the new race (p. 42).

What is significant about Sen Kenlin's explanation of his genealogy is that it is ambiguous: is he the son of a genius, or is he "an experiment"? In one sense he has no father; as the first of the new race, he is himself the father of the "new race." In another sense, not only he but the whole race is beholden to his father.

Campbell's story accepts the genetic idea of genius, but at the same time gives voice to a desire to be self-made, to be independent of parental inheritance. In part this second motive may owe something not to the demand that one be judged by one's accomplishments but to an adolescent psychology which wants to reject parental influence. At this level the SF hero partakes of the developmental issue that seems to motivate Rand's heroes. Roark is an orphan, and it is part of his integrity never to believe he is owed anything at all by right of birth. The insistence that he earn whatever he gets repeatedly gives him dignity denied those other "smart" people who fall back on their "inheritance."

A striking rendering of the Oedipal difficulties of the hereditary genius occurs in Simak's "Huddling Place," from which I quoted at the beginning of this chapter. This story begins with Jerome Webster, the descendant of a line of brilliant men and the world's greatest specialist on the Martian brain, burying his father. Like Ralph and Sen Kenlin, Webster is acknowledged as a great and irreplaceable scientist. His book on Martian physiology is praised a number of times, and a Martian specialist says that no one else could have written it. The world admires him, but the story finds that Webster cannot enjoy his mastery. Webster discovers that, like his father, he has what the story terms "agoraphobia" and is terrified of leaving the family house. When he learns that he is the only person in the world who can save his dying friend, the Martian philosopher Juwain whose "concept" is so essential to the world's future, Webster finds that he is afraid to take the trip to Mars.

In this fantasy of the dilemma of the good genius, the inhibiting "agoraphobia" is less a psychotic state than an overwhelming sense of class affiliation and a dread of other classes. And this narrow class identification is, in its turn, a debilitating identification with the father and the genealogical tradition. The aristocracy of intellect which defines the genius here is imagined in terms of the conventional formulas of class aristocracy—a butler, a large house, brandy in the study—and Webster finds himself trapped in his father's house.

The story reads very much like a dream. As we have already observed, the value of Juwain's "concept" is overdetermined. Webster himself is made irreplaceable: no one else in the world can save Juwain. And the "agoraphobia" is an irresistible attachment to the imagery of the family. When at the end Webster finally resolves to leave despite his fears, he is foiled because Jenkins, the robot butler who also served his father, has sent away the ship that was to take Webster to Mars. As Jenkins puts it, "I finally made them understand you could not possibly want to go to Mars." The verb *want* here catches a crucial dilemma in the fantasy of being a genius: the genius is the one who can do whatever he "wants," but there is a conflict of wants. He can want to leave home, which would be to surpass his father, and he can want to stay home, which is to admit how thoroughly he is his father's son. By acting on Webster's deepest fears, the robot sabotages his genius. Whereas Sen Kenlin obscures the parental issue to make himself doubly important, Webster finds himself overwhelmed by his parental influence. The son of a genius is finally no more than the son of a genius.

"Microcosmic God"

Theodore Sturgeon's "Microcosmic God" (1941) finds itself sucked into the social contradictions that Gernsback avoided in his depiction of the innocent genius. Sturgeon tells about a genius, James Kidder, who, after some brilliant inventions of his own, increases his output by developing a race of tiny, intelligent creatures, "Neoterics," He keeps the Neoterics in a large, complex laboratory and makes them evolve rapidly. By making them solve catastrophic crises that he, the "god" of their tiny world, originates, he forces them to invent materials and techniques that he then offers to the human world. Kidder's banker, Conant, who begins as an ally, later tries to use Kidder's invention, a power transmitter, to take over the United States government. When Kidder tries to stop him, Conant attacks Kidder's island with an armed force. Kidder and his Neoterics finally defeat Conant and, with an engineer named Johansen, retreat from the world beneath an impenetrable dome. The story ends with an anxiety, familiar from horror tales, about what may happen when the Neoterics decide to leave their dome.

The language describing Kidder at the beginning of the story places us squarely in the Gernsback tradition; we note that a certain care is taken to distinguish this tradition of genius from other, less optimistic ones:

> Kidder was quite a guy. He was a scientist and he lived on a small island off the New England coast all by himself. He wasn't the dwarfed little gnome of a mad scientist you read about. His hobby wasn't personal profit, and he wasn't a megalomaniac with a Russian name and no scruples. He wasn't insidious, and he wasn't even particularly subversive. He kept his hair cut and his nails clean and lived and thought like a reasonable human being. He was slightly on the baby-faced side; he was inclined to be a hermit; he was short and plump and—brilliant. His specialty was biochemistry, and he was always called *Mr.* Kidder. Not "Dr." Not "Professor." Just Mr. Kidder (p. 115).

This paragraph, with its voice of cheerful, colloquial admiration—"quite a guy"—encourages us to accept Kidder as just a brilliant kid. But, having assured us of Kidder's healthy conventionality, the story in the very next paragraph begins to tilt toward seeing Kidder as neurotic and dangerous. The third paragraph of the story states, "He was an odd sort of apple and always had been." It is possible to read this as harmless, but later, after a long list of his brilliant inventions and a description of the Neoterics, we will hear, "Lord, how he hated *people!*" (p. 130, emphasis in original) When Conant argues that "the masses of people who are now paying exorbitant power bills" will benefit from Kidder's invention of a power transmitter, Kidder exclaims, "I hate the masses!" (p. 131) Such a development into neurosis, certainly unexpected given the opening description—"inclined to be a hermit" has become "I hate the masses!"—is generated, not by the oedipal issues that haunt Webster, but by the inadequacy of the initial image of the brilliant boy as a social hero. If Kidder is successful as an inventor, he will be powerful and his actions will have consequences.

It is in its depiction of Kidder as the god of the Neoterics that the story works itself into the most compromised view of him. If his childish mind invents for the sheer pleasure of invention, Kidder is also capable of inflicting the most calculated atrocities on his Neoterics to keep them obedient and to motivate them to invent. And yet the sinister quality of this sadistic imitation of natural selection is almost entirely overwhelmed by the admiration for the ingenuity of the "toy," the miniaturization of which invites the reader to dismiss the moral dilemmas it raises as inconsequential. Here is a passage describing Kidder at work, and while there are moments, as in the second sentence, that imply that Kidder is cruel and demonic, the prose continues to ring of thorough admiration:

> They were completely in Kidder's power. Earth's normal atmosphere would poison them, as he took care to demonstrate to every fourth generation. They would make no attempt to escape from him. They would live their lives and progress and make their little trial-and-error experiments hundreds of times faster than man did. They had the edge on man, for they had Kidder to guide them. It took man six thousand years really to discover science, three hundred to put it to work. It took Kidder's creatures two hundred days to equal man's mental attainments. And from then on—Kidder's spasmodic output made the late, great Tom Edison look like a home handicrafter (pp. 121–122).

In its muted way, such a passage renders a complicated vision which is never quite brought to full consciousness. The delight in mastery, a severe domination, a pride in his own and his creation's accomplishments, a deep-set competitiveness with previous genius—we are drifting into an area of ambiguities and of contradictions that Ralph could never imagine, much less begin to acknowledge.

Sturgeon's style is rhapsodic and spontaneous. It cannot resist fantasies of success of any sort. Typical of the almost free-associational quality of the fantasy is the long line of gratuitous inventions the story attributes to Kidder. At one point, midway through the description of Kidder's developing the Neoterics, the story momentarily sidetracks itself and considers the invention of "a colorless elixir that made sleep the unnecessary and avoidable waster of time it should be" (p. 120). It is the detail of "colorless" that is most tellingly gratuitous here. Often the story contradicts itself as it accumulates victories. Thus, after a page telling us how Kidder put together a fortune from various inventions, the story turns and asserts that Kidder has absolutely no interest in money. Or the genius can follow contradictory methods: "He made mistakes, but only one of a kind, and later, only one of a species. He spent so many hours at his microscope that he had to quit work for two days to get rid of a hallucination that his heart was pumping his own blood through the mike. He did nothing by trial and error because he disapproved of the method as sloppy" (p. 119). After praising Kidder's efficient trial and error method, the story seems to rethink the matter and decides that a real genius wouldn't make any errors at all.

This same spontaneous admiration for all aspects of genius leads the story to treat Conant's machinations with the same intense interest it gives to Kidder. Though Conant seems to have been introduced as simply the villainous foil for the innocent Kidder, the dynamics of the opposition lead to developments and rationalizations that do not seem part of the original intention. Just as a Sherlock Holmes must finally find a Moriarity who is his match, or a Roark must find a Dominique, the competitive logic of the genius fantasy causes the antagonist to develop until Conant is almost Kidder's equal. At first the story can use Conant as a simple mechanism to rescue Kidder from responsibility. Conant, the agent of social, economic power, is the villain who will corrupt the world of Kidder's playful brilliance: social problems are caused by bankers, not inventors. In Ralph's world one can be innocently brilliant, but in Kidder's world inattention to the uses of inventions will lead to catastrophe.

The problem such an innocent fantasy creates for the narrative is revealed by an awkwardness at the point in the story when Kidder seems the innocent dupe of the conniving Conant. When Conant goes into a fiendish monologue about what a "crazy fool" Kidder is, we are abruptly told that much earlier, before he has been given any reason to distrust Conant, Kidder has installed a listening device so that he can monitor Conant. Suddenly Kidder is granted a retrospective caginess that is hardly appropriate to his boyish innocence. We have here a glimpse of the contradiction involved in the very idea of innocent genius.

When, about midpoint, the story takes time to describe Conant, it draws our attention to the parallels between him and Kidder:

> Conant's mind was similar to Kidder's in that its approach to any problem was along the shortest distance between any two points, regardless of whether that approach was along the line of most or least resistance. His rise to the bank presidency was a history of ruthless moves whose only justification was that they got him what he wanted (p. 124).

And a bit later we learn:

> Conant and money were like Kidder and knowledge. Conant's pyramided enterprises were to him what the Neoterics were to Kidder.

Each had made his private world; each used it for his instruction and profit. Kidder, though, disturbed nobody but his Neoterics. Even so, Conant was not wholly villainous. He was a shrewd man, and had discovered early the value of pleasing people. No man can rob successfully over a period of years without pleasing the people he robs (p. 125).

These comparisons do not clarify; they point to a deep confusion about the admiration of power and genius. Like General Turgison, in Stanley Kubrick's *Doctor Strangelove*, who lets his chauvinistic raptures betray him into a fantasy of destroying the world, this story repeatedly lures itself into enthusiasms that it then finds uncomfortable. The problem of the relation between Kidder and his Neoterics is clearly not as simple or as moral as the second of these passages wants to claim. The argument that Conant is not wholly villainous because he pleases the people he robs suggests a much more complicated idea of social usefulness than the simple terms of the story will allow.

At one level we are observing a confusion arising from the overlap of two aspects of capitalism. The entreprenurial banker and the inventor, both essential to the mythography of technological development, represent different phases of it. The story evades the contradiction involved in admiring both of them by seeing Kidder as a social hero and Conant as a selfish villain. The good-evil dichotomy solves at the narrative level what is a moral puzzle: as Fredric Jameson puts it, how can my enemy "be thought of as being *evil* (that is, as other than myself and marked by some absolute difference), when what is responsible for his being so characterized is quite simply the *identity* of his own conduct with mine."[16] This sort of split, as Jameson argues, is characteristic of romance. The romance narrative, which SF is often considered, with its absolute oppositions based on identity, serves an important ideological function by validating on moral grounds an antipathy whose real origin is political. After all, though Sturgeon's story seems to subscribe to the idea that Conant is a social leech while Kidder is a producer, at another level, hidden from all the world, the genius, secretly manipulating and robbing his Neoterics, is just as parasitical as the banker.

The confusion about values implied by the parallels between Kidder and Conant derives from a confusion about the nature of brilliance itself. In the first passage quoted on Conant, the story claims that directness characterizes the intellects of both men. But no sooner has the claim been made of Conant than we read, "Like an over-efficient general, he would never vanquish an enemy through sheer force of numbers alone. He would also skillfully flank his enemy, not on one side, but on both. Innocent bystanders were creatures deserving no consideration" (pp. 124–125). And then follows a paragraph describing in lengthy and admiring detail how in order to buy a thousand

acre property, Conant ruins the owner's airport and then, to prevent the revenge of the wealthy man, takes over his bank at a loss and causes it to fold.
Far from being direct, Conant is elaborate and redundant, a creature of rage
and obsession.

We are now in a position to see how much the narrative excess of the story
does more than advance the plot: it allows it to move over a set of fantasies
that reveal deep contradictions. Much as it hates the conventional figure of
the parasitical banker, the story has to admire his accomplishment and his
suavity. Its dream of a clean, "direct" intellect leads it to praise redundancy
and psychological motive. And, try as it will to keep power innocent, it finds
that it always has to patch in ways that deny the innocence. The childish
dream of having one's own miniature world, far from leading to the moral
inconsequence suggested by the claim that Kidder "disturbed nobody but
his Neoterics," brings us closer to large questions about the order of the universe, and certainly makes us ask if the genius can be tolerated as simply
brilliant.

For all its enthusiasm for the genius and his benefits to society, the story
also imagines a mode of invention that has absolutely no need for the individual genius. The Neoterics invent marvelously, not by depending on the
flashes of individual geniuses, but by evolving a whole race capable of such
invention. While the story will explicitly claim that what distinguishes Neo-
teric civilization is its evolutionary speed (that is, its biological difference
from humanity), at a deep and probably unconscious level the story has for-
mulated a social alternative to Kidder's capitalism. Where he is an individual
entrepreneur, they are a collective society. Where he does what he wants,
they do what they are told. Where he invents for pleasure, they invent from
fear. Where he pleases only himself, they institute an absolute rule of social
need. Kidder's exclamation "I hate the masses" is the exact antithesis of the
spirit that the Neoterics must enforce to insure that no eccentric individual
endangers them. In the Neoterics' world invention is necessary for survival.
From the little we know about them, they live under extreme psychological
pressure. In the human world, by contrast, the progress the genius offers is
gratuitous and haphazard. Invention is free play, the benefits to society are
essentially a luxury, and all inventions are more or less equal: a better paint
remover gets as much credit as an energy transmitter. The Neoterics represent, if you will, a materialist reading of progress which calls into doubt the
values of Kidder's world. After all, though Kidder's inventions make a profit,
society seems quite able to get along without them. If one strain of the myth
of genius celebrates the biology that has bred the Sen Kenlin or the Jerome
Webster, here is another which admires not the individual genius, but the
species. The confusion as to whether we should admire Kidder's genius or

the racial accomplishment of the Neoterics is at the center of the story, and the story does not resolve the issue.

The deep ambiguity in Sturgeon's story, whether conscious or not, enacts a crucial dilemma. While it cannot give up the idea of genius—after all, Kidder, with his little world, is much like a young SF author—the story also acknowledges the socially destructive aspect of the genius. By using the psychological device of "splitting" the character into Kidder and Conant, the author manages to give the destructive aspect play without destroying the idealization. In the fantasy of the neoterics, the story invents a form of social progress that escapes the dilemma of the genius, but the story also abstains from pursuing the social implications of this idea. In the fantasy of the Neoterics we can see hints of an idea that neither American SF enthusiasts nor scientists themselves have much encouraged: that progress is a cultural (rather than individual) product. Recently one can find this idea argued explicitly by Paul Feyerabend in "Creativity—A Dangerous Myth" and, in a slightly different form, by Robert Weisberg in *Creativity: Genius and Other Myths*.[17] I do not mean to suggest that Sturgeon's story makes such an argument, but that at some level it is aware of it. In such a story one observes a process of cultural (rather than individual) thought.

"The Little Black Bag" and "The Marching Morons"

The dilemma posed by the attempt to imagine the genius reaches a crisis in two stories written by Cyril Kornbluth, "The Little Black Bag" (1950) and "The Marching Morons" (1951).[18] In these stories Kornbluth poses a future in which the general intelligence of the human species has dropped significantly and a fake technology is maintained by the enormous effort of the "supernormal" minority. "The Little Black Bag" tells the story of a doctor's bag from this future filled with moron-proof tools which will cure any illness, which slips back into our own time and changes the lives of an alcoholic doctor and an ambitious adolescent street urchin. "The Marching Morons" elaborates much more fully the original idea about the degeneration of intelligence and the way the supernormals sustain civilization. A man from our own time, "Honest John" Barlow, is awakened in the future and, using the skills he learned in the Evanston real estate market and from the Nazis, he teaches the supernormals how to exterminate the morons. The atrocities that these stories confusedly sanction can be rationalized as "black comedy," but as we study them further we find that the humor conceals the contradiction we see elsewhere in the idealized figure of the genius. Kornbluth seems to

reject the egalitarian aspiration of genius, and he ends up defending a paradoxical vision in which the genius is at the same time both master and victim.

Kornbluth puts genes at the very heart of his myth of genius. The future
as it is envisioned in these stories is shaped as it is not because of any social
or technological imperative but because of a fluke in natural selection. As
one of the "supernormals" of the future tells "Honest John" Barlow, "While
you and your kind were being prudent and foresighted and not having children, the migrant workers, slum dwellers and tenant farmers were shiftlessly and short-sightedly having children—breeding, breeding. My God,
how they bred!" (p. 149). We learn later that the average IQ of the morons,
who constitute more than 99.9 percent of the future population, is 45. It is a
part of this easy snobbery that the morons are identified throughout by their
accented speech, as if standard English were a genetic function.

It is telling that Kornbluth's fantasy seemed so natural when it was written
and that, as far as I can determine, no one objected in print to the politics of
these two stories until their ideology and science were strongly criticized by
D. West in a 1981 essay, "The Right Sort of People."[19] Since then, Malcolm
Edwards has defended the stories—unconvincingly to my mind—as a de-
spairing criticism of the brutality of the present.[20] Even more recently,
William Sims Bainbridge, enthusiastic about the value of SF for its "ideas,"
seems able to read "The Marching Morons" without irony as a story which
"dares to speak openly of this unmentionable but critical problem."[21]

At one level Kornbluth has attempted to demystify the conception of genius he has inherited by subordinating social-political issues to material and
biological fact. The future is the way it is simply because of the biology of
intelligence. And looked at quickly, Kornbluth's reading of the degeneracy of
the future looks like a commonplace of SF. But the major antecedents of this
idea, such as Wells's *The Time Machine* or Campbell's "Twilight," attribute
the decline, not to the simple overbreeding of inferior stock, but to the more
dialectical, though still problematic, reason that evolutionary success breeds
weakness and dullness. By subscribing to a positivist commonplace and to
the basic SF faith in genius, Kornbluth has concealed the social dialectic.

No sooner has the social been denied, than it is reintroduced, though now
as a paradox that is never recognized as such. The future world of "The Marching Morons" is a spectacular parody of the SF future, a sort of Disneyland
filled with the illusions of power and speed, but created by quite ordinary,
contemporary technology. What look like rockets are just fancy airplanes.
Car speedometers say 200 kph, but the cars travel at an easy 25 kph. Clearly
Kornbluth is satirizing a sort of singleminded SF enthusiasm for the iconography of technology and perhaps attacking—though, as we shall see, this to-
nality is unclear—the ideals of a technocratic utopia. But the condescension

of the satire distracts us from the dynamics of the enthusiasm: the morons are being deceived by the supernormals. It is a paradox rather like Groucho Marx' country club which would prove itself unworthy of him by admitting him. What is initially pictured as a biological tragedy becomes a lament that the privileged are not more privileged than they are. The story complains that the morons are in control, and yet the morons are blamed for being taken in by the fraudulent technology manufactured by the supernormals.

Such a situation might be defended by the same reasoning used by the automobile producer who claims to give the public "junk" because that is what the public wants. But magnates and performers who profit from their audience's gullibility usually feel satisfied with the situation they find themselves in; they happily derive profits from the foolishness of others. Kornbluth's supernormals show no such sense of satisfaction. When the morons happily sit through grotesque propaganda films against having children and seem apparently uninfluenced by the message, it is taken as a further sign of their unworthiness—as if it were the consumer's moral and intellectual duty to be manipulated by an advertisement. The supernormals in Kornbluth's future add a further twist to this situation by seeing the state of affairs as an instance of enormous injustice. While they impose an illusion on the morons, they see themselves as the victims because they feel if they break the illusion "civilization" will collapse. Such a sense of injustice is perhaps not uncommon, but it needs to be examined. John Rawls can pose as a model of justice a situation in which better endowed people support the more poorly endowed.[22] Kornbluth's two stories put us in an inverted version of Nisbet's civilization which depends on its geniuses. Kornbluth with a neat and acrobatic logic is able to create a world in which the geniuses are entirely in control but are also the victims. The morons are stupid, helpless tyrants. By inversion, in "The Little Black Bag" the social ambition of the disadvantaged is seen as corrupt.

If at one level Kornbluth's stories seem to be asking large social questions about the future of humanity and of civilization, at another level they are simply transposing the familiar riddles of the genius from the individual to the group. By a circuitous route, we are back to a system of social discrimination that is thoroughly familiar. All aristocracies rationalize their ascendancy by an appeal to merit, and all tell tales which show why they are superior. Here in Kornbluth, the merit is simply IQ. The conventional class distinctions are never far from the story's consciousness. Honest John suspects that "You and the rest of the aristocrats live in luxury on the sweat of these oppressed slaves" (p. 148). In *The Time Machine* such an hypothesis leads to a rethinking of the dialectics of domination. Here in "The Marching Morons" the surprise is not that Honest John, who has all along been a happy victim of the stereotypes of SF, is wrong, but that he is right and only has the values reversed. Tinny-Peete, his supernormal guide, replies, "The actual truth is that the millions of workers live in luxury on the sweat of a handful of aristocrats" (p. 148). "Aristocrats" and "workers"—the visions may differ about which is the productive class, but they agree entirely on the appropriateness of the class language and division. Once we learn that it is the aristocrats who are productive, the story simply attacks the morons.

Having set up this conventional opposition and inverted it, the stories then undergo some easy transformations. The "millions of workers" who are the descendants of the "migrant workers, slum dwellers, and tenant farmers" who were "shiftlessly and shortsightedly having children" get no credit for their evolutionary success. They are even demoted below the human. When Barlow is informed that "the just-average, they'll-get-along majority took over the population," he asks, "But who are *you* people?" The answer is, "Just people—real people" (p. 150). By a strangely democratic logic, Tinny-Peete can argue that there are only three million "real people" and five billion morons, "so we are their slaves."

Such a system in which the mere level of a person's IQ is sufficient to categorize him or her would, one might expect, be very neat. But there are in both stories anomalous figures, Angie in "the Little Black Bag," and Honest John Barlow in "The Marching Morons," who will not fit into either the moron or supernormal categories. Honest John, a sleazy real estate broker from twentieth-century Evanston, is as enthusiastic as any moron about the fake "rockets" and streamlined cars he finds in the future, but he is clearly not a moron. He is repulsed by the morons' games and advertisements. Although Angie has the poor, ethnic background associated with the morons, she is clearly able to take advantage of opportunity in a way no moron could. If allowed their freedom, these two outlaws would, by their very being, destroy Kornbluth's system, so he seeks revenge on them by invoking a moral system to punish them for violating the genetic one, thus ending the story.

Barlow is the more difficult character to understand. Insofar as he is crude, aggressive, selfish, and an offense to all the aesthetic and moral values of the supernormals, he is the object of Kornbluth's satire. Yet he is also valued as a reservoir of "precious vicious self-interest." And his solution to "The Problem" of the domination of the morons is to imitate Hitler—to commit genocide. It is unclear as to how we are to read this "solution." Certainly it must be intended as a piece of cynical dark humor, but the humor indulges its anger in ways that make one wonder whether the unthinkable solution may not also be a wished one. Throughout "The Little Black Bag" there are ominous references to "crossing that bridge," by which is meant somehow exterminating the morons. And the seemingly admirable supernormals play a totally contradictory game. On the one hand they complain that they are trapped by their own feelings of responsibility for the well-being of the morons and their civilization. On the other hand they claim that the only reason they have not simply left the morons to their own self-destruction is the problem of disposing of so many corpses. In "The Marching Morons," Barlow's "genius" is unhampered by moral scruples and, from his experience as a shyster selling worthless real estate, he also learned how to manipulate people. Given the history and traditions of SF, one has ultimately to see such double-edged contempt as a form of self-hatred on the part of the genre.[23]

"The Marching Morons" ends by assuming a moral attitude, but this closing does not resolve the dilemma that has been posed. While the outcome renders a clear judgment on Barlow, it seems to free the supernormals from guilt. The morons are sent off into space, and the last person to go is Barlow who thought he had bargained for great rewards for setting up the extermination scheme. The story closes:

> Lying twisted and broken under the acceleration, Barlow realized that some things had not changed, that Jack Ketch was never asked to dinner however many shillings you paid him to do your dirty work, that murder will out, that crime pays only temporarily.
> The last thing he learned was that death is the end of pain (p. 163).

The comment "that some things had not changed" repeats the opening line of the story. There it referred to the craft of pottery. In the end it seems to refer either to an unchanging justice that finally catches up with Barlow, or more cynically, to the ability of even admirable people to finagle their consciences—to accept the dirty work of people they despise and yet continue to despise them. But the moral judgment is selective. Just as the supernormals are the creators of the contemptible technological culture, they are also the perpetrators of a colossal murder, for which Barlow is the scapegoat. Yet, except for the one who "couldn't live with his conscience" and commits suicide, the supernormals go unpunished and unjudged. Is it really true that "murder will out" and that "crime does not pay?"

That single suicide poses a difficult interpretative problem. It shows that at some level the story is clearly aware of the atrocity being imagined. But at the same time, given the magnitude of the atrocity, the one suicide is a small gesture of outrage. If someone were to respond by arguing that, on the contrary, the suicide of a supernormal is tremendously significant, one would be balancing the life a single genius against those of millions of morons. Such an argument would therefore be resubscribing to the very value system that has rationalized the atrocity in the first place. Another way to read the suicide would be to see it as a morally sensitive gesture but out of place given the technical problem confronting this society. So the story seems to say that someone must take responsibility for removing the danger confronting the race. I suspect this latter reading is a common one. It is also a technocratic one in that it has subordinated a host of moral difficulties to the solution of the single, overriding technical problem of how to improve the race.

I see no other way of interpreting this story except as saying that a drastic solution, such as that devised by Barlow, is necessary for the problem of the "morons." By subscribing to the myth of genius and attaching it to IQ, Kornbluth has contradicted the very social concern that generates the story's satire. Dark comedy becomes the only way of holding this contradiction together, and even as the comedy succeeds, it self-destructs. The contradictions, which are at first limited to the attitudes of superior condescension to the monstrous future, finally become those of the story itself: genocide is both a discovery beyond genius and a real estate scam, both a horror and a final solution. The logic of the story cannot see any way out. The bitterness of the humor has a grim pleasure to it; the story delights in making its audience face the implications of its attitudes.

The idea of genius generates in these two stories the political dilemma inherent in the values of technocracy and in the way the SF community thinks about itself. Kornbluth, who died in 1958 at age thirty-five, is a legendary figure in SF history. In the forties he was a member of the group of young SF writers and fans clustered in Manhattan who called themselves "The Futurians." At the time they considered themselves leftists of an anarchist sort. A tremendously witty and inventive man, Kornbluth was treated as a genius by the group, and the title generates an aesthetic dilemma for him. A fellow Futurian, Damon Knight could say: "No working stiff, or slob either, [Kornbluth] has had deliberately to suppress the sensitive, cynical, philosophical, irreverent top slice of his mind in order to counterfeit the tribal conventions of the boobs around him. The result is as craftsmanlike, well polished and hollow-sounding as a tin dollar."[24] If we can hear in this praise of Kornbluth a recapitulation of the situation that underlies his two most famous stories, we can also hear in it the embittered consequences of "Doc" Smith's happy and self-congratulatory praise of the SF community itself. The Gernsbackian reverie of the happy genius has discovered the alienating nightmare inherent in the fantasy.

The Sturgeon and Kornbluth stories have a cheerful tone that hides and complicates any strong thematic statement and therefore leaves them open to contradictory interpretations. The fact that these stories have generally been read as celebrations of intelligence tells us much about the SF subculture. That common reading can be sustained only by denying or ignoring many of the implications of these stories. The important aspect is not how we interpret these stories, but how their unsettling aspects have been handled. Have they just not been seen? That seems to me implausible; the stories themselves repeatedly draw our attention to their own refutation. It seems to me more likely that we see here one of the powers of ideology: it can look right at difficulties which should lead to alarming questions about the values being promoted and then dismiss them. These are texts which embody knowledge of great importance and at the same time claim to be ignorant of that knowledge even as they speak it.

"Flowers for Algernon"

The knowledge that these stories repress begins to be unfolded in a different way in Daniel Keyes's "Flowers for Algernon," (1959) a late story in the anthology. The story of the genius usually sets the exceptional person apart from ordinary people and finds a way of indulging the satisfactions of superiority without openly acknowledging feelings that are seen as socially reprehensible. Without ever quite giving up its admiration of the idea of genius, "Flowers for Algernon" manages to understand the injustice implicit in it.

In the tradition of American SF, this story treats genius as a simple matter of a mysterious brain-power which is measured by IQ. Following an operation, Charlie Gordon's IQ, formerly 68, triples, and within a month he is condescending to the scientists who changed him. Such a fantasy sees intelligence as simply a void waiting to be filled. In itself it has no psychological dimension—Charlie's "motivation" exists before the operation. Once he is smart he cannot help but be a genius, "accomplishing in days and weeks what it takes normal people to do in half a lifetime" (p. 621).

Charlie explicates a new dimension of the by now familiar idea of genius when he sees his own former situation mirrored in that of a restaurant busboy who is mocked for breaking dishes. In accordance with the ideology of biological IQ, this seems to imply that education is futile. Intelligence is a blunt given; attempts at self-improvement miss the point. But the attempt to reconcile genius and humanity leads to a curious meditation on what it means to *know*:

> Only a short time ago, I learned that people laughed at me. Now I can see that *unknowingly* I joined with them in laughing at myself. That hurts most of all.
> I have often reread my progress reports and seen the illiteracy, the

childish naiveté, the mind of low intelligence peering from a dark room, through the keyhole, at the dazzling light outside. I see that even in my dullness *I knew* that I was inferior, and that other people had something I lacked—something denied me. In my mental blindness, I thought that it was somehow connected with the ability to read and write, and I was sure that if I could get those skills I would automatically have intelligence too.

Even a feeble-minded man wants to be like other men.

A child may not *know* how to feed itself, or what to eat, yet it *knows* of hunger.

This then is what I was like, I never *knew*. Even with my gift of intellectual awareness, I never really *knew* (p. 626, emphases added).

By the end of this passage *to know* has come to mean *to sympathize, to feel*. Yet, if such a humane empathy demands a kind of social awareness unavailable to the supernormals of Kornbluth's stories, it also seems to demand that one *know* ones inferiority and, it would seem to follow, be properly ashamed. IQ marks a rigid social category that does not allow for movement. Only the miracle of the new scientific technique can change the "natural" state of things.

While "Flowers for Algernon" consciously worries about the humanity of scientists and the social value of science, it does not doubt the social value of the genius. The dangers posed by genius belong to psychology. Charlie realizes that one of his mentors, Dr. Nemur, is not a genius. He notes that "he has a good mind, but it struggles under the spectre of self-doubt. He wants people to take him for a genius. Therefore, it is important for him to feel that his work is accepted by the world." In this vision, the true genius has no self-doubt; like Roark, such a person never worries whether his or her "work is accepted by the world." But in this story such security risks an intense alienation. Keyes's theme of alienation is a complex one since the moron is also in his way alienated. The theme is adumbrated by Miss Kinnian whose fear for what Charlie may become is tempered by her assurance that he is a "fine person." At one level the anxiety is entirely the one of social acceptance that famously plagues young people; the worst fault is to be conceited. Charlie is saved from this disaster by seeing the moron being mocked and realizing that he too was once like that person: a "but for the grace of god" awareness humanizes his genius.

But there is also a deeper anxiety that knowledge itself is inevitably alienating. In a complex exchange one of Charlie's co-workers, Fanny Girden, the only person who defends Charlie when he is fired, also voices a deep suspicion about his new intelligence:

"Which don't mean to say," she remarked, "that I don't think there's something mighty strange about you, Charlie. Them changes. I don't know. You used to be a good, dependable, ordinary man—not too bright maybe, but honest. Who knows what you done to yourself to get so smart all of a sudden. Like everybody around here's been saying, Charlie, it's not right."

"But how can you say that, Fanny? What's wrong with a man becoming intelligent and wanting to acquire knowledge and understanding of the world around him?"

She stared down at her work and I turned to leave. Without looking at me, she said: "It was evil when Eve listened to the snake and ate from the tree of knowledge. It was evil when she saw that she was naked. If not for that none of us would ever have to grow old and sick and die."

Once again now I have the feeling of shame burning inside me. This intelligence has driven a wedge between me and all the people I once knew and loved. Before, they laughed at me and despised me for my ignorance and dullness; now, they hate me for my knowledge and understanding (pp. 622–623).

Two themes overlap here. First the idea that intelligence corrupts and its corollary that a simple person is an honest person hover between being instances of antiintellectual prejudice and, as Doctor Nemur and even Charlie himself reflect, a truth. And this theme then shades into a more general idea that there is knowledge and knowing that humans ought to leave alone. The reference to Eden, which could lead to a large social meditation, is here apparently just nostalgia for an earlier innocence. Fanny's unease with Charlie seems to arise from a distrust of change itself. Charlie then converts Fanny's anxieties back from a social theme to a personal dilemma. Yet, the theme of knowledge as personal exile depicted in the shape of the Fall itself is given a brief departing chord later when Charlie, in his intellectual decline, finds that he can no longer understand *Paradise Lost*.

Regardless of the personal social anxieties that may accompany the fantasy of suddenly being a genius, Keyes leaves no doubt that the genius is still beneficial to society. Even after Charlie's moment of revelation on the situation of a moron, he sees the extraordinary benefits the operation offers: "There is so much that might be done with this technique. If I could be made into a genius, what about thousands of others like myself? What fantastic levels might be achieved by using this technique on normal people? On *geniuses*?" (p. 627, emphasis in original). For a moment the mechanical idea of intelligence is seen in the service of an idea of social justice, of helping the mentally feeble. But quickly the familiar fantasy of superiority reasserts itself, and Charlie indulges in escalating thoughts of efficiencies beyond imagination, of geniuses engeniused. And later, for all the extraordinary pathos of Charlie's decline, his scientific achievement remains. Miss Kinnian, with the most insight into human needs, concedes from the start that, as Charlie in an early phase puts it, "at werst you will have it [i.e. intelligence] for a littel wile and your doing somthing for sience" (p. 614). The comic exuberance of Kornbluth and the insouciance of Sturgeon have been converted to tragic irony here, but despite the change in mode the idealization of the superior genius persists.

An Economy of Reason:
The Motives of the
Technocratic Hero

4

AS TECHNOCRACY IDEALIZES INSTRUMENTAL
reason, it poses emotion as the antithesis of reason and perceives it as a purely
disruptive force. Science Fiction stories spend an enormous amount of energy handling the problems emotion seems to cause and developing psychological and social models which will in some way defuse emotion. The usual
solution is simply to dismiss all emotional reasons as irrational, or at least
irrelevant. When that fails, the next best solution is to channel the energy of
personal emotion into social emotion which, by subordinating personal emotion, disguises its character as emotion. A third solution is to claim that an
emotional response is actually a purely rational response. This last mode,
while allowing for powerful emotions, especially hatred and envy, rationalizes the emotion as a necessary, logical reaction. In the next three chapters I
will examine these strategies by which the genre salvages reason in the face
of powerful, sometimes overwhelming emotional claims. The first of these
chapters, on the technocratic hero, will treat the way emotion is explicitly
repressed or rechannelled. The second chapter will examine ways that the
figure of woman, who in this male-dominated literature is the bearer and
symbol of emotion, can be modified or interpreted so as to make her emotionality acceptable to technocracy. The third chapter, on imagining the alien
and the monstrous child, will show how emotion is rationalized.

While fantasies of power certainly inspire much SF, there is another important facet of the fantasy that envisions the hero, not as the genius elevated
and apart, but as the technician-manager, a superior everyman whose virtues derive from his harmonious adjustment to the needs of science and
technology. This fantasy is often identified with the subgenre of "hard-core
SF." The supernormals in Kornbluth, were they not so superior to the mass
of the population, could be considered in this category. Such heroes work in
concert with others and manage a technology which they have not invented,
which has been in place before they arrived on the scene, and which demands not the genius's unique creativity but a dependable competence. In
the hands of a writer like Heinlein such competence itself becomes an aspect
of charismatic heroism.

In the case of the technocrat hero the psychic rewards of the fantasy are less obvious than in the case of the genius. The rhetoric of such narrative gives pleasure, not by indulging directly in grandiose visions of power and success, but by depicting a mastery which often entails a condescension toward those people who cannot live by this same psychic code. In the stories of Heinlein and Godwin, the two paradigmatic versions of this fantasy in the *Science Fiction Hall of Fame* anthology, the heroic act is to remain "rational" in the face of disorienting and traumatic temptations to emotion. But such rationality is always in the service of an emotion. Details of the texture of Heinlein's "The Roads Must Roll" show how persistent contradiction functions in the SF text to deny emotion in the name of emotion. In Godwin's "The Cold Equations" the adherence to a strict rationality can be the excuse for indulging in a deeply problematic fantasy about punishing a woman. In Cordwainer Smith's "Scanners Live in Vain" we see the dilemma of emotion taken up explicitly—the story is in some ways a direct response to Heinlein's—but at the end it hides any critique of technocratic rationality in irony. Even such an outwardly anti-technocratic story as Ray Bradbury's "Mars is Heaven" shares with these more hard-core stories an illusion of technocratic rationality, though the veneer is awfully thin. In all these stories the illusion of stability offered by rationality is a screen, not only allowing the reader to indulge the emotions that the hero explicitly controls, but covertly expressing attitudes of which the story itself is unaware.

The figure of the technocratic hero is a development in SF that is only possible when the genre has reached a certain phase. Though a strain of SF has always insisted on the virtues of "hard core SF," those virtues have changed between the beginnings of the genre with Verne and Wells and the period we are studying. While to certain fans and writers, hard-core SF has always seemed to be a clear and unambiguous form, analysis reveals it to be more intricate and less pure than the casual, and usually spontaneous, theories of the form would allow. The illusion of science which so identifies the form of the hard-core story is, like all other fictional devices, in the service of a narrative fantasy. In order to understand the attraction of the technocrat's cool rationality we need to understand how the terms of the scientific illusion have developed and changed.

The Idea of Hard-Core SF

The enthusiastic readers of hard-core SF have always been emphatic in their disapproval when a story fails to meet their criteria for the form. Letters to SF magazines belligerently complaining that certain stories are not SF constitute clear evidence of a strong, popular instinct about the genre. That instinct is evident as early as Verne's indignant attempt to distinguish his writing from Wells's:

> "It occurs to me that [Wells's] stories do not repose on very scientific bases. No, there is no rapport between his work and mine. I make use of physics. He invents. I go to the moon in a cannon-ball, discharged from a cannon. Here there is no invention. He goes to Mars in an airship, which he constructs of a metal which does away with the law of gravitation. *Ca c'est tres joli*," cried Monsieur Verne in an animated way, "but show me this metal. Let him produce it."[1]

Verne's literalness in demanding that Wells produce the metal may sound quaint to our ears, but it addresses a central issue of the plausibility of much SF. A half century later, in his address at the University of Chicago, Robert Heinlein would propose in much the same spirit that we divide literature into realism and fantasy and that we place SF within the realm of realism.[2] He tolerates fantasy; he even admits to writing it himself in books such as *Magic, Inc.*, but finally his impatience with the form breaks out:

> It is not enough to interlard an old plot with terms like "space warp," "matter transmitter," "ray gun," or "rocket ship" with no knowledge of what is meant (if anything) by such terms, or how they might reasonably work. A man who provides Mars with a dense atmosphere and an agreeable climate, a man whose writing shows that he knows nothing of ballistics nor of astronomy nor of any modern technology would do better not to attempt science fiction. Such things are not science fiction—entertainment they may be; serious speculation they cannot be. The obligation of the writer to his reader to know what he is talking about is even stronger in science fiction than elsewhere, because the ordinary reader has less chance to catch him out. It's not fair. It's cheating.[3]

When he insists that the SF writer "know what he is talking about," Heinlein echoes Verne's anxiety that SF ground itself in what scientists will say is real. Both writers praise a literature that relies, not on "invention"—by accusing Wells of *inventing*, Verne seems to mean that he simply fantasizes—but on a strict adherence to a reality principle certified by hard science.

After we have observed the broad similarity of realistic criteria in these two statements made more than half a century apart, we need to acknowledge that they envision very different ways of attaining scientific realism.

While Verne appeals to an elementary empirical standard of plausibility ("let him produce it"), Heinlein points to the centrality of a strong sense of generic conventions. The very idea that a story can play "fair" is a generic one; it implies a set of literary rules, in this case rules based on a notion of scientific plausibility. A SF story, like a certain kind of detective story, is supposed to play in such a way that a reader can hope to "solve" it. As some thought will easily show, however, one has to be acquainted with the generic rules (not simply scientific facts) before one can even begin reasoning about any story's world. After all, what is so plausible about Verne's cannon as a way of getting to the Moon? As in the cases in which someone guesses the murderer in a detective story, a correct anticipation of an SF story's puzzle solution is based, not on pure deduction, but on a good knowledge of the probabilities and possibilities of the genre.

We should observe that this combination of empirical reference and generic familiarity is common to much literature. And it is especially important to our understanding of hard-core SF to recognize that even the language of science itself can succeed by playing by generic rules of fairness as it appeals to empirical fact. The generic conventions that validate scientific discourse are difficult to separate from "facts" and logic, but the conventions begin to become evident when the other elements of the discourse are abused. By skillful use of the scientific language, unscrupulous scientists can create the illusion of science while in fact promulgating fictions. Thus, a Cyril Burt, while fabricating his data, can create a credible presence that for years can silence almost completely all critical thought simply by making adroit use of the conventions of scientific discourse. Even more revealing of the conventional generic basis of scientific language are the recurrent instances of self-delusion in science. Stephen Jay Gould's *The Mismeasure of Man*, depicts how investigators of intelligence have used scientific language to justify sloppy and uncontrolled experimental techniques and to validate highly dubious theories about the racial bases of IQ. My point in recalling such notorious instances of the misuse of science is not to debunk science itself, but to remind us that no language is in itself simply "true" or realistic. By showing how scientists have resorted to the language of science to justify prejudice and culturally determined expectations, Gould's book testifies to the significant rhetorical dimension of the scientific language itself.[4]

The hard-core SF that Heinlein defines is a unique fictional form because it has discovered how to put the rhetorical aspect of scientific language to fictional use. Most fiction has allied itself with poetry and has traditionally asserted that it is different from science. Following Sidney, it has excused its lie on the grounds that it never claimed to tell the truth in the first place. But hard-core SF represents a special literary case; unlike this other fiction, it has asked to be judged by the same criteria we use for science. We judge hard-core SF, not by an appeal to our experience of the world, but by the scientific language it uses. In SF the rhetorical allusion to a system of ideas outside of our experience overwhelms all other criteria of validity. The flimsiness of empirical standards in this world of thought appears when Heinlein tries to discriminate between valid and invalid ideas. After rejecting as "fantasy" stories "which have the lizard men of Zlxxt cross breeding with human females [and] stories which represent the surface conditions of Mars as being much like those of Earth" (p. 19), Heinlein a little later can allow as "possible" and therefore "realistic" stories which entail "faster than light [movement], time travel, reincarnation, ghosts" (p. 20). For Heinlein some theories (those of biology and astronomy here) designate "fact," while others (Einsteinian physics, psychology) are just "tentative hypotheses." Given the shifting and arbitrary criteria for reality in Heinlein's world, we readers are positioned exactly as we are with Cyril Burt: we accept a fiction, not because it is tested or it has some solid, recognizable empirical basis, but because of the illusion the scientific language itself generates. Heinlein's "realism" and his ideal of fairness boil down to writers sounding like they know what they are talking about. This is, of course, a familiar observation; what Heinlein neglects to observe is that in hard-core SF this is essentially a rhetorical ploy.

As the genre of hard-core SF establishes itself and the rhetoric of the scientific language it uses shifts from Verne's empiricist emphasis ("show me the metal") toward Heinlein's ideal of generic coherence ("it's not fair"), an important change takes place in the way the hard-core ideal appeals to its audience. Intrinsic to Verne's imagination is the refusal to acknowledge the operation of imagination itself. With Verne we are in the same historical-aesthetic situation as we are with Conrad when, in the preface to *The Nigger of the Narcissus*, he says that his object is to "make you see."[5] Such an empirical ideal results in a fiction which, while it is capable of fantasy, never acknowledges its movement into fantasy. Verne goes to great lengths to obscure the line between the real (scientific) and the fantastic.[6] For instance, in *The Journey to the Center of the Earth*, the travelog descriptions of Iceland and of the ascent of Sneffels are mundane enough, but at some unmarked point we cross a border and find ourselves in a world capable of producing giant shepherds and an ocean deep in the earth, a world in which you can ride the thrust of an erupting volcano. And even in the midst of such obvious fantasy Verne repeatedly invokes the language of scientific explanation. Similarly, *Twenty-Thousand Leagues Under the Sea* has a regular litany of classificatory rituals which anchor that extraordinary fantasy in a scientific base. Within this tangible world of categorized fact the Vernean heroes shape their monomaniacal private and fantastic destinies.[7]

By the 1940s when the genre of hard-core SF had become established in the United States, narratives such as Heinlein's own future history stories can casually begin in a mode we might term "plausible fantasy." In this period the generic game consists of playing "fair" according to the agreed upon rules of the genre. While it may be often overlaid by a philosophy of libertarian individualism, the ideology implicit in this generic imperative tells us to leave moral and social difficulties to the "scientific" experts. The generic perspective often can become so overwhelming that all issues and questions that do not fit the genre's concepts of fairness are seen as trivial and forgotten. This misplaced concreteness, this technological monomania, is then called "realism."[8] The values implicit in this attitude are bluntly summarized by Heinlein in his 1957 talk. After some lengthy, vigorous, and bad-tempered denunciations of the literary mainstream's concern with psychology, he asks, "Can James Joyce and Henry Miller and their literary sons and grandsons interpret the seething new world of atomic power and anti-biotics and interplanetary travel? I say not" (p. 42). This rejection of psychology in favor of technology is basic for Heinlein. For him, the great accomplishment of SF is that it has prepared the public to accept space flight. In place of Verne's ideology of individualist empiricism we have the ideology of technocracy.

"The Roads Must Roll"

Such a denial of psychology derives from a psychological dynamic essential to the technocratic scheme. Technological imaginings do not satisfy because they produce results—after all, for all the claims to technological prescience few popular SF stories, even the most detailed and accurate, have managed to design machines that *work*. But such imaginings satisfy readers because, by their restrictions, they exclude ambiguities and thereby suggest a world in which choice and responsibility are freed of anxiety. The technocratic hero is rewarding precisely because he or she seems to be able to make decisions purely "rationally." Such an illusion of rationality is not based on logic. Like the illusion of science in this literature, it is a rhetorical effect. To adapt Heinlein's ideal, it is the technocrats sounding as if they know what they are talking about. Often, as in the case of Heinlein's own work, the effect of rationality is generated by a rather daring indulgence in contradiction. To be sure, some degree of contradiction is common to all literature: thematic explication which implies that a story is consistent is always a reduction of a complex texture and awareness. But in Heinlein we often find blatant contradiction around the central didactic issues. While such contradiction may well be unconscious, it is not therefore irrelevant. In fact, it is the very spontaneity of such contradiction that makes it important.

Gaines, the hero of Heinlein's own *Hall of Fame* story, "The Roads Must Roll," is typical of the technocratic hero who, by embodying an ideal of rationality, manages to suggest that politics is free of psychological complications. He is the director of the military organization that monitors the rolling road between Reno and Los Angeles, and he appears as a self-controlled, public spirited, sensitive, and generous man. In the story he copes with the sabotage of the fast-moving roads by a striking union led by Van Kleek, a "functionalist," union-guild leader who is selfish, power mad, envious, hypocritical, anti-social, and the victim of his own overpowering and childish emotions. Given this opposition, the politics of the story are not obscure. But we may examine the ways these politics are made persuasive. In fact, each of the positive political values that is asserted in the story is also denied. Although that denial might seem to raise a problem in the abstract, it does not. By obscuring the precise politics at the surface, the text renders a deeper politics more undebatable.

The attitude toward the union in the story is a paradigm of the way this rhetoric of contradiction works. Throughout the story we find elements that would seem pro-union. The opening scene reflects union solidarity; Harvey, the "honest" union man who later aids management, never denounces the union, only the "bad apples" who have attained control. Even Gaines talks about how he supported the union's cause in the "strike of '66." Yet by the end of the story the union has been completely disqualified. Its leaders are murderous and selfish, its job actions thoroughly anti-social, and its members are at best dupes. The occasional pro-union attitudes announced in the story do not modify the basic stance; they simply serve to disqualify the objection that the story is anti-union. The method is one we are used to in political agitation. Contradiction is used, not to work out a complex point, but to disqualify logic altogether. Like Orwellean doublethink and newspeak, the story's explicit statements are simply false leads that confuse the careful thinker, while the story's plot conveys a simple, unambiguous stance unaffected by these surface statements.

We can see this process in miniature and yet in clear detail in a short passage from "The Roads Must Roll" which raises the questions of freedom of speech and belief. Let me frame this discussion with the observation that Heinlein's politics have always claimed to be libertarian. The Jubal Harnshaws, Lazarus Longs, and D. D. Harrimans are what they are because they are free to dream, think, speak, and act as they please. The thought police, whether in the form of stifling convention or of totalitarian censors, are frequently villains in Heinlein's work. With these libertarian values in mind, how do we handle the following passage? Harvey is a union man who believes the union has gone too far (they have stopped a road moving at 100 mph, thereby killing and maiming hundreds of people). He has come to offer his aid to Gaines. When Gaines asks him, "How long has this been building up?" Harvey replies:

> "Quite some time, I guess. You know how it is. There are a few sore-heads everywhere, and a lot of them are Functionalists. But you can't refuse to work with a man just because he holds different political views. It's a free country."
>
> "You should have come to me before, Harvey." Harvey looked stubborn. Gaines studied his face. "No, I guess you are right. It's my business to keep tabs on your mates, not yours. As you say, it's a free country. Anything else?"
>
> "Well—now that it has come to this, I thought maybe I could help you pick out the ringleaders" (p. 101).

Heinlein's depiction of such Abdielian loyalty raises questions which he never analyzes but that, so it is implied, are understood and settled by the end of the passage. At the center of this exchange lie two opposed "truths," both of which the story seems to sanction. "It's a free country," and "It's my business to keep tabs on your mates." The passage renders the issue of "keeping tabs" easy by placing it in a context of terrorist violence that makes us impatient with the complications of freedom. We may even find ourselves praising Gaines for taking the time in the midst of the crisis to acknowledge Harvey's point.

If at one level we may see the story as defending both freedom and surveillance, at a deeper level we may see the gesture toward freedom as false. Harvey makes the gesture of help so that he could then, with a clear conscience, become a spotter. The issue of surveillance recurs later in the story when Gaines raises the question, "Qui custodiet ipsos custodes?" though he treats it simply as a matter requiring a more laborious screening of personnel. When he observes that "even he, Gaines, should be watched in that respect," he holds off the really difficult issues by using the passive and thereby not considering who should watch him or who should watch those watchers. He leaves it entirely ambiguous as to what kinds of control are implied by the terms *to watch* and *to keep tabs*. By making us accept flat contradiction, Gaines's early exchange with Harvey has prepared us to read through these later difficulties without question. Harvey is both staunch union loyalist and spotter. Gaines can advocate freedom as well as "keeping tabs." There is something of the magician's sleight-of-hand in the passage: it treats some of the most difficult issues of social cooperation so easily and so quickly that they hardly seem problems at all.

In Heinlein's narration it is part of the hero's competence and privilege to surmount intellectual difficulties with this serene ease. Where lesser characters get stranded on contradiction, Gaines is able to be on both sides at once and still be "right." An extraordinary example of this doubleness occurs following the situation recounted in the passage above. After a cadet has been ruthlessly murdered by the strikers, Gaines asks the assembled cadets "You saw Hughes brought in. How many of you want a chance to kill the louse that did it?" When three cadets respond eagerly to this provocative challenge, Gaines has them disarmed on the grounds that this is not "a matter of private revenge." But a little later, when Harvey is shot in cold blood while trying to negotiate with the strikers, "the cadet captain beat Gaines to the draw." Having denounced the motives of "private revenge," Gaines, in this instance, acts on them. We may note the legalism that Gaines himself, thanks to the speed of the cadet captain, never actually kills anyone for "private revenge," but we should also note that his gesture of private anger seems to be sanctioned.

The Heinlein text raises problems of interpretation that will not be solved by simply discovering the author's intention. The contradictions exist whatever the author's private ideas. The issue is not which of the two forms of behavior offered is the right form, but rather the issue raised by Rabinowitz of *how to read*. What kind of detail does one want to pay attention to? To use again the model of the visual arts, what distance from the text does one need in order to visualize a meaningful picture? I think of a gold chain by Rembrandt: the art here is to suggest intricacy by deft use of texture. If observed too closely the chain shows up as a mere jumble of paint. But this model again fails us, for where the painter's image turns into nonsense when viewed too closely, the prose passage retains meaning as we move in on it. It appears as contradictory, but it is not meaningless.

In the case of Heinlein we can be reasonably sure that the readers who have appreciated his work and made the story popular, if they were aware of the contradiction at all, were certainly not bothered by it.[9] In fact, it seems reasonable to suppose that an aspect of Heinlein's "art," his "profundity," may derive from such an illusion of mastery over a complex issue. Such bold and unmediated contradiction is essential to the feeling of clear-sightedness and to the air of wisdom that Heinlein's voice and his heroic characters exude. If certain strong political positions are defended in Heinlein's work, they are not evolved logically but rather are imposed on a basically contradictory narrative. And at the heart of this narrative confusion is the honoring of the technocratic hero whose greatest virtue is a certainty that transcends political difficulty and controls emotional pressure.

The story concedes a place for emotion, but it also insists that it be repressed. When Blenkinsop, the Australian ambassador who is being shown the road system, inwardly worries that Gaines seems unmoved by the mayhem that has followed the stopping of one lane of the road, we are told how emotion fits in:

> On the surface, Gaines' exceptionally intelligent mind was clicking along with the facile ease of an electromechanical integrator—arranging data at hand, making tentative decisions, postponing judgments without prejudice until necessary data were available, exploring alternatives. Underneath, in a compartment insulated by stern self-discipline from the acting theater of his mind, emotions were a torturing storm of self-reproach. He was heartsick at the suffering he had seen, and which he knew too well was duplicated up and down the line. Although he was not aware of any personal omission, nevertheless the fault was somehow his, for authority creates responsibility.
>
> He had carried too long the superhuman burden of kingship—which no sane man can carry lightheartedly—and was at this moment perilously close to the frame of mind which sends captains down with their ships. but the need for immediate constructive action sustained him.
>
> But no trace of this conflict reached his features (p. 91–92).

This is an elaborate argument. Once released the praise of Gaines's emotional responsiveness pushes him almost to breakdown. The "heartsick" feeling shifts rapidly from a response to what he is seeing, to a response to suffering he knows is going on elsewhere, and finally concludes as a willing acceptance of responsibility and guilt. At this point the emotion is no longer "feeling" but an intellectual judgment—"the fault was somehow his." From this point the issue is how to avoid a sense of excessive responsibility, "the frame of mind which sends captains down with their ships." Throughout the story we are told that Gaines, by an enormous effort of will, manages to remain calm in situations that would unnerve others, but that underneath he is feeling the emotions of anger and pity more fully than anyone else. He is at once the coolest and the most passionate person in the story.[10]

Such contradiction can be found in much popular fiction. The heroes of romances and detective stories often share with Gaines the honor of being extravagantly passionate and self-controlled, though it is rare in more sophisticated literature to find the contradictions posed so bluntly and in such close conjunction. My point in drawing attention to such a device is not to disqualify the story, but to show what kind of rhetorical complexity any interpretation must account for and how textual signs may complicate more than simplify an interpretation. The "competent" reader of Heinlein is able to put these conflicting clues in their hierarchical places and to derive pleasure from a reading experience that the "incompetent" reader, trained only in high literature, will possibly find merely annoying.

"The Cold Equations"

It is the efficient technology that in the end justifies Gaines's behavior, and we should be always aware how much such an environment shapes our expectations of the technocratic hero. In most hard-core SF stories the "science," however bogus, is invoked, not to teach science, but to operate a narrative fiction. Frequently, the rhetoric of science is a sop to reason, allowing the reader to indulge in a fantasy which may be entirely irrational. Such an imaginative economy is clearly apparent in works of technological landscaping like *Ringworld*, that after establishing their "ideas," indulge in extravagant, picaresque fantasies. Other stories more subtly integrate the science and the fantasy. But in all such cases we need to ask, not simply does the science work, but what has the author gained by the illusion of science? By challenging the scientific illusion we place ourselves in a good position to see what are the real issues of the fantasy. The illusion of rationality, while it may serve as a sleight of hand by which an explicit political agenda can be hidden, can also conceal more aggressive and less clearly enunciated political fantasies.

To explicate these dynamics, let us examine Tom Godwin's extraordinarily popular story, "The Cold Equations" (1954).[11] Here is a story that presents as its clearly reiterated thesis Heinlein's hard-core demand that a story play "fair."[12] In addition, the "cold equation" on which the story depends is a ballistic one: to Heinlein ballistics is the epitome of the pure, realistic science, the science of unchallengeable fact. The story describes the dilemma of the pilot of an EDS (a small, emergency spaceship) which is bringing needed serum to a colony stranded on a distant planet. He discovers Marilyn, a teenage stowaway, whose weight has not been calculated in the EDS's fuel allotment. After repeated explanations by the narrator and by the pilot that the craft cannot land with her additional weight, the girl and the reader are convinced that the only solution is for her to be expelled into space to die. The girl accepts this fate bravely, and we are impressed by the logic of the "cold equations" of physics that "killed with neither hatred nor malice" (p. 569). It is a sign of the story's success in conveying its thesis that Gregory Benford can use it in the classroom to teach the objectivity of science: in "The Cold Equations," he argues, we see "society's institutionalized delusions set against the overwhelmingly, absolutely neutral point of view of the universe."[13]

Since in what follows I will be challenging a number of aspects of the story, let me make clear that I do not disagree with the argument that the universe is "neutral." I also agree that what is now called "triage" may well be a necessary and regrettable consideration in some circumstances. I will thus not be questioning the truth of the story's thesis, but I will be asking what purpose that "truth" is being made to serve in this case.

Until its end the story hovers between two incongruent ideas of SF. One idea promises liberation by means of an ingenious solution to what seems an irresolvable problem. The other promises a rigorous holding to the rules of plausibility. The storyline is completely clear. Yet by repeatedly insisting on its unavoidable end, the narrative raises the reader's hopes for a more humane solution. All of us are familiar with fiction which uses repetition of difficulty as a way of heightening tension and rendering the anticipated "solution" all the more amazing and relieving. Yet here such repetition constitutes a lecture designed to make it absolutely clear and unambiguous that there is no way out and to insist on the essential hard-core point that science and nature are "neutral." Because we have faith in the genre, we persist—in a way we might not were we reading another genre—in waiting for an invention that never arrives. At the end we realize (perhaps with some dismay) how extraordinarily hard-core the story is—this is playing "fair" with a vengeance!

But while the story plays "fair" scientifically, it also raises the possibility of a different criterion of fairness and thereby directs our attention to the very standards and values that the scientific illusion obviates. At one point, just after the pilot discovers that his stowaway is a girl, the story allows him to consider an alternate melodramatic formula:

Why couldn't she have been a man with some ulterior motive? A fugitive from justice, hoping to lose himself on a raw new world; an opportunist, seeking transportation to the new colonies where he might find golden fleece for the taking; a crackpot, with a mission—

Perhaps once in his lifetime an EDS pilot would find such a stowaway on his ship; warped men, mean and selfish men, brutal and dangerous men—but never, before, a smiling, blue-eyed girl who was willing to pay her fine and work for her keep that she might see her brother (p. 548).

This conventional figure of the man of resentment could relieve the fiction of the need for any more complex analysis by supplying a completely sufficient object of hatred and violence.[14] Yet the story invokes this figure only to reject him. Thus, the fiction raises as a real question something that has no place in "science": how can the murder of the stowaway be morally justified? The story then solves the problem it has raised by rejecting the "moral" criterion of fairness and by appealing to the criterion of absolute hard-core SF: to play "fair" is to obey the scientific formulae, regardless of morality and emotional demand.

But let us step outside the generic game for a moment to ask if the girl really has to die? The equations are certainly cold, but do they really justify the pilot's behavior? Throughout the story items have been mentioned on the spaceship that are dispensable: there is the door of the closet, the blaster, the people's clothes, the pilot's chair, the closet itself, its contents, the sensor that registers body heat, the bench she sits on. Do they still need the radio? Once one's mind gets on this track, the story becomes quite frustrating. In stories of sinking ships and falling balloons, the first thing anyone thinks of is what can be thrown out instead of a human. But in "The Cold Equations" no one even begins to consider such possibilities. These "scientific" men, tragically wise about the "cold equations" of physics and space, immediately take a favorite SF stance: they feel greatly, but they master those feelings and go on to do "what they have to do."[15]

Of course the story does not want such piecemeal and conventional solutions as I am here suggesting. I am being a spoilsport. But am I really? Am I not holding up to the story the very kind of standard that is always held up to soft-core SF by hard-core addicts? The fact that most critics accept the story's conclusion is ample testimony to the hard-core illusion, but we have to admit that it is an illusion. This quintessential hard-core story, a story that even appears to regret its own rigors, its obedience to the "cold equations," can be shown to be just as much a "fantasy" as the soft-core stories it rebukes.

It might be objected that my unsympathetic complaint is trivial and that we could easily rewrite the story in such a way as to answer it. Perhaps. But let us first admit that such a rewrite amounts to a concession that the story as it stands is seriously blind to some quite common realities and possibilities. And I suspect that in the process of such a rewrite we would lose more than we would gain. As we "purify" the story we would deprive it of its imaginative texture. Without the blaster, the clipboard, the heat sensor, and so forth, what do we have? Surely, the effect of the story depends in part on the sense of the wonderful technological cornucopia implied by these casual details. Without them the EDS is just another sinking ship.

And as we "purify" the story we come up against another hard-core contradiction: if the story insists on the "realism" of the equations, it nevertheless participates in a fantasy about machines. As we try to make it more hard-core we will have to account for the idealization of technology that dreams of a space ship so precise, so perfect, so exactly adjusted to the weight of a specific crew that it has no margin of safety, no reserve fuel, no back-up system. Curiously, elsewhere in the story's universe machines can be cranky and undependable—the EDS cannot contact Marilyn's brother in his helicopter because "some printed circuits went haywire" and the radio wouldn't work. But on the EDS itself the machine matches the equation exactly. This is a fantasy of utopian technology.

The important thing for us to realize at this point is, not that the story has faults, but that its details are not inevitable. Once we have rid ourselves of the illusion of inevitability, we are in a position to see its details in a new way. Marilyn is a particularly helpless scapegoat. In the passage mentioned above describing the kinds of vicious man the pilot expected and hoped for, it is clear that in the moral economy of this story a woman cannot be guilty; only a man can be guilty. It is remarkable that once he sees she is a girl, the pilot never thinks—and the story certainly supports him in this—that she might do something desperate to save her life (seduce him, grab his blaster, become a creature of resentment herself). Marilyn is pure innocence, a pure victim, an object incapable of self-defense.

Paradoxically, this pathetic innocence, this state of being a defenseless object who has no guilt except weight, may be instrumental in making us accept Marilyn's death even as it increases the sense of injustice. She herself invokes the proper analogue when she recalls a kitten she once owned which her brother replaced after it died. Rhetorically, this little anecdote is a complex parable, and I do not here claim to do it justice, but at least one of its implications is that for certain innocent but expendable and replaceable creatures death is not real. At one level the anecdote raises our hopes by suggesting that a competent man, inspired by crisis to the point of violence, can overcome death (her brother threatens to beat up the pet store owner if he doesn't open his shop at three AM and sell him a new kitten). But such hope is illusory, and the final force of the parable is to suggest that Marilyn is expendable. Perhaps she, like the kitten, is renewable, but only by replacement.

The pity that such a creature inspires may hide a more basic rage at innocence and incompetence. The moment Marilyn, unaware of the cold equations of the situation, cheerfully and smugly asks, "I'm guilty, so what happens now? Do I pay a fine, or what?" seems designed to elicit anger. She is, after all, guilty of trespassing: the sign said clearly in extra large letters, "UNAUTHORIZED PERSONNEL, KEEP OUT!" Women, so this stereotype goes, expect to get away with things. They think they can cruise along, doing what they want, seeing whom they want, never really taking responsibility, paying token fines when they get caught. But if rage is generated by Marilyn's act, the story never acknowledges this emotion as such. Instead its anger is concealed by an elaborated pity. But the anger, however hidden, is acted out, and Marilyn is killed. So while the story is an exercise in punishing a woman, at the conscious level it tries to hide that real activity and avoid responsibility by claiming deep sympathy with the victim.

The issues of responsibility and irresponsibility figure prominently in an important passage describing the tornado that destroyed one of the camps on the planet the EDS is approaching.

It had been in the Western Sea that the tornado had originated, to *strike* with such *fury* at the camp and destroy half their prefabricated buildings, including the one that housed the medical supplies. Two days before the tornado had not existed; it had been no more than great gentle masses of air out over the calm Western Sea. Group One had gone about their routine survey work, unaware of the *meeting* of the air masses out at sea, unaware of the force the union was *spawning*. It had *struck* their camp without warning; a thundering roaring destruction that *sought to annihilate* all that lay before it. It had passed on, leaving the wreckage in its wake. It had destroyed the labor of months and had *doomed* six men to die and then, as though *its task* was accomplished, it once more began to resolve into gentle masses of air. But for all its deadliness, it had destroyed with neither malice nor intent. It had been a blind and mindless force, obeying the laws of nature, and it would have followed the same course with the same fury had men never existed (pp. 558–559, emphases added).

The assertion that the tornado is "blind and mindless" is surely true, but the dramatic vocabulary used to describe the storm (fury, sought, doomed, its task, etc.) suggests just the opposite, that the tornado was conscious and intentional. In the very process of denying motive to nature, the prose personifies and thus motivates nature. This is an act of destructive malice for which all responsibility is denied by an appeal to an inanimate, neutral nature.

The disavowal of responsibility that takes place in this passage is a version of the disavowal that pervades the whole story. After it has been made abundantly clear that "there could be no alternative" to Marilyn's death, the story announces repeatedly and extravagantly that no one can change things. It is worth quoting the most prominent of these disavowals just to make it clear how insistent the story is about this point:

"I'm sorry," he said again. "You'll never know how sorry I am. It has to be that way and no human in the universe can change it" (p. 550).

"It's not the way you think—it isn't that way, at all," he said. "Nobody wants it this way; nobody would ever let it be this way if it was humanly possible to change it" (p. 552).

"Everyone would like to help you but there is nothing anyone can do" (p. 553).

He swung around to face her. "You understand now, don't you? No one would ever let it be like this if it could be changed" (p. 555).

A little later we are told that even Marilyn's brother, an experienced man "of the frontier," "would know there had been nothing the pilot could do." We have already seen how hasty is this conclusion that nothing can be done, but we can also ask whether the voice repeatedly denying responsibility here is accurate even if there were no other solution possible. After all, there is one person "in the universe" who could change things, and that is the author himself.[16] This pathetic story of unavoidable death is a completely gratuitous exercise, chosen by the author and engineered by him. It is he, after all, who has worked so hard to try to make sure there is no way to save Marilyn, and it is he who has created men who, obedient to the cold equations, never try to improvise some mode of salvation for her.

All through the story, from Marilyn herself with her pathetic cry, "but I didn't do anything," to the tornado whose "fury" is declared to be unmotivated, to the pilot and the other men in the story who easily accede to the equations' conclusions, to, finally, the author who has made up the story, we find people disavowing responsibility for what is happening. And it is science and its neutral mathematical language which justifies such evasion. The victims and the victimizers adjust themselves to their roles of passivity and irresponsibility by appealing to the cold equations.

Thus, in this paradigmatic SF story, behind the unchallengable assertion of the "neutrality" of the universe lies a fantasy about punishing a woman who tries to use her innocence to avoid responsibility. As evidenced in the passage in which the pilot regrets she is not a man, the author faces a problem in justifying her punishment. The "scientific" explanation comes to the rescue in two ways. It says she must be severely, fatally punished even for a minor violation of the law. At the same time it allows all the men in the story and the fantasizing author himself (and perhaps the fantasizing reader) to assure themselves, even as they perform this rationally satisfying act of obeying the equations, that they do not want it this way, that they would change it if they possibly could. As a way of hiding the blame attached to the murder of such innocence, the scientific equation has all the brilliant efficiency of dream.

"Scanners Live in Vain"

While, as we shall see, it has its specific social rendering in figures of women, the problem of the place of emotion in technocratic society is also part of a more general problem that runs through all the literature we are studying. The problem is posed and answered neatly in Heinlein's "The Roads Must Roll." Van Kleek, the villain who takes control of the union and threatens to destroy the road system unless given power, is seen as a man driven by envy. It is his emotionality that distorts his social vision and, in the end, proves his weakness: Gaines can overwhelm him by teasing him. In a broad way, the story shows reason's conquest of emotion.

Gaines's heroism is his self-control.[17] It is his unemotionality which becomes a model for his subordinates. When Gaines calls his office, we see this suppression of emotion spread:

> "It's you chief! Thank God! Where are you?" Davidson's relief was pathetic.
> "Report!"
> The senior watch officer repressed his emotion and complied in direct, clipped phrases (p. 92).

Once men have been shown to have emotions, they can deny them. After this point in the story, the narrative can praise Gaines's heroic self-control and ridicule Van Kleek's emotional vulnerability without any sense of grotesqueness. What needs to be noted, however, is that while the character system of "The Roads Must Roll" seems to repress and devalue emotion, emotion is nevertheless a powerful charge loose in the story needing grounding. The emotional energy, so powerfully regulated in Gaines, finds expression, not in any single character, but in the broader *brudershaft* of the cadet corps, with its enthusiastic marching songs based on "The Caissons Go Rolling Along," to its passionate and selfless devotion to the honor of the corps itself, and to the rituals of organizational cooperation. The emotion gathered here becomes a source of energy that transcends any individual character or motive.

This Heinleinian paradigm, in which emotion is channeled into this kind of public ceremonial expression, dominates the SF genre throughout the period we are studying. But it is a paradigm that is always under strain. Cordwainer Smith's "Scanners Live in Vain" (1948) is a clear instance of how the paradigm is challenged and how that challenge is recontained. The story begins as if in repudiation of the emotional values of the Heinlein story. The scanner is so distant from his own feelings, both emotional and sensual, that he must "read" them on his internal dials. Only when he is "cranched," that is, when he enters a temporary, self-induced state of vulnerable and unregulated emotionality, does he "feel." The story's scanner protagonist, Martel, is a kind of anti-Gaines who seeks out this feeling state even though he knows it can be dangerous if overindulged.

In Smith's story the ability to segregate and compartmentalize the mechanical and the emotional, considered a virtue in Gaines, becomes deeply problematical. The scanners themselves are not just a literal rendering of the split, but by their ability to cranch they define a paradox. On the one hand they are unfeeling habermen—humans who have had their sensations cut off so that they can endure the pain of space. In the world of the story, the habermen seem to be considered contemptible creatures who are simply allowed to become extinct when no longer needed; a source of labor, valuable only for their mechanical skills. The scanners have the advantage that they can read their own feelings and, by going "under the wire"—a kind of electroshock therapy—they can temporarily return to the state of normal human feeling.

If the story poses the virtues of a mechanized humanity, it also poses a world which cannot do without the human. Habermen, although unfeeling, are, after all, humans at the start. The core fantasy here, explicated by Adam Stone, the inventor who has rendered the scanners irrelevant, is that "life" must protect life from the pain of space. Stone's great discovery is that by insulating a spaceship with oysters he can make space flight possible for ordinary humans with feelings.[18] We need to appreciate the elaborate negotiation this fantasy undertakes to mediate between a feeling state which is both emotionally necessary and yet vulnerable and a mechanical state which is emotionally sterile yet efficient and strong.

Emotion in "Scanners Live in Vain" is an urgent necessity, but it is not offered as the opposite of scanner control. Just as in Heinlein's story, emotion has its dangers and weaknesses. When cranched Martel smells a cooked lamb chop and his recollection of the burning flesh in a spaceship fire sends his body into a panicked excitement that is itself dangerous. When cranched a Scanner is unable to bear the pain of space. Like Van Kleek, Vomack, the villain of the story, is a figure of disruptive emotionality who employs an otherwise admirable group to further his own ambitions.

Once we begin to see parallels between "Scanners Live in Vain" and "The Roads Must Roll," many others appear. Both honor the individual who turns against the group in the name of a higher social imperative. Next to Gaines and Blenkinsop, Harvey, in "The Roads Must Roll," is socially insignificant, but he is a central element for the story's politics: he is a staunch unionist, loyal worker who turns against the union when it is taken over by "bad apples," and innocent martyr to union violence. In "Scanners Live in Vain," Martel covers the same series of linked postures, but he is the central figure of the story and, as we see when we compare villains, the group he betrays has a different meaning.

Smith's story diverges from Heinlein's in its ambivalences about the inner group. Just as he neatly splits Gaines and Van Kleek, Heinlein distinguishes between the good cadet corps and the corrupt functionalist union. In Smith, the two groups are one. The guild is a working union intent on protecting its honorable employment as well as an elite corps of self-sacrificing volunteers essential to transportation.

A particularly interesting aspect of the story is the complex way the scanner's guild manipulates the intricacies of emotion. At its core is a futuristic medieval structure, dominated by hierarchy and ritual, and tinged with the aura of traditional romance, which is also authoritarian and, because of its narrowly self-serving motivation, socially destructive. As in other stories we have studied, this displacement is, at the same time, cognitively liberating and profoundly ambiguous. The guild picks up an idea of honorable tradition that is much like that of the cadet corps in "The Roads Must Roll" and a commonplace throughout Smith's own work. The young hero of Smith's novel, *Norstrilia*, learns at the end "never to discount ceremony as the salvager of difficult or painful occasions" (p. 272). In "Scanners Live in Vain" we see various rather intricate ceremonies between Martel and Vomack which prevent their emotional conflict from ever getting out of control. When Vomack summons Martel, there are ceremonies by which Martel, because he is cranched, can refuse Vomack's summons and ceremonies by which Vomack can overrule that refusal. At the meeting an elaborate ritual of signifying stances keeps a volatile situation orderly.

But this admirable ceremonial order is also open to misuse. Vomack, who even as a scanner exhibits the emotional expressions conventional for a villain, manipulates the meeting to his private and paranoid purposes. What is curious here is his anxiety that if Adam Stone's invention of spaceflight without scanners succeeds, then "scanners live in vain." The phrase is ambiguous. On the one hand it is a fear of being outmoded and thereby rendered insignificant. This fear is shown to be baseless at the end: "You don't think the Instrumentality would waste the Scanners do you?" (p. 389). Since the

scanners are being transformed back into ordinary humans, we must presume that scanners are valued, not for their mechanical nature, but for their
knowledge and especially their discipline. The other source of Vomack's fear
is his belief that if the scanners disappear, social anarchy will occur. "The
Discipline of the Confraternity may relax if this kind of nonsensical heresy is
spread around" (p. 375).

The end of "Scanners Live in Vain" has the potential for ambiguity that
does not exist in "The Roads Must Roll." As he awakes in a hospital after
having foiled the scanner plot to assassinate Adam Stone, Martel is told by
Luci, his wife:

> "Scanners. Oh, yes, darling, they're all right. They had to arrest some
> of them for going into *High Speed* and running away. But the Instru-
> mentality caught them all—all those on the ground—and they're happy
> now. Do you know, darling," she laughed, "some of them didn't want
> to be restored to normality. But Stone and his Chiefs persuaded them"
> (p. 390).

It is difficult to know how to read this. It may be innocuously happy, but
there is an ambiguity radiating from it that gives a phrase like "they're happy
now," or the word "persuade" a disturbing quality. Is this cure ironic, like
that at the end of *1984* (published the same year) when we are told that
Winston Smith loved Big Brother? Certainly when we hear that Vomack has
arranged to become Chief of Space with the rest of the scanners as his depu-
ties, we may harbor some skepticism about the political system that so rewards those who have recently sought to promote their own interests by
assassination. The final "happy" twist is that Martel's murder of the assassin,
Parizianski, has been publicly misinterpreted as death from an unguarded
moment of joyful emotional excess. However intentional such potential ambiguities are, the cluster of them suggests a deep irresolution on the author's
part about the emotional "solution" that the plot of the story has achieved.

Heinlein does not entertain such confusion. At the close of "The Roads
Must Roll" we observe a complex transaction as Gaines, after arranging for
his devoted secretary, Dolores, to call his wife and "calm her down," heads
for Stockton. As he leaves his office,

> the sight of the rolling strips warmed him inside and made him feel
> almost cheerful.
>   He strode briskly away toward a door marked "Access Down," whis-
> tling softly to himself. He opened the door, and the rumbling, roar-
> ing rhythm from down inside seemed to pick up the tune even as it
> drowned out the sound of his whistling.

> "Hie! Hie! Hee!
> The rotor men are we—
> Check off your sectors loud and strong!
>   ONE! TWO! THREE!
> Anywhere you go
> You are bound to know
> That your roadways go rolling along!" (pp. 113–114).

The movement, the rhythm of the machine, and the working comradeship of the rotor men and their song here combine in a moment of aliveness and pleasure. This is the emotion that the technocracy can put to use.

"Mars is Heaven!"

The claim to scientific rationality that the hard-core SF story makes must always be in a problematic relation to the deeper motives that inspire the narrative. It does not follow, however, that a less rigorously scientific story will better integrate rationality and emotion. In the genre of this period there is a rebellion against the technocratic code and its repressions even more explicit than that given voice in "Scanners Live in Vain", but it can express itself only by regression. A story like Ray Bradbury's "Mars is Heaven!" (1948) comes from the other end of the generic spectrum from "The Cold Equations," "The Roads Must Roll," and "Scanners Live in Vain," yet it also opposes reason and emotion. Again we find the same discrepancy between explicit theme and essential fantasy. This may be the story Heinlein had in mind when he contemptuously asserted, "A man who provides Mars with a dense atmosphere and an agreeable climate, a man whose writing shows that he knows nothing of ballistics nor of astronomy nor of any modern technology would do better not to attempt science fiction" ("Science Fiction: Its Nature, Faults, and Virtue" p. 30). Though Heinlein's description could refer to a number of stories, it fits Bradbury's rather neatly. Yet, the scientific fuzziness of "Mars is Heaven!," while extreme, still carries some of the aura of the science that identifies the form of SF. Bradbury, like Godwin, sees science as "cold" and sees the "frontier" as demanding rigorous obedience. But rather than reveling in the hardship, Bradbury plays against it and emphasizes the pleasures of emotional indulgence.

If the Godwin story overdoes its clarity, the Bradbury story poses a difficult problem for any interpretation because its fairly blunt thematic conclusion is at odds with much of the emotional texture of the story. The story tells of an exploratory mission on Mars which discovers a midwestern town that dates from before the great depression and is inhabited by deceased relatives of the rocket's crew. The illusion is constructed by the Martians to separate the Earthmen from each other and to make them careless. In the night, thinking they have found home again, they are easily murdered. Clearly, the story can be read as a warning against relaxing discipline. When the rocket from Earth lands on Mars, Lustig, a crewman whose very name suggests undisciplined desire, asserts that the crew should immediately go out to see the town they have found. Captain John Black reminds him forcefully that "Nobody gave any orders."[19] Later, after the three officers have surveyed the town, the Martians lure the rest of the crew out of the ship. The Captain is outraged:

> "Abandoned!" cried the captain. "Abandoned the ship, they did! I'll have their skins, by God! They had orders!"
> "Sir," said Lustig. "Don't be too hard on them. Those were all old relatives and friends."
> "That's no excuse!"
> "Think how they felt, captain, seeing familiar faces outside the ship!"
> "I would have obeyed orders! I would have—" (p. 403).

Associated with this military obedience is a skeptical attitude that distrusts emotional attraction. Disguised as humans, the Martians break down the Captain's rational defenses: "Why go around questioning?" (p. 402) asks one. His own "mother" suggests that to doubt at all is to show a lack of faith: "We're here. Don't question. God is good to us. Let's be happy" (p. 405). Finally, just before he figures out the trap the Martians have laid, Captain Black, thinking "logically," claims that "it had all been emotion." He finally concludes, "What better way to fool a man, by his own emotions" (p. 407). Since the Martian trap works and the humans are destroyed, it is plausible to accept these warnings and to read the story as a cautionary parable against emotion and disciplinary slackness. In this thematic aspect, the story fits neatly with the Godwin story.

But clearly this story is very different from the hard-core story, and one has to wonder whether the ending is not rather like dream censorship and a final gesture to cover up what is actually an expression of deep, though unacknowledgeable, pleasure. Unlike the Godwin story, the Bradbury story's energies are centrally devoted to imagining an irresistible and, in itself, unqualified happiness. More than any other story in the collection, "Mars is Heaven!" makes reference to a historically and geographically specific situation: small-town middle America in the spring of 1926.[20] It also restricts its relationships to childish ones with parents (or grandparents) and siblings.

Sweethearts are mentioned, but peripherally, and wives and lovers are entirely absent. The fantasy is, thus, both personally and socially nostalgic—a reverie of an unconflicted time, of the self-sufficient town, and of the cared-for child. There is no sense that the life is claustrophobic, emotionally limited, or politically repressive. Though the beloved figures are Martians in disguise, they are not seen as bad in themselves. Parents, grandparents, and brothers are *good*; it is their very goodness that makes them such an irresistible temptation.

In this story the scientific language, rather than restricting the possibilities of action as in the Godwin, is transformed into a source of further reverie. The suggestiveness of the opening paragraph is typical of the whole story:

> The ship came down from space. It came from the stars and the black velocities, and the shining movements, and the silent gulfs of space. It was a new ship; it had fire in its body and men in its metal cells, and it moved with a clean silence, fiery and warm. In it were seventeen men, including a captain. The crowd at the Ohio field had shouted and waved their hands up into the sunlight, and the rocket had bloomed out great flowers of heat and color and run away into space on the third voyage to Mars! (p. 391).

This is prose that would undoubtedly outrage Heinlein. But although it is easy to point to its scientific emptiness, we need to understand what it actually does. The second sentence "poeticizes" rocket flight. Heinlein might point out, with some irritation, that the ship never left the solar system, so it does not come "from the stars." The poetic figure of the displaced epithet, which puts the adjectives "black" and "shining," which compliment the concrete nouns "space" and "stars," with the abstract nouns "velocity" and "movement," manages to strip the essentially scientific vocabulary of its descriptive function. By creating a blur, the second sentence sets in motion suggestions that in the third sentence become maternal next to the abstract and slightly threatening distance of space. The ship itself is "new," "clean," "fiery and warm." It has a "body." In the last sentence the elaborate metaphor—"bloomed out great flowers of heat and color"—turns technological violence into a gardener's triumph, and the phrase "run away into space" strangely converts the voyage into a childish escapade. Finally, having begun with the conclusion of the voyage, the passage ends with its commencement, but that surprise is more complex than we can yet comprehend because the takeoff from the Ohio field will be closely followed by the inexplicable *landing* in what seems to be a similar field. The prose itself confuses end and beginning and, like the Martians themselves, creates a sense of reality which, even in its science, is already deeply infused with the values and attractions of childhood, family, and the small town of an earlier era.

The important psychological device for Bradbury is an accumulating overdetermination. By offering more explanations of the crew's Martian experience than are needed, the story renders any explanation suspect. And if the explanation that the Martians have somehow constructed a world based on human projections in order to destroy the expedition seems to be the final one, it is still unsatisfactory because in the story's epilogue the charade goes on longer than it should. After the astronauts are dead and there is no audience for the deception, the Martians, still more or less in their earthly roles, perform a funeral ceremony complete with band, mayoral speech, tears, and tombstones. The final gesture of the story is both Martian and human: "After the funeral the brass band slammed and banged into town and the crowd stood around and waved and shouted as the rocket was torn to pieces and strewn about and blown up" (p. 409). This closely recapitulates the crowd described back on Earth at the launch. The final phrases of the story describing the destruction of the rocket are redundant in a way that is typical of the whole story. The ritual is not only excessive, it is contradictory: how can you "blow up" something that has been "torn to pieces and strewn about"? What no longer exists cannot be exploded. This final act of childish narrative rage paradoxically preserves the childish small-town idyll. Though this is a "rational" story about Martian deception, the underlying fantasy of regressive Earthly pleasures continues.

In the figure of Captain Black, Bradbury acknowledges the technocratic virtues of obedience, repression, and rationality. Yet the story takes pleasure in thwarting these virtues. The final lines side with the Martians, who are at this point identical with the old-fashioned hometown crowd. Heinlein's outrage at such strategies is justified, not just because the science is weak, but because the technocratic values that allow a Gaines to remain heroically active in the midst of ambiguous and contradictory imperatives are here subverted. Bradbury's story is a denunciation of the very adult reality principle that the rocket represents. This dynamic is neatly expressed in the epigraph to *The Martian Chronicles*, in which the story appeared: "'It is good to renew one's wonder,' said the philosopher. 'Space travel has again made children of us all.'"[21] Renewal here entails historical and psychological regression.

The Bradbury story poses a puzzle for our understanding of SF, for whatever manifest themes it presents, in its deep structure it seems to deny the value of the self-control that characterizes hard-core SF. But, as our study of the Heinlein, Godwin, and Smith stories shows, that self-control is demanded only in certain areas of life; in other areas the stories permit an extravagant indulgence of emotion. A struggle between self-restraint and self-indulgence characterizes all technocratic fantasy. To be sure, the casualness of Bradbury's gestures toward the language and rigor of scientific and technological thought is uncharacteristic of much of the genre, but the enjoyment of childish emotions, far from being generically irregular, leads us toward the extravagantly satisfying fantasies of stories about the monstrous child that we shall look at in chapter six.

Reason and Love:
Women and Technocracy

5

THE IDEOLOGY OF TECHNOCRACY IS
fueled in part by a dream that machines can, somehow, fulfill all of men's
desires. We see this fantasy occur in a number of ways, but most crucially in
the thought that a machine might replace a woman.

It is a commonplace to note that in the SF of this period women play a
minor role or that, when they do appear, they are devalued. It is not sufficient simply to say women are treated this way in SF just because they have
been denied important roles in technocratic society. While limitations in
women's roles in society are undeniable, it seems clear that other reasons
lead this fiction to see women as a difficult problem. In "The Little Black
Bag," Angie can be punished because she is active and aggressive, in "The
Roads Must Roll" Gaines's wife can be dismissed as a comic burden. These
stories express the familiar double bind that entraps woman: she is condescended to when weak and seen as corrupt when strong. Sometimes, as in
Leiber's "Coming Attraction" and Knight's "The Country of the Kind," we
see traces of what might be termed "social sadism": it is the very powerlessness and marginality of women in these societies that is stimulating to
men. Godwin's "The Cold Equations" shows how this powerlessness can
stimulate sadistic anger.

Women appear fairly frequently in the role of the mother.[1] Casual attention to the maternal presence is understandable and to be expected in a
literature devoted to the male adolescent's issues of establishing an independent identity. It is also understandable, for much the same reasons of adolescent development, that the woman should not figure prominently in SF as
erotic object of male aspiration the way she does in the other popular genres.
But it would be naive of us to suppose that because the erotic is muted it is
absent or that the values associated with motherhood involve merely adolescent issues. Even when women are attacked it is often because they stand for
an aspect of experience and possibility that the technocratic code does not
address. Eroticism is an important aspect of this missing area, which can be
extended to include emotion in general. Gaines's rigorous suppression of

feeling is a model for a categorical rejection of the area of experience that women represent.

Scott Sanders has made a strong case for the existence of a pervasive split in the SF imagination: "woman," "nature," and "intuition" are clustered and devalued, while "man" and "reason" are linked and elevated.[2] As Sanders observes, the paradigm is traditional, going back through Milton to St. Paul, and is not limited to the western tradition. The paradigm is so ideologically basic that even explicit challenges to it, as in stories by Marion Zimmer Bradley and Ursula Le Guin, can only invert it. Such an attack can, while demolishing local expressions, leave the essential opposition intact and, by showing its persistence even in negation, reinforce it.

On the other hand, the split and devaluation that Sanders explicates can be maintained only by intense imaginative effort. The reason, so honored by technocracy, can easily fade to a thin, sterile, and frustrating logic. Intuition and emotion are no sooner denounced in women than they show up as essential to male behavior. The fiction that struggles to outline a set of technocratic values finds itself repeatedly compromised and forced into ambiguity lest it blatantly contradict itself. The struggle to make the technocratic ideology coherent takes place throughout the genre; the effort to figure out a place for woman and the values she is made to represent is one crucial element of the whole. The puzzle that woman represents for the genre is posed implicitly in the passage from the end of "Surface Tension" that we looked at in chapter two. On the one hand, rescuing the maiden in distress justifies the whole technological effort. On the other hand, that same maiden calls forth a realm of experience and value that renders the technological enterprise irrelevant.

"Helen O'Loy"

"Helen O'Loy" (1938) attempts to work out a mechanical solution to the problem of how a technocratic culture can handle emotion and eroticism. It tells of a robot made in the form of a woman who at first frightens her creator by her amorous aggressiveness but finally proves to be the perfect wife. In many respects the story bears comparison to *Ralph 124C 41+* for the simplicity of its technocratic commitment. But unlike *Ralph*, by putting the issue of the woman at the very center of the meditation, "Helen O'Loy" forces consideration of the relation of woman to the machine. The image of the robot as the perfect woman raises two puzzles: How the perfect machine differs from a human being; and how a man deals with emotion—what does a man really want? This second question is the more explicitly tormenting one, and the story is never able to resolve it. The machine puzzle appears to be solved in the story but if it finally seems to say that the perfect machine is the perfect woman, at the same time it can never quite imagine the actual consequences of such a credo.

The story's opening lines raise the first puzzle: when Dave says of the robot he and his friend Phil have just unpacked, "Man, isn't she a beauty?," (p. 62) he might be speaking as a male appreciating a woman, but the language is also that of a mechanic appreciating a machine. The next lines further entangle the two languages: "She was beautiful, a dream in spun plastics and metals, something Keats might have seen dimly when he wrote his sonnet" (p. 62). The sentence begins by suggesting clearly the machine reading, but then, by the allusion to Keats—since the next thought is about Helen of Troy, they must be thinking of the lines about Helen in Marlowe's *Doctor Faustus*—the dialogue returns to the theme of female beauty.

The interchangability of the aesthetic-erotic and the mechanical languages is mirrored in the double protagonist of the story. Phil is a doctor— he repairs humans. Dave runs a robot repair shop. Somehow the two men go into business together. Over the course of a year Phil teaches Dave all about endocrinology and Dave teaches Phil how to make and repair robots. Phil, the doctor, treats emotions mechanically: he uses a pill to turn off the love affair between Mrs. van Styler's son and a servant. Dave at one point demands Phil correct Helen: "You're the surgeon of this family. I'm not used to fussing with emotions." Despite this claim, and though he specializes in machines, Dave is the one who reacts with violent emotion to Helen.

The most vigorous line in the story derives its peculiar energy from this overlay of the mechanical and the human. Phil, pitying Helen's lovelorn suffering, tells Dave, "Things can't go on the way they are, Dave. I've made up my mind. I'm yanking Helen's coils tonight. It won't be worse than what she's going through now" (p. 72). In the midst of sentimental cliches comes the language of the auto-mechanic—callous, yet precise, concrete, and energetic. The effect is difficult to describe; some of the liveliness of the line "I'm yanking Helen's coils tonight" may come from the sadism suggested by the violence of "yanking," some from the eroticism hinted at by the gratuitous "tonight," and some simply from the mechanic's pride in mastery. The line is, after all, a claim to be in complete control of the robot-woman. The mechanic's erotic relation to the machine is not just proximity, but intimacy; it is the sense of control and power derived from taking something apart, putting it back together, knowing it and making it work.

If the men tend to let the language of mechanics speak for human realities, Helen, though never denying her robothood, asserts her humanity by her actions. She repeatedly behaves in ways that are perfectly normal for a human but unnecessary, irrelevant, and even harmful for a machine. We have been prepared for her emotions; they are, according to the "theory" proposed early in the story, a prerequisite for critical thought and therefore necessary for a truly advanced robot. But Helen does more than just act emotionally: She eats, she gets tired, and, in a central passage, she implies that she is a sexual being.

> "I'd make him a good wife, really I would, Phil."
> I gulped; this was getting a little too far. "And give him strapping sons to boot, I suppose. A man wants flesh and blood, not rubber and metal."
> "Don't, please! I can't think of myself that way; to me, I'm a woman. And you know how perfectly I'm made to imitate a real woman . . . in all ways. I couldn't give him sons, but in every other way . . . I'd try so hard, I know I'd make him a good wife" (p. 70, ellipses in original).

The 1938 coyness obscures just how sexual this sterile woman is, but the passage strongly implies that she is sexual well beyond the needs of emotion or robot service. While the men mechanize the woman, Helen literally humanizes the "dream in spun plastics."

If the mechanical and the human languages are really describing the same thing, or if either language is adequate to describe both the machine and the human, then there should be no problem: one can treat humans as robots and robots as humans. In fact, that is the solution with which the story seems to end. But in the middle of the story the identity of human and machine is seen as an antithesis, and both sides are seen as inadequate in their special ways. The crux is not sexuality as such, but emotion: a non-emotional being (the primitive robot) is prone to mistakes, unable to correct itself, and, therefore, inefficient. But the emotional being (the woman) is unpredictable and uncontrollable. Emotions are disruptive and offensive, but they are necessary for self-conscious thought.

The contradiction inherent in emotion, which reaches its height when Helen makes amorous advances on Dave, is depicted simply and explicitly early in the story in the experiment on Lena, the "housemaid mech." After the men have given Lena emotions she becomes a self-correcting machine able to cook "a perfect dinner with six wires crossed." But she also throws a tantrum at being meddled with, and the men, "not taking any chances," "cut out her adrenal pack and restore her to normalcy" (p. 64). From the start emotions are set up as a source of self-consciousness and as a source of discomfort.

The fear of emotion is not made theoretically explicit the way the need for it is, but the pattern of the story repeatedly underlines that emotion gets in the way. Dave and Phil's romance with a pair of twins breaks up over a disagreement as to whether they should go watch "the latest Venus-rocket attempt" or "see a display stereo starring Larry Ainslee." The elaborate balance of this opposition—the men are fascinated with the Venus-rocket, an eroticized machine, and the women with the display stereo, a mechanized depiction of a man—renders the problem irresolvable.[3] Later, when Phil has to leave for three weeks to make Mrs. van Styler's son stop loving a "servant girl," we may see evidence of a simple fear of emotion, but the balance is there still: emotion should be introduced into machines and repressed in humans.

Helen does not throw tantrums like Lena; her emotional responses are more complex, but they are also more disturbing to the men. When, hurt by Dave's brusque rejection of her, Helen ducks into the kitchen with tears in her eyes on the pretense of washing the dishes, Phil complains, "Lena in her heyday had been nothing like this." The story begins by being very explicit about the problems in connection with Lena. But when Helen, awakened to full robo-womanhood by "Larry Ainslee, that same cute emoter who'd given us all the trouble with the twins," tries to embrace Dave, the story becomes evasive:

> Dave came home in the best of spirits. The front alcove was neatly swept, and there was the odor of food in the air that he'd missed around the house for weeks. He had visions of Helen as the super-efficient housekeeper.
>
> So it was a shock to him to feel two strong arms around his neck from behind and hear a voice all a-quiver coo into his ear, "Oh, Dave, darling, I've missed you so, and I'm so *thrilled* that you're back." Helen's technique may have lacked polish, but it had enthusiasm, as he found when he tried to stop her from kissing him. She had learned fast and furiously—also, Helen was powered by an atomotor.
>
> Dave wasn't a prude, but he remembered that she was only a robot, after all. The fact that she felt, acted, and looked like a young goddess in his arms didn't mean much (p. 68).

The assertion that it is Helen's status as a robot that upsets the men is clearly a rationalization. The intensity of Dave's response to Helen's advances—he leaves home, stops eating, starts drinking, and lets his business collapse—is completely out of proportion to Helen's threat as a robot. It is Helen's womanliness that offends these men, and their claim that the problem is that she is made of metal and rubber is simply a way of displacing this anxiety.

The truth that Helen is "only a robot" is contradicted by Dave (and Helen's) argument that to turn her off would be murder. If she is "only a robot," like Lena, then her emotions and feelings need not be considered. But it is her emotional unhappiness that leads Phil to decide to "yank her coils"—a form of euthanasia.

The fear of woman and the emotion she represents is not in itself particularly remarkable. What is remarkable is the thoroughness of the story's evasion of this issue. We have already looked at the coy ellipsis that obscures the nature of Helen's sexuality. When Dave changes his mind and decides to come back to Helen, the passage again coyly, but stubbornly, refuses to say what is happening:

> "I've changed my mind," [Dave said]. "I was packing when you called."
>
> Helen jerked around me, her eyes glued to the panel. "Dave, do you . . . are you—"
>
> "I'm just waking up to what a fool I've been, Helen. Phil, I'll be home in a couple of hours, so if there's anything—"
>
> He didn't have to chase me out. But I heard Helen cooing something about loving to be a rancher's wife before I could shut the door.
>
> Well, I wasn't as surprised as they thought. I think I knew when I called Dave what would happen. No man acts the way Dave had been acting because he hates a girl; only because he thinks he does—and thinks wrong (p. 72).

"Fool" seems an inadequate word to describe Dave's hysterical behavior. Helen leaves gaps where crucial words should be. Phil avoids saying what Dave does feel and simply tells us that it is not hate. And Dave's emotions are further obscured by the verb *thinks*: all Phil really comments on are Dave's thoughts about his emotions.

The ambiguities here may be the honored ones of soap opera, but in this story they have a depth of meaning they usually lack, for, after all, despite the word "girl" and despite the emotions and the passion, Helen is not a woman. Everything that is said here in avoiding the declaration of love, can be read as a statement that Dave has decided to be "rational," remembering that Helen is a robot he can control. In its quiet way the remainder of story confirms this reading by praising Helen, not for her emotional presence, but for her "flare for cooking and making a home." These are the virtues of a Lena.

The last time Dave is mentioned, he is dead, and Helen plays her final emotional tour-de-force by asking to be destroyed with him. But the problem she represents lives on, and Phil can only deal with it by offering us further contradictions: "Dave was a lucky man, and the best friend I ever had. And Helen—Well, as I said, I'm an old man now, and can view things more sanely; I should have married and raised a family, I suppose. But . . . there was only one Helen O'Loy" (p. 73). The story has made it clear that Helen cannot reproduce, so the implication that Phil wanted to raise a family with Helen is an evasion. The final words blatantly erase the real miracle of Helen by denying that she is a robot and therefore not unique. There were the fatal two hours during which Helen watched TV and learned about love, but even that was a kind of recreatable experience. There was one Helen only because Phil and Dave did not make more. My point here is not to fault the story. The confusion in the final paragraph is accurate in terms of the whole story's ambivalence. In the story's psychological framework, a robot is a bore, and a woman is frightening. The story threads its way between these unacceptable opposites, and while it gives the illusion of having settled something, in fact both sides of the antithesis are still alive in active contradiction with each other.

Such an antithesis is always a social construction. The dilemma in "Helen O'Loy" is an artificial one and would have shown up as such had Dave declared his love for Helen. The evasions of the last part of the narrative, however, show that the story, for all its claim to a happy ending, does not quite accept the solution that a life-like robot is as good as a real woman. I would argue that it is simply racial mysticism to say that the machine cannot be human. As Turing argued almost at the same time as this story was written, the line between the human and the machine is one we impose. As in Turing's test of whether a machine can think, if we cannot perceive the difference between the human and the machine, then for social purposes the difference does not exist. Of course, it might be argued, the problem remains that Helen cannot bear sons. But this characteristic is not confined to robots; it also applies to many real women. Therefore, this is not a universal problem of human versus machine, but simply one constructed by a particular society that can value women only as housekeepers or as the bearers of the male lineage.

"That Only a Mother"

"Helen O'Loy" solves the problem that the emotional woman represents by having her become, as Phil once remarks in praise of Helen, "as sensibly silent as a man." The robot woman can touch on issues that the SF culture uses women to represent, but because she is a machine she can also always slide away from them. A story of a decade later, Judith Merril's "That Only a

Mother," poses a similar dichotomy between reason and emotion. Again this story associates reason with man and emotion with woman. Resolution of the sort offered by the robot, however, is now impossible, and the story manages the difficulties of its theme by suggesting rather than saying, by encouraging misunderstandings, and by consciously promoting ambiguity.

"That Only a Mother" engages the monstrous child motif that we will explore in the next chapter. The infant, Henrietta, is explicitly precocious and deformed, but by the end of the story she is also forgotten. By using the parent's point of view, first the mother's and, at the end, the father's, Merril has deprived the monstrous child motif of its egoistic core. We see the child as exceptional, but we do not see her pleasures. And, while there is certainly an element of horror at the end of the story when the child's deformity is confirmed, the technique of the story has taught us to reread and reassess. So like the title, which alludes to a cliche about an ugly child but also focuses on the powerful emotion of mother-love, we are also presented with provocative rational issues of parental responsibility. The story manages to hold to its serious thematic subjects—the dangerous effects of atomic radiation, the distorting power of love, and the (perhaps) murderousness of rationality itself—by remaining ambiguous at crucial moments about what its actual theme is.

Ambiguity in this story seems clearly intended, but there remains a problem about how the reader should handle it. This story, the first part of which is told largely with letters from an expectant mother to her absent husband about her fears of having a deformed child and her pleasure in their child once it is born, ends with a complex revelation as the father, home for the first time since the child was born, picks her up:

> His left hand felt along the soft knitted fabric of the gown, up towards the diaper that folded, flat and smooth, across the bottom end of his child. No wrinkles. No kicking. *No . . .*
>
> "Maggie." He tried to pull his hands from the neat fold in the diaper, from the wriggling body. "Maggie." His throat was dry; words came hard, low and grating. He spoke very slowly, thinking the sound of each word to make himself say it. His head was spinning, but he had to *know* before he let it go. "Maggie, why . . . didn't you . . . tell me?"
>
> "Tell you what, darling?" Margaret's poise was the immemorial patience of woman confronted with man's childish impetuosity. Her sudden laugh sounded fantastically easy and natural in that room; it was all clear to her now. "Is she wet? I didn't know."
>
> *She didn't know.* His hands, beyond control, ran up and down the soft-skinned baby body, the sinuous, limbless body. *Oh God, dear*

God—his head shook and his muscles contracted in a bitter spasm of hysteria. His fingers tightened on his child—*Oh God, she didn't know* . . . (p. 353, ellipses and emphases in original).

The confirmation that the child is limbless throws us back to the earlier letters and we realize there is a deep strain of ambiguity running through them that deflects suspicion away from the consciousness of the baby's deformity.

But the confirmation of intended ambiguity at one level may itself distract us from a number of crucial and confusing ambiguities that arise in the last passage. First, is the father committing infanticide? Earlier parts of the narrative have repeatedly warned us that it is the fathers who kill deformed children, and one plausible reading of the line "His fingers tightened on his child" is that he is killing her. But the child hardly seems the center of his attention at this moment. The "spasm of hysteria" that causes his muscles to contract is stimulated, it seems, not by the revelation of the baby's limblessness, but by Maggie's statement, "I didn't know." And this statement, which in the last paragraph seems to suggest that she didn't know the baby was deformed, has been lifted from a much more innocent statement that she didn't know the baby was wet. But the issue of wetness is a misreading of Hank's panicked question as he begins to realize the fact of the child's deformity, "why didn't you tell me?" Throughout this last scene Maggie has been willfully innocent. Her emotional attachment to the baby has led her to play a psychological double game by which she denies (even to herself) any knowledge of the baby's deformity and at the same time skillfully protects that innocence. How do we untangle such a skein of misunderstandings which may be subconscious understandings?

Merril's story has worked by ambiguous suggestion from the start. Margaret's pregnancy is no secret, but the reader must construct an awareness of it from hints: Margaret is pleased at her increasing bulkiness; her mother writes a worried letter which talks around the issue of genetic damage from radiation; Margaret, while reading the newspaper, recalls a geneticist's claim that the worst mutations could be "predicted and prevented." This oblique technique has a pleasure in itself and can be traced to aspects of modernist aesthetics. But the technique is open-ended: one builds up a picture from tangential hints.

Is everything in the story a clue? For instance, from the fragments of the story we can construct the picture of a world at nuclear war with devastated and radioactive areas. But what are we to make of the short meditation that immediately follows Margaret's recollection of the geneticist's consolation that mutation could be "predicted and prevented"? "'Predicted and prevented.' We predicted it, didn't we? Hank and the others, they predicted it. But we didn't prevent it. We could have stopped it in '46 and '47. Now . . ." (p. 345, ellipsis in original). This is a deeply enigmatic passage. First, there is a shift, much like that which takes place at the story's end, between different realms of consciousness: the phrase "predicted and prevented" has to do with mutations, but here it shifts to the issue of nuclear war. How could such a war be prevented? And who is the "we" at the end here? Humans? Americans? The technocratic class? "Hank and the others?" By this ambiguity the story pairs nuclear war and the birth of a mutation with infanticide. If we follow out the parallel we might presume there is some equivalent on the international level to abortion on the personal level. (I interpret "prevented" to mean abortion, though that too is not entirely clear. It could possibly mean that by this future time a mutating embryo could be corrected.) And given the line of thought the geneticist suggests, we may feel we are being asked would it not have been better had Henrietta never been born? Certainly, by emphasizing the baby's limblessness at the end, the story encourages us to forget her extraordinary intellectual precocity. On the other hand, the argument can clearly be made, and not just by doting mothers, that Henrietta's mutation is not just deformity.

By relying throughout on ambiguous gestures and statements, Merril creates a simple, suggestive structure which can be read in many ways, some of them diametrically opposed to each other. Certainly the story can be seen as broadly anti-nuclear, but it remains an open question whether it defends male rationality (subject, perhaps, to murderous spasms) or female self-deception. Merril uses technique to hold together ideologically conflicting ideas and to remain neutral in politically weighted situations. There is, to be sure, a serious question whether in the late forties issues such as the genetic effect of nuclear radiation could be considered "political." But confusion about the range of political choice may be exactly what we need to be aware of in the story. It envisions both responsibility ("We could have stopped it") and powerlessness ("We could have stopped it in '46 and '47. Now . . ."). There is no way to resolve the story's riddles on the basis of the text alone; we must treat it, like Maggie's letters, as an unconsciously willed attempt to deny what one knows. And such an act of repression is seen both as grotesque and as generous.

How one reads "That Only a Mother" depends very much on ones own culture and values. When I first taught the story fifteen years ago, classes generally treated the possibility that Hank is killing Henrietta as ingenious but secondary to the overwhelming revelation of Maggie's maternal self-delusion. In that early-seventies phase of feminist awareness, the women in the class often felt betrayed by the story and wondered how a woman could have written it. More recently classes seem less distressed by Maggie and more concerned with Hank's actions: they tend to see the story as an ironic stand-off, though I hear occasional questions as to whether the mere presence of foreshadowing statements that fathers kill deformed babies necessarily "means" that Hank is killing Henrietta. And it is with some surprise and pleasure that I find Albert Berger recently argued a reading that *approves* of Maggie's delusion.[4]

If "That Only a Mother" is ambiguous in its actions and its political conclusions, it is nevertheless clear and conventional in its gender stereotypes. Maggie, whether we honor her or commit her, represents an interpretation of reality based on feelings. Hank, whether a murderer or just a distraught father and husband, sees clearly. However, in just allowing for the possibility that Hank's rationality is murderous, Merril's story differs from other SF of its era. One cannot imagine Gaines in "The Roads Must Roll" or the EDC pilot in "The Cold Equations," or even the supernormals in "The Marching Morons" being viewed as pathological. It is not until Knight's "The Country of the Kind" that one finds in this literature a conscious criticism of the lethal possibilities of rationality. If ambiguity in this story is a mode of evasion, it is also a way of suggesting meanings that are ideologically unthinkable.

"Coming Attraction"

It would be difficult to claim that the attitudes we find in "Helen O'Loy" and "That Only a Mother" are special to SF. What distinguishes the stories is, not the feelings about women, but the way those feelings are handled. In the first the machine offers a special mediating image by which the story is able to absorb and defuse the sexual presence of the woman. The cheerful interchange at work is, at least in part, an aspect of the utopian expectations for technology that characterize, even define, the SF of this period. In the second story a much more explicit anxiety concerning the reasonableness of rational technocracy gets a muffled voice, and the story leaves the anxiety afloat at the end. Both stories handle what appear as contradictions by leaving possibilities open. But Fritz Leiber's "Coming Attraction" (1951) attempts a definitive closure. "Helen O'Loy" can find an evasively muddled yet comfortable solution in the humanized robot. "Coming Attraction" lacks the optimism to achieve such a compromise and must end by violently punishing the erotic woman who, in her forced victimization, arouses emotions in a man. This story, in effect, yanks her coils.

"Coming Attraction" describes a grim futuristic New York in which a few elements of fifties technology (automobiles, for instance) have become slicker and more dangerous. In this world emotion appears in perverse forms: erotic attention has been displaced from genital areas to the face, and women wrestlers who defeat men appear as objects of fascination. Having women display their bodies and mask their faces is a way of satirizing current prudishness about the display of the body. And the wrestling matches challenge conventional ideas of male domination, though, since the main effect of such matches is a masochistic humiliation of the man, it might well be argued that this particular violation of convention finally serves only to reinforce it. The story's knowingness about prudery and masculinity leads to a profound·ambivalence.

The story itself is aware of its complicated attitude toward the place of emotion in the American future it depicts. A policeman's confused response to "Girls going down the street bare from the neck up"—an act of almost pornographic self display in the story—is exactly the reaction we would expect one of the story's readers to have to a woman bare from the neck down: "It was not clear whether he viewed the prospect with relish or moral distaste. Likely both" (p. 447). Like the masks themselves, which the narrator observes may be "heightening loveliness or hiding ugliness," (p. 448) fear is double valued. The frightened woman is both attractive and offensive. The protagonist's British conservatism—he comes from a society that does not seem much different from England in the mid-twentieth century—is seen as both morally straight in a world of American perversions and perhaps as foolish, cowardly, and stodgy.

The insecurities behind this ambivalence are made clear in a gratuitous scene midway through the story:

> The street was almost empty, though I was accosted by a couple of beggars with faces tunneled by H-bomb scars, whether real or of makeup putty, I couldn't tell. A fat woman held out a baby with webbed fingers and toes. I told myself it would have been deformed anyway and that she was only capitalizing on our fear of bomb-induced mutations. Still, I gave her a seven-and-a-half cent piece. Her mask made me feel I was paying tribute to an African fetish (pp. 447–448).

Contradictory responses of sympathy, distrust, contempt, fear, and shame pose an interpretive dilemma here: How are we, the readers, to respond to a narrator who tries to evade the beggar's plea for her deformed child by asserting that "she was *only* capitalizing on our fear of bomb induced mutations"? Are we to agree that in a world of extravagant symbolic fantasies, beggars alone are not to "capitalize" on our fears? And what does he mean by "it would have been deformed anyway"? The attitudes here are common enough; the question is are we to accept or to challenge them? Is the British narrator, the representative of a familiar world, to be understood as morally sound or as hypocritical? The whole story is riddled with this sort of dilemma. Is Theda, the enigmatic woman who engages the narrator, victim or "capitalizer"? If the latter, what is her profit? And by befriending her, is the narrator acting as a good samaritan or a conned sucker? And if the latter, is it his fault or hers?

The essential moral displacement that characterizes "Coming Attraction" would seem to allow these questions to remain open. After all, this story is different from the other two stories we have looked at in this chapter because it makes a change in sexual relations the explicit thematic issue of the story. The changes in "Helen O'Loy" are scattered inventions (the Venus rocket, the display stereo, the pill to prevent love, and, of course, the humanized robot), which have not caused any noticeable change in social relations. "That Only a Mother" makes a point of depicting the relation of Hank and Maggie in terms of a typical World War II marriage. "Coming Attraction," by contrast, imagines new sexual relations and emotional values, thereby at least potentially disqualifying conventional judgments and responses. The interpretative problem posed by the story is whether we are to read the kinky future as an emancipation from our own inhibitions or as a degeneration from the "wholesomeness" of our own, however limited, system of gender roles.

Despite the potential interpretive complexity of these problems, I think it is clear that moral displacement finally succumbs to genre in this story. At the end, though the narrator has had moments of confusion, he is outraged when Theda offers to let the man he has just defeated "hurt" her, and he suddenly seems to know where he stands. The familiar "hard-boiled" narrative voice gives us the unambiguous answer that the woman is at fault. The whole genre from which this voice originates may be a device for blaming the woman.

The scene of Theda's unmasking puts us firmly in the tradition of exposure of the ugly sorceress. A model would be the humiliation of Duessa at the end of Book I of the *Faerie Queene*. And yet, even as it seems to want to be absolutely explicit, "Coming Attraction" cannot say exactly what it means. It is a sign of the dependence on genre that this crucial moment is conveyed, not by detailed description, but by sarcastic tone and elaborate metaphor. If Spenser gives us the visual icon, the serpent's tail, to tell us how to read his devilish hag, Leiber slides into a metaphor which is vivid but, finally, entirely obscure:

> I really don't know why I should have expected her face to be anything else. It was very pale, of course, and there weren't any cosmetics. I

suppose there's no point in wearing any under a mask. The eyebrows were untidy and the lips chapped. But as for the general expression, as for the feelings crawling and wriggling across it—

Have you ever lifted a rock from damp soil? Have you ever watched the slimy white grubs?

I looked down at her, she up at me. "Yes, you're so frightened, aren't you?" I said sarcastically. "You dread this little nightly drama, don't you? You're scared to death" (p. 457).

As in so many of these stories, at the point where one expects something precise—an explanation of this woman's feelings—we get a complete enigma; the image of the grubs is clear only in its aversion. The sarcasm of the narrator's next words is no more exact. In part, he is just lashing out when he realizes he has been the woman's stooge. But the attack is not effective if she is the demon he imagines, and it is deeply inhumane if she is not such a demon. In this second case his sarcastic remarks to her are not to be read as the opposite of what is true, but simply as the truth in an unsympathetic tone.

It is tempting to try to read this whole scene ironically and to see the narrator as a coward at the end, but such an interpretation leaves the story with no point at all. The narrator's return to England in the final paragraph of the story seems to confirm the unmasking as a righteous denunciation of the woman and of the whole American future she represents. Theda symbolizes a complicated and, though for a while fascinating, ultimately terrifying possibility for a change in the emotional relation of the sexes. What is, perhaps, most frightening is the awareness of how eroticism of a variety of sorts—the story is filled with hints of cross-dressing and homosexuality—has modified conventional power relations in this future society. Even the masochistic woman has become potent in such a world. But there is no satisfactory way to humiliate someone who seems to take pleasure in fear. Theda's repeated line in the story is "I'm so frightened," and if at one level this fear suggests emotional need and makes her attractive to the narrator, at another it marks a state of affairs that a conventionally rational and potent man is unable to affect. If fear is her pleasure—and if it is the pleasure of the whole society— then all heroic attempts, either at rescue or at exposure, will merely contribute to that fear and therefore to the sustenance of the emotionally perverse future that is an abomination.

"A Rose for Ecclesiastes"

If we look back at the scene in which Helen O'Loy first surprises and embraces an unwilling Dave, we may note that the real sexual potential of the scene has not been dealt with, either in the story—which after this moment turns Helen into an emotionally distraught but docile robot—or in our analysis. To "remember that she was powered by an atomotor" (p. 68) is to see her as a figure of quite extraordinary power. In "Coming Attraction" the woman's sexuality gives her a power that, as in the conventions of much fiction—and much film too for that matter—even a controlled, "rational" man cannot resist. In "Coming Attraction" this power is linked with technological change, but it is rendered demonic and the male protagonist does his best to destroy it. "A Rose for Ecclesiastes" (1963) also acknowledges the emotional stimulation of female sexuality, but now that power is linked to an alien alternative to technocracy. In this late story, the emotional excess which can be generated by erotic involvement is identified with the man rather than the woman. Gallinger, a beatnik poet-scientist, falls in love with Braxa, a Martian priestess, only to find that she is motivated by a rational understanding of her duty to the continuation of Martian culture rather than by love. While seeming to accept and enjoy female eroticism in a way that is not possible for earlier stories, "A Rose for Ecclesiastes" nevertheless finally finds such emotional intensity uncontrollable, allied to interests the man cannot join, and therefore dismaying.

The concluding image of "A Rose for Ecclesiastes" was seized upon when the story appeared as marking an extravagant "poetic" voice that in 1963 seemed absolutely new to the field.[5] Prevented from seeing Braxa, Gallinger has attempted suicide: "But when I awakened I was in the dispensary, and alive. I felt the throb of engines as I slowly stood up and somehow made it to the port. Blurred Mars hung like a swollen belly above me, until it dissolved, brimmed over, and streamed down my face" (p. 672). Unlike Leiber's image of the grubs, this image resonates with allegorical meaning. Braxa is pregnant, but Gallinger, the father, has been rejected by her. Fecund femininity is a cosmic and, for the man, alienating presence.

Compared to the other stories in the anthology, "A Rose for Ecclesiastes" offers a genuine range of women's roles, though most of them are stereotypical. M'Cwyie, the Martian matriarch who teaches Gallinger the High Tongue and the protocol for reading the Martian holy books, is a forbidding mother. Betty, the Terran linguist, is the female sidekick. If we can trust Gallinger—and while his assertion never receives firm confirmation, there is no reason to doubt his egoistic intuition —Betty is in love with him. Gallinger, however, does not find her tempting: a number of times he exclaims how he hates blonds, and he describes her as "bovine." The fantasy of the attracted woman and the overstated reasons for rejecting her put us in a situation reasonably similar to that in "Helen O'Loy." Gallinger almost snatches his hand back when Betty takes it to lead him into the matriarchal temple, and then, strangely, he compares himself to Samson. Despite his slangy and knowing language, Gallinger is afraid of a willing and powerful woman.

Braxa mediates between these two antitheses represented by M'Cwyie and Betty. Though she looks young, she is hundreds of years old, like M'Cwyie, but she is also erotic and fertile, like Betty. If Betty and M'Cwyie represent more or less fixed and familiar positions, Braxa offers a new possibility, both to Gallinger and to SF's conception of woman. But Braxa, while acting according to mores different from those that shape "Helen O'Loy" and "Coming Attractions," remains an emotionally charged figure who finally baffles the male. Her service to the higher, racial mission as set forth in the prophetic books of Mars is structurally the same as Theda's service to the sadomasochistic men in "Coming Attraction." Both women put their sexuality in the service of groups that exclude the stories' protagonists. Gallinger's suicide attempt at the end of "A Rose for Ecclesiastes" is an inverted rendering of the narrator's verbal assault on Theda in "Coming Attraction." Both stories end with the conventional return of the betrayed, disillusioned male to a safe "home."

In "A Rose for Ecclesiastes" this suspicion that eroticism is a tool used by a woman for her own ends is repeated in Gallinger's memory of his earlier attraction to Laura:

Laura. Laura and Braxa. They rhyme, you know, with a bit of a clash. Tall, cool, and blonde was she (I hate blondes!), and Daddy had turned me inside out, like a pocket, and I thought she could fill me again. But the big, beat word-slinger, with Judas-beard and dog-trust in his eyes, oh, he had been a fine decoration at her parties. And that was all (p. 658).

The rhyme between the two women is finally more than aural. In this story women use men for their own purposes. Erotic feelings, regardless of how generously they are entertained, are still a trap for the male.

That Braxa has acted the way she did without loving Gallinger is but one of many divorces of words and deeds that occur in the story. The whole first page is an exercise in the sarcasm of alienated adolescence: Gallinger plays roles ("Hamlet to Claudius, 'I was working.'") that only he knows and that hide his true feelings from his companions. Gallinger can declare that his invocation of *Ecclesiastes* and of the creativity of blasphemy is a "gospel" that he himself does not believe. At the center of the story is a lengthy and irrelevant episode in which Gallinger, to conceal his feelings about Braxa, lies about why he is searching the desert.

Given the sophistication implicit in such self-conscious complexity, it is significant that Gallinger unquestioningly accepts M'Cwyie's statement that Braxa was acting out of duty rather than love and that she does not want to see him. In other literary traditions such a statement from a maternal guardian would be extremely suspect. In those other traditions the hero, urged by the force and purity of his own passion, would break through to see the beloved herself and to hear the prohibition from her own lips or to rescue her if she is a prisoner. Gallinger's readiness to accept defeat at this point, his inability to think that anybody but he himself can lie, signals his commitment to the alienated state he bewails at the end. As in "The Cold Equations," a premature closing of options is a sign of desire. Though Gallinger claims that Braxa and the Martian Matriarchy used him and left him, in his failure to challenge his fate we may see signs of collaboration. Despite the attempted suicide at its end, "A Rose for Ecclesiastes" is really not much different from other genres in which the hero, instead of marrying, rides off into the sunset.

The technocratic imagination has occasionally acknowledged the limits of rationality and the need for emotion and eros, but while it has tried various ways to think about the issue, it has not succeeded in bridging the gaps created by its own ideology. "A Rose for Ecclesiastes" marks an advance of sorts, but it is made possible, not because it transcends the dichotomy, but because it abandons technocracy and its genre. Gallinger's genius is far removed from that of Ralph 124C 41+ or James Kidder. His science is linguistics. He is an outsider, a cynic, by his own confession psychologically "turned inside out." The outpost on Mars is indistinguishable from familiar encampments on the Gobi or the Sahara. And it is the alien woman, Braxa, a generic descendant of H. Ryder Haggard more than of H. G. Wells, who acts according to a rational, unemotional code. It is tempting to see a series of structural transformations at work here, but I suspect the new tolerance of female emotionality, such as it is, results from generic interbreeding rather than a logical breakthrough.

Feeling the Unthinkable: Imagining Aliens and Monsters

MODERN FEMINISM HAS TAUGHT US
to be aware of the political implications of the ways male desire resolves itself. We have seen how the figures of women can be used in SF to think about some possibilities of emotional—as opposed to rational—experience for men. But women do not figure prominently in this literature, and the emotions they represent tend to be avoided. More commonly the emotional charges that SF fantasy indulges in are hostility and rage, and the figures that most coherently generate these emotions are the alien and the monstrous child.

IMAGINING THE ALIEN

The alien, a frequent, even obsessive, motif in SF of this era, does not present itself immediately as an integral or natural element of the technocratic vision. To be sure, insofar as technocracy is a function of imperialism, it will imagine contact, for trade or plunder, with other peoples. But the relation between humans and aliens in SF is seldom commercial. The alien is more commonly a focus of hatred (or, on rare occasions, attraction). While they claim moral and ethical rationality, the protagonists' deeply emotional and instinctual reactions to the alien give authors and readers an outlet for violent emotions that technocratic values would otherwise repress. The issue of the alien is clearly linked at a deep structural level to the overvaluation of rationality and the anxiety about emotion that characterize other SF stories we have looked at. And stories about aliens, while they may posit a political situation at the start, do not analyze the politics but, instead, find the source of difficulty in the alien itself. By such a practice, the story about the alien can reinforce the technocratic claim to have transcended politics.

As we saw in the case of Godwin's "The Cold Equations," disclaimers of responsibility at one level can conceal strong emotions at another. Thus, in SF stories, if aliens often seem to pose an inescapable and unwelcome dilemma, we have to remember that these aliens have not simply appeared or been discovered; they have been *imagined* by an author, and their presence, despite its manifest discomfort, suggests the writer's *desire* that the alien exist. By imagining the alien the author has justified an emotional reaction.

Two very different senses of "imagine" are involved here. In a broad and benign sense, a writer imagines an alien by creating it—inventing something unlike anything we know. In this sense, "imagining" refers to the creative powers of the human mind and the possibilities of originality. But after that initial creative gesture, a more problematic sense of "imagining" becomes possible in which the strangeness of the alien is emphasized and its otherness enforced. In this sense, "imagine" almost means "exclude." These meanings—to conceive and to differentiate in order to exclude—are not easily or neatly separated. The second is often substituted for the first. No one readily admits to projection; even while promulgating baseless stereotypes, bigotry will insist on the truth and depth of its perception.

At the start, this second sense of "imagine" (to exclude) can be more useful than the first because its logic is relatively neat. While we may argue at length about what original invention means, we can quickly agree about what it means to exclude. In popular SF, imagining the alien often consists of including or excluding it from the narrator's sense of what is normal. There is, of course, literature in which beings somehow alien to the author—like Mrs. Moore and Dr. Aziz in *A Passage to India*—may develop in complex ways because their alienness is not their essence, but in SF "alien" is often a defining and sufficient term.

"Arena"

For obvious reasons, war especially inspires the hostile alien story. However, I suspect the pleasure derived from such stories is to some extent independent of the exigencies of war propaganda. Certainly Fredric Brown's "Arena" (1944) has remained a popular story long after the allusion to the Japanese flag in the tentacled red roller was forgotten. Such persistence tells us not that SF is more vicious than other literary forms but that the emotion of righteous hatred has its satisfactions.

"Arena" is a classic rendering of the exclusionary mode in which a surface emphasis on rationality conceals a powerful irrational hatred. It is a simple, reiterative narrative in which various justifications of genocide overlap. Carson, the story's protagonist, is chosen by a God-like "Entity" to be the gladiatorial champion of humanity and placed in an arena to fight a faceless, tentacled, red creature that moves by rolling. The loser's race will be exterminated by the Entity. The rules of the game allow for no compromise or negotiation.

We can learn much about the dynamics of a story like "Arena" by comparing its methods to those of a truly subliterary genre, the harangues of the racist agitator. Readers interested in this body of text can refer to Leo Lowenthal and Norbert Guterman's classic analysis of antisemitism, *Prophets of Deceit*, in which all the devices we find in Brown's story can be found. Lowenthal and Guterman argue that the agitator, while pretending to advocate social change, avoids any authentic analysis of present social problems. "He always suggests that what is necessary is the elimination of people rather than a change in the political structure."[1] As in the technocratic approach to history, imagining the alien can be a way of treating an essentially political situation without confronting its politics. The agitator appeals, not to facts or logic, but to our intuited need for someone to blame and hate. What the agitator poses as a proof is not a proof at all, but merely a trigger for subrational feelings and impulses. The harangue is not even a call to action; it is a "seduction" designed to bind the audience to the agitator. The relationship between agitator and auditor is not the normal relationship of teacher and student, or doctor and patient, or even politician and constituent, but that of leader and follower. In this relationship the audience, by successively feeling pain, dependency, and satisfaction, becomes addicted to the agitator, who addresses what Lowenthal and Guterman call "malaise," a vague but real social complaint, like a skin disease which we instinctively want to scratch:

> If [the patient] follows the orders of a competent doctor, he will refrain from scratching and seek a cure for the cause of his itch. But if he succumbs to his unreflective reaction, he will scratch all the more vigorously. This irrational exercise of self-violence will give him a certain kind of relief, but it will at the same time increase his need to scratch and will in no way cure his disease. The agitator says: keep scratching (p. 16).

The agitator understands the "itch," reacts to it powerfully, but cures nothing. Yet such discourse may be more gratifying than a more reasonable political analysis, because it offers the audience a release from inhibition. The agitator intimates that unrestrained violence against the supposed cause of the malaise is not only permitted but approved.

"Arena" encourages our itch for violence against the alien in a number of ways. The image of an invertebrate animal, a combination of insect and octopus, implies a permission for violence common to much fantasy: just as the lower animals may be exterminated without moral qualms, the murder of such an alien evokes neither pity nor outrage. A more intricate rationalization of violence assumes that the alien lacks a moral sense. The roller is depicted as cruel and uncompromising, driven by a boundless and essential malice. Carson's "humane" attempts at communication are rebuffed by "hatred and lust-to-kill." When the roller pulls the legs off a lizard for no apparent reason, Carson can hardly bear to watch, much less do the same. But in a remarkable paragraph that very revulsion turns to sadistic pleasure:

> Carson shuddered and wanted to turn his eyes away. But he made himself continue to watch; anything he could learn about his opponent might prove valuable. Even this knowledge of its unnecessary cruelty. Particularly, he thought with a sudden vicious surge of emotion, this knowledge of its unnecessary cruelty. It would make it a pleasure to kill the thing, if and when the chance came (p. 292).

Carson first sets himself apart from the roller, but by the end of the paragraph he is anticipating murder. It is the roller's perverse and monstrous violence that permits, even demands, that Carson indulge his murderous rage.

Finally, violence is encouraged by a paradox essential to imagining the alien: though the alien is depicted as extraordinarily dangerous, it is also seen as a weak and ready victim. The danger demands immediate and total action, while the weakness promises vicious pleasure. Through most of the later part of the story the issue is not the danger posed by the roller, but the penetration of the invisible barrier that for a time prevents Carson from getting at the roller for what turns out to be a fairly easy slaughter.

These various rationalizations for violence coalesce in the final statement of the roller's alienness just before Carson kills it:

> He felt sheer horror at the utter *alienness*, the *differentness* of those thoughts [that the alien projects on him by telepathy]. Things that he felt but could not understand and could never express, because no terrestrial language had the words, no terrestrial mind had images to fit them. The mind of a spider, he thought, or the mind of a praying mantis or a Martian sand-serpent, raised to intelligence and put in telepathic rapport with human minds, would be a homely and familiar thing, compared to this (p. 307).

The equation of differentness and horror is predictable, but note the absoluteness of language like "sheer horror," or "utter alienness." "Differentness," a word that in other contexts might allow for arbitration, here justifies absolute enmity.

In this passage an essential contradiction in the whole situation becomes apparent: the roller, if it were as utterly alien as the story claims, would be outside Carson's cognitive view altogether. Clearly, it is not "utter alienness" that offends, but comprehensible alienness. And even as the sentence declares incomprehension, it admits to repressed awareness: "things that he felt but could not understand and could never express . . . " The alien is horrible, not because it is wholly incomprehensible, but because it stimulates difficult, inexpressible feelings in the protagonist. The alien's qualities are related to Carson but in ways he cannot accept, and he punishes them by externalizing and attacking them.

In "Arena" the universe is defined as an evolutionary struggle that can be won only by one race eliminating the other. Such logic says that difference is unassimilable; conflict is inevitable and imperative. This theme is invoked and reinforced at all levels in "Arena." At the beginning the Entity who sets up the combat declares it as a truth. When Carson later abandons his attempts at compromise, he acknowledges the inevitable struggle, and at the end he even understands it intuitively: "Man or roller, and the universe was not a place that could hold them both. Farther apart than god and devil, there could never be even a balance between them." Even the greatest moral antitheses of Western myth do not approach the hostility between human and roller.

The story provides no reason for such drastic all-or-nothing antipathy except Carson's own feelings. The Entity asserts that an inevitable war between humans and rollers will destroy both races, but it never explains why such a war must take place or why it will be so thoroughly disastrous. A little thought about the politics of the situation shows how strange the competition is: if the two species are as different as they seem, they are going to require very different environments. The universe, which the story claims will not hold both human and roller, is surely a good deal larger and more various than this intensely paranoid vision can admit. The overdetermined motive for killing the roller—its danger and repulsiveness, the gratifying justice of its destruction—is made to sanction an act that neither political nor evolutionary logic would condone.

From the start the story has defended itself against the charge of illogicality by claiming for intuition an absolute sagacity that makes proof superfluous. Though at one level "Arena" is a parable of inductive reasoning (how Carson learns to penetrate the barrier),[2] at a deeper and prior level it sanctions an irrational, nonempirical mode of understanding. Early in the story Carson *knows* without any evidence. When he first looks around the arena, "Somehow he *knew* it was circumscribed and finite even though he couldn't see the top of it" (298); when the Entity speaks to him, Carson thinks it "had to be a nightmare," "but he *knew* it wasn't" (p. 286); and the shape of the roller immediately represents its mind—"*Instinctively, somehow, he knew* its mind was as alien as its body" (p. 289, emphases added). One might be able to reason from body-shape to some idea of mental process, but Carson's intuition is explicitly prerational.

Along the same lines, Carson's sense of this alien depends entirely on the perception of his own emotions. Even before the Entity explains the situation, Carson shudders "unaccountably" in the presence of the roller and experiences a "vague feeling of horror" (p. 285). And later he apprehends the telepathic hatred projected by the roller as "a paralyzing wave of nauseating, retching, horrid hatred," as "wave upon wave of fierce emotion" (p. 287). He understands the alien by reading his own feelings.

The story thus affirms a trust in intuition which absolutely nullifies empirical reason. While the story overtly praises rationality, it covertly advocates unexamined emotion. And while at one level it does reward compassion for an alien (Carson's kindness to lizards pays off when they give him the clue to breaching the force field), at its deepest level it sanctions paranoid intuition. The story cloaks a fantasy of violence against a mirrored alter ego in a parable of rational, scientific induction.

The barrier between Carson and the alien turns out to be impermeable only to conscious matter. It is fitting that Carson finally passes through the barrier by knocking himself out—in "Arena" the epitome of rational activity is to be unconscious. With the thoroughness of a dream, the story directs us to the unconscious and irrational even as it praises the conscious and rational. Similarly, it praises the hero for his moral sensitivity but enlists that virtue in the cause of brutal murderousness. The story thus expresses xenophobic rage, but masked as rational deduction and tolerance.

"First Contact"

Even stories that make a conscious effort to bridge the alien gulf can exhibit the same structure of instinctive exclusion rendered as rational inevitability. In Murray Leinster's "First Contact" (1945) also published at the end of World War II, the alien turns out to be friendly, and the problem is posed as a purely logical (as opposed to evolutionary) issue. Here even the differences between the human and the alien point toward mutual understanding. When a spaceship from earth encounters an alien ship in the Crab Nebula, both species want to negotiate, but both are wary of revealing their home base lest the other destroy or occupy it. The standoff leads to a tracing of similarities within differences. At the center of Leinster's story lies the paradox, implicit but emphatically denied in "Arena," that the alien is dangerous because it is *like* the human. The more the aliens resemble us and our "way of thinking," the more suspicious we have to be. As we shall see, this logic rests on a racial premise, and at the end, after a mode of negotiation has been found, the exclusionary impulse reasserts itself by reorganizing the bases of exclusion.

By showing that even similar (and, as it turns out, friendly) aliens cannot trust each other, "First Contact" wants to claim that the "logical issue" is the whole issue, and a universal one. But early in the story a short passage undermines such claims to a universal logic. The Captain of the *Llanvabon* explains his dilemma:

> What are we going to do about them? Maybe these creatures will be aesthetic marvels, nice and friendly and polite—and underneath with the sneaking brutal ferocity of a Japanese. Or maybe they'll be crude and gruff as a Swedish farmer—and just as decent underneath. Maybe they're something in between. But am I going to risk the possible future of the human race on a guess that it's safe to trust them? (pp. 315–316).

Creatures, according to his analogy, are either trustworthy (like Swedes) or not (like Japanese). Thus, the need is not to establish a universal basis of trust but to identify the racial or cultural type. Given the Captain's presuppositions, trust is impossible until the type is identified; all signs of friendship may be only more elaborate deceptions leading to the final betrayal. What "First Contact" holds up as a disturbing logical dilemma is also a fantasy of racist paranoia.

A true paranoid, of course, never feels safe; treachery is always possible. Yet "First Contact" finally allows humans and aliens to trust each other. They solve their problem by exchanging spaceships. Each race disarms its own ship's tracking mechanisms. A paranoid might ask, how can either be sure the other did not leave some kind of bug or tracer on the ship? It is to its credit that the story rests happy with this elegantly simple solution. Once the ingenious trade is worked out and the humans feel safe from alien betrayal, they can acknowledge the evidence that dissolves the paranoia: "'Oh, we'll get along all right, sir,' said Tommy. 'We've got a good start toward friendship. After all, since they see by infrared, the planets they want to make use of wouldn't suit us. There's no reason why we shouldn't get along. We're almost alike in psychology'" (p. 343). Though this is spoken as a promise and a consolation, it also confesses the irrationality of the fear and distrust that started all the trouble.

But just when trust is established, a new exclusion emerges, though one that the story fails to recognize in any explicit way. Tommy notes that both ships are "manned" by womanless crews. And as final evidence that humans and aliens will get along, he and his new alien friend, Buck, during a lull in final preparations sit around telling dirty jokes. This gesture of comradely union is also a gesture of male exclusivity; sexual difference is pointedly acknowledged as the racial gulf is bridged. Dirty jokes, while a mode of bonding, are also a mode of sexual assault; a form by which men, often rivals, collaborate against women.[3] In aligning themselves as males against their common alien, the absent female, Tommy and Buck enact what we might call, half facetiously, the law of conservation of exclusion. One alien can be accepted as benign only when another alien is discovered to ground the xenophobic charge. As Freud observes, "It is always possible to bind together a considerable number of people in love, so long as there are other people to receive the manifestations of their aggressiveness."[4] Freud calls this phenomenon "the narcissism of minor differences," a phrase he admits does not do much to explain the phenomenon. We can see this psychological mechanism at work in Stephen Spielberg's film *E. T.* when as the alien gains our sympathy by behaving in recognizably human ways, hostility is generated against such adult authorities as scientists and policemen.

"First Contact" shows that in imaginative structure the story of the friendly alien is not necessarily the opposite of the story of the hostile alien. The two story types are often in agreement about the racial basis of concord or strife, and such agreements tend to prevent more precise thinking about authentic political issues. The way this situation is treated owes something to the historical circumstances under which the stories were written. Certainly "Arena" and "First Contact" carry a heavy freight of wartime assumptions which would last into the cold war. But the main problem lies in the very act of trying to imagine the alien. The story of the benign alien, while in conscious, thematic opposition to the story of the hostile alien, by the very act of positing alienness enters an imaginative territory also occupied by racist projection.

We may hope that when we meet real aliens they will prove friendly, but in fiction the idea of the "friendly alien" poses a paradox. In the dynamics of imagining the alien, the friendly alien must achieve benignity by approaching the familiar and conventionally valued, that is, by not being truly alien. Thus, in much "enlightened" SF, women are valued for their approximation to male values, non-Western humans for their approximation to Western values, non-Caucasians for Caucasian, and non-humans for human. In such stories alienness is superficial, a distracting costume covering a familiar person.[5]

In addition to transferring the exclusionary impulse to a new creature, "First Contact," if it is to depict the alien as benign, must also deny the alien's "foreignness." Despite the differences between the aliens and the humans, the species merge at the end. An exchange of dirty jokes confirms their biological and cultural similarity: between creatures of different sexual processes or even different sexual customs, sexual badinage or jocularity would not be possible. The absurdity of biological aliens exchanging smut is wittily shown in William Tenn's short story "Party of the Two Parts," in which an amoeba pornographer is pursued by the galactic police for selling sexually explicit pictures of a dividing amoeba to the publishers of a high-school biology text for humans.[6] Leinster may not have considered the ramifications of such jokes—he may have simply wanted an image of fellow sailors having a good time—but the conclusion of "First Contact" suggests in a particularly telling way that the friendly alien is not different at all.

"A Martian Odyssey"

"Arena" and "First Contact" do not imagine different-yet-friendly or similar-yet-hostile aliens, subcombinations which, while they may not affect the basic issues in an important way, nevertheless by their different dynamics raise special issues. The different-yet-friendly alien has at its core a social fantasy of radical individualism that would deny the meaning and power of social groups altogether. The similar-yet-hostile alien story, especially the story of the monstrous child, by a kind of inversion of affect can render feelings of rage that are denied by the rational technocratic code but that probably play a more important role than is usually acknowledged.

In an essay attacking the xenophobia of American SF, Ursula Le Guin credits the "invention" of the "sympathetic alien" to Stanley Weinbaum's "A Martian Odyssey" (1934).[7] While the social dynamics of this elementary story are complex, the plot is extremely simple. Jarvis, a human separated from his expedition on Mars, saves the life of Tweel, a tall, birdlike alien. They become friends of sorts and have a series of adventures. When the humans arrive to save the day, Tweel disappears. Tweel is a charming character who verges on the incomprehensible. His language seems to keep changing; a thing is never called by the same word twice. He displays pleasure by soaring seventy-five feet into the air, descending like a javelin, nose first, to stick quivering in the earth. But behind such comic eccentricities, we see an essentially human figure: bipedal, rational, tool-using, capable of emotion and loyalty. Toward the end of the story, when Tweel has helped him escape the Martian barrel people, Jarvis says, "Thanks, Tweel. You're a man!" Out loud he wonders whether that is really a compliment, but in the next breath he acknowledges that it is the highest form of praise he can conceive.[8] Like other friendly aliens, Tweel is an eccentric who, despite his oddities, is valued for the way he approaches a human ideal.

But "A Martian Odyssey" is unlike "First Contact" in that it continues to try to see Tweel as different. He is admittedly odd, and if we grant him his difference, we find that "A Martian Odyssey" pays for its generosity toward him by an excessive anxiety about all other differences, even differences which seem absurdly trivial in the Martian context. The humans in the story are men of different nationalities, and while their comradeship is acknowledged, the story repeatedly points to the differences in their language and understanding. The difficulty even humans have understanding each other is rendered by confusions of pronunciation at the beginning of the story: Harrison (American) tells Jarvis to "spill it, man." Leroy (French) asks, "Speel, . . . Speel what?" To which Putz (German) easily answers, "He means 'spiel'. . . . It iss to tell" (p. 114). A clumsy understanding is attained here, but it is by false etymologies and mispronunciations. Throughout the story Leroy and Putz mangle idiomatic English. One has to be struck by Weinbaum's attention to this level of ethnic difference when the main theme of the story seems to be the areas of identity between aliens. This sense of the minor gaps between people can shade easily into hysterical and exclusionary discriminations.

The other forms of Martian fauna (the living grass, the silicon bricklayer, the dream monster, and the barrel people) involve common cliches of alien exclusion of the sort we expect to find in hostile alien stories. The dream monster is the most conventionally hateful: like the roller in "Arena," it is tentacled; it can be described a number of times simply as "one of those writhing, black rope-armed horrors." Like the roller and like the Martians in "Mars is Heaven!", it has a telepathic capability that renders it particularly dangerous to the open, good-natured human. The only way to deal with it is to destroy it. The barrel people belong to a slightly different set of clichés. They are laborious, self-oblivious, organized automatons who learn from Jarvis two phrases, which they repeat frequently: "We are v-r-r-riends. Ouch!" The final revelation that Jarvis has stolen the shining thing that removes warts and may cure cancer places us casually in the imperialist tradition. It is taken for granted that Jarvis is in the right and that his theft is heroic; the barrel people's hostility turns out to be justified, but it is also disregarded.

We can observe here how casually a story that at one level has tried to be sympathetic to the alien can settle back into conventional postures. The effort to appreciate Tweel cannot entirely change underlying discriminatory structures, and the more generous the story is toward Tweel, the more necessary it is for it to reinforce its essentially chauvinist base at other points in the story. Here again we see the law of conservation of exclusion at work.

If differences in language and pronunciation remind us of the potential distances between humans, they do not thereby settle the issue of friendship, for distance here may be a source of affection as well has hostility. On the one hand, there is a superficial bad-temperedness in the story: Harrison, the captain, repeatedly accuses Jarvis of being crazy; Jarvis himself makes a crack about the apparition of a woman being "as solid as Putz's head" and simply ignores Putz's confused "Vot?" Such moments, while denotatively hostile, are also rituals of friendship. As the stereotype of the slow foreigner is developed, it is also being transformed from a simple exclusionary mechanism into a language of a kind of affection. It is an affection, however, made possible by condescension. Just as the humans' seemingly hostile banter covers affection, so does the barrel people's rendering of "We are friends" conceal indifference and hostility.

The affection-hostility confusion parallels a confusion between superior and inferior intelligence. Harrison keeps trying to attribute Tweel's actions to craziness and to see his intellect as inferior. Jarvis prefers to see him as sane and intellectually superior: he observes that Tweel is able to learn some English while Jarvis himself can learn nothing of Tweel's language. The possibility that nouns keep shifting in Tweel's language may be evidence of confusion or of a superior antinomian awareness of radical individualism. Jarvis has a typical Western condescension to thought processes he cannot follow. He plays with (and discards) the idea that Tweel's language may be like that of the Negritoes who have "no word for food or water or man—words for good food and bad food, or rain water and sea water, or strong men and weak men—but no names for general classes. They're *too primitive to understand* that rain water and sea water are just different aspects of the same thing" (p. 22, emphasis added). To our post-Lévi-Straussian understanding, such condescension is entirely unjustified; though it is not clear how, in the context of 1934, we should interpret Jarvis's speech. Jarvis himself points to this specific problem of interpreting someone else's evaluation of intelligence when he argues that Tweel's description of the barrel people's intelligence is ambiguous. "Their intelligence was not of our order, but something different and beyond the logic of two and two is four. Maybe I missed his meaning. Perhaps he meant that their minds were of low degree, able to figure out the simple things—'One-one-two—yes!'—but not the more difficult things—'Two-two-four—no!'" (p. 34). Though Jarvis finally concludes that Tweel meant the first, there is good reason for the reader to see these perhaps intelligent creatures as limited, comic, mechanical zombies. They imitate language without attaining it. In a late scene we see them sacrifice themselves dispassionately.

These apparently epistemological problems (How can we evaluate alien intelligence? How can we tell affection from hostility?) may be misleading, however. Clearly, Jarvis' affection for Tweel exists regardless of the level of his intelligence, and, just as clearly, his affection for Putz and Harrison exists despite the hostile language. The difficulty is not one of knowing affection but one of expressing it openly. As in other SF stories we have studied, desire is again the issue, and again it is repeatedly blocked. In the scene in which Jarvis sees the image of Fancy Long, motives become deeply confused. As in a nightmare, behind the woman Jarvis finds the "black rope-armed horror" of the dream monster. But although Jarvis has a deep dread of the woman, he also desires her. The conflict leads to some bizarre moments. When Jarvis lets Tweel shoot the vision of the woman, we get one of a number of instances of narrative indecision, "I don't know why I stood there watching him take careful aim, but I did" (p. 30). Clearly, Jarvis has realized that the image is false, that this is not really Fancy Long. His declaration of ignorance about his motives is necessitated by the atrocity his abstention sanctions: he has to deny that he allowed a woman to be shot. But he is also caught in a moment of passionate desire so strong that even in its retelling it threatens to distort his rational understanding of the situation even in the retelling.

The dream monster apparently "uses its victim's longings and desires to trap its prey" (p. 31). Jarvis cautions the crew to watch out. "We can't even trust our eyes," he warns. "You might see me—I might see one of you—and back of it may be nothing but another of those black horrors" (p. 31). Such a conviction justifies repression of all affection. The danger of the dream monster is that it might lure the men by their desire for one another. The important issue here is not anxiety about homosexuality but anxiety about all desire. The difficulty is most palpable toward the end of the story when Tweel disappears and Jarvis exclaims, "He'd gone, and damn it! I wish—I wish he hadn't!" What strikes one here is the quite extraordinary flatness of the obviously deeply felt line. In part, the hesitation after "I wish" and the tepid "hadn't" are formulas of the era, but they are also further signs of difficulty with feelings. Friendship is a relationship with ambiguous potential. Though the barrel people's claim to it is clearly to be seen as shallow and ironic, when Jarvis says of Fancy Long, "just friends, get me," it is difficult to determine just what kind of a relationship is to be understood.

We see another instance of Jarvis' inability to say what he really feels and means when he stops himself in midsentence:

> "Yet, in spite of all difficulties, I *liked* Tweel, and I have a queer certainty that he liked me."
> "Nuts," repeated the captain. "Just daffy."
> "Yeah? Wait and see. A couple of times I've thought that perhaps we—" he paused, and then resumed his narrative (p. 21).

This last incomplete sentence is different from the usual narrative device in which the reader is able to fill in the words the speaker cannot say; here it is impossible to determine what Jarvis might have said. The break does not reveal what meaning the character is repressing. We can nevertheless speculate on some of the issues he might discuss at this point. His concern with liking Tweel may lead him to generalizations about human affection. Or Jarvis might be responding to Harrison's accusation of craziness and intending to generalize about sanity and alienness. Or he might be about to comment on Harrison's general attitude and language, on the slandering of those we actually like. Whatever the subject of his meditation, it breaks off on the enigma of the pronoun "we." The ambiguity of the "we" leaves it open whether his comment would be restricted to just Tweel and himself, or would include Harrison, to whom he has just responded, or the rest of the crew, or perhaps larger generalizations (we men, we humans, we communicators, we explorers). By breaking where it does, the sentence emphasizes the problem of the constitution of the group, the "we."

This enigmatic gap in the story is a moment at which the story encounters the real social dilemma posed by imagining the friendly alien. Try as it will to imagine forms of desire independent of social groups and conventions, the story finds itself inevitably forced to confront the crucial issue of the group. Even the unique couple, odd as it may be, constitutes a social group and thereby changes or distorts the larger social field. We may recall the extraordinary moment in Zamyatin's *We* when, as the revolutionaries surge into the city, one jubilantly exclaims, "We are acting!" D-503, caught between his love for I-330 and his still deeply social allegiance to the Benefactor, can only wonder in dismay, "Who are we? Who am I?"[9] The fantasy that we can define ourselves outside of the group is a powerful one, but it rather quickly comes up against the fact that the individual is defined, is only meaningful, against the background of the group. No sooner has the group been transcended than it must be reconstituted. Jarvis' dilemma is that he cannot— nor can any of us—"think" the contradiction of the individual and the group.

The question that arises is how much of the elaborate economy of love and hate in "A Martian Odyssey" is inherent in the formula fiction of America in the thirties and how much is structurally inherent in the act of imagining the friendly other? It would be naive to think that we could settle the question precisely and finally. Clearly some of Weinbaum's mechanisms are historically local. But if, for the historical contrast, we consider Le Guin's "Nine Lives," a much more self-conscious story published thirty-five years later, we can see that some aspects of this system of balances are common to efforts to imagine the sympathetic alien.[10]

Le Guin's story is conscious of the difficulties we have been examining. In it two miners, Martin (Argentine) and Pugh (Welsh), who have spent two years of irritable isolation on a volcanic planet, greet their assistance team, a "tenclone" consisting of five men and five women, all nearly identical. Relations between the two miners and the highly integrated tenclone are tense. When nine members of the tenclone are killed in an eruption, the survivor has to learn to trust and to gain emotional strength from men different from himself. Roughly the story's thesis is that the harmony that exists among members of the tenclone shows up as a kind of isolation ("Incest is it, or masturbation?" asks Pugh when two members of the clone make love), while the friction caused by the difference between Martin and Pugh shows up as a negotiated contact which can achieve love. By the dialectical process that Le Guin makes explicit, the gruff words that seem to point gratuitously to differences, initially signs of disharmony in the human ranks, finally become signs of affection.

We all know perfectly well, however, that differences do not necessarily breed affection. Le Guin's squabbling humans can finally declare their love for each other, but in other situations and with other people such petty nagging can be the obvious expression of deep antipathy. In "A Martian Odyssey," the system remains explosively undischarged of both possibilities. The love of the alien, whether Tweel or Martin, is in part a fantasy of overcoming obstacles to love.

But if both stories are in favor of "love," we should also note that in both stories it is the harmonious group that is a major object of distrust. The tenclone, while admirable for its efficiency, is too narcissistic (if one can use that term for a group) to engage in genuine social interaction. It substitutes good manners for true engagement with others. In "A Martian Odyssey," the barrel people are an allegory of social coherence; their mindless greeting, "We are v-r-r-riends! Ouch!" is in the same social category as the tenclone's good-mannered obliviousness to Pugh and Martin.

Tweel is, so far as we know, not part of a larger group. He is the only creature of his type Jarvis ever meets. The humans in the story seem to take it for granted that Tweel is a Martian, although he may be no more aboriginal than they are. After Jarvis tries to signify that Earth is his home, "Tweel set up such an excited clacking that I was certain he understood. He jumped up and down, and suddenly he pointed at himself and then at the sky, and then at himself and at the sky again. He pointed at his middle and then at Arcturus, at his head and then at Spica, at his feet and then at half a dozen stars, while I just gaped at him" (p. 20). This is a confusing message, but after it one might expect Jarvis to investigate Tweel's origins more thoroughly. Instead, he just repeats the message about his own origins. We, in the meantime, may well suspect that Tweel is not Martian at all, and that he is more alone than Jarvis. The bond between Tweel and Jarvis is, therefore, not a sign of social integration, but rather the opposite: they represent individuals free from all social bonds and definitions who, in this state of isolation, find meaningful connection. At the moment Jarvis is reunited with his human comrades, Tweel is lost to him. Both Le Guin and Weinbaum aspire to finding bonds of loyalty and affection between individuals apart from and unrelated to the larger groups to which they belong. If "A Martian Odyssey" runs up against the problem of who "we" are, it also fantasizes a friendship that makes questions of "we" irrelevant.

We observe here a dialectical process that will belong to any consideration of the alien. The story of the hostile alien is often an exercise in excluding individuals because of their group type; the story of the benign alien is often an exercise in finding a bond that transcends groups. In "First Contact" it is on this ground that Tommy, deep in the midst of space, finds his alien friend, Buck. Such a story isolates the individual and emphasizes his or her difference from the rest of the species. This rejection of the group, while it may lead to a readiness to accept the individual alien, may also lead to a disregarding of social factors that generate discrimination in the first place. Just as the phrase, "Some of my best friends are X," is often the preface for a discriminatory generalization about X, this claim to transcend group categories by finding the alien individual friendly, far from obliterating the categories, allows them to operate with impunity, beyond the control of rational awareness.

I would therefore suggest that the story of the benign alien may not be any more socially constructive than that of the hostile alien. The Freudian bond of "the narcissism of minor differences" is based on a strict emotional economy. Freud argues that the injunction to "love thy neighbor as thyself" entails a disastrous contradiction: I can love so indiscriminately only if I disregard or devalue the very qualities and virtues that earn love.[11] Similarly, I can love the extraordinary alien only by abandoning the social conventions that allow for rational exchange and understanding.

THE PLEASURE OF THE MONSTROUS CHILD

There remains one further permutation of alienness, a sort of inversion of the structure of exclusion, in which the reader is placed in the position of the alien. One story in particular from *Science Fiction Hall of Fame*, Matheson's "Born of Man and Woman" (1950), epitomizes this particular structure, though we see aspects of it in "Mimsy Were the Borogoves" and "It's a *Good* Life." This type of story presents a paradox: how can I be alien, since the alien is the other, the not-I? Insofar as these are fantasies of superiority and of unjust exclusion, they can also be considered as a transformation of the genius story. These stories express the condescension and rage that we find in Rand but that are usually denied in SF genius stories. However, what links these "monstrous child" stories with the alien is the rationale they give to such destructive emotions.

Though there are occasional SF stories that focus on limitations—Simak's story of the son's failure to escape the shadow of his father—most commonly SF tries to grant all wishes. The "monstrous child" motif, while it may pretend to find its meditation fearful, indulges in childish fantasies of being powerful. Underneath its facade of horror, such a story delights in the child's grotesque domination of its world. The monstrous child is the agent of pleasurable violence and therefore is unlike the hostile alien itself, which, while perhaps at a deep level a reflection of the self, must be externalized, distanced, and punished.

In Latin, *monstrum* means both *divine omen* and *unnatural growth*, both *miraculous portent* and *abomination*. In the motif we are examining this double sense is common. We see it clearly at the end of such classic SF novels as *Childhood's End*, when the children evolve into the Overmind, and *A Canticle for Liebowitz*, when Rachel, Mrs. Grales' childish second head, comes alive. In both cases these grotesque childish presences betoken a future which is both horrible and redeemed. In part this contradiction renders a psychological dilemma: we dread the transformation that, while destroying us, will advance the species. But, in the stories we will study, the ambivalence is also an expression of a fantasy of vengeful triumph which must be hidden because, at some level, it is socially intolerable.

Charlie learns in "Flowers for Algernon," that people don't "like" geniuses. The disguises desire must undergo in the monstrous child stories are evidence of the pressure on these stories to conceal the selfishness that lies at the heart of fantasies of triumph. The social stigma functioning at the story's surface allows the story to disavow the fantasy that motivates it even as it enjoys it. But that stigma also suggests a genuine social issue by encouraging conventional reactions to monstrosity, so that the motif itself is a union of opposites. The genius wants to be seen as the central figure in society and, at the same time, as exceptional to that society. By a complex series of negations the story of the monstrous child manages to satisfy this contradictory demand.

"Born of Man and Woman," by its restricted point-of-view technique, clearly satisfies this subgenre. The reader shares the experience of an eight-year-old, who seems to be a human spider chained in the cellar of a suburban house by its parents. The monster is as pathetic as it is grotesque. Like the monster in *Frankenstein*, it wants to be liked, but its gestures of sociability—coming to see the laughing people upstairs, looking out the cellar window at playing children—arouse the antipathy of the people to whom it appeals. It murders a small dog in self-defense. But what is most interesting is that its grotesqueness—it is many legged, strong, slimy, drips green blood, and hisses—is finally not just a source of hostility and isolation, but a kind of power. The story's final lines ring, not just of terror, but of justice and revenge: "I will show them. I will do what I did that once. I will screech and laugh loud. I will run on the walls. Last I will hang head down by all my legs and laugh and drip green all over until they are sorry they didn't be nice to me. If they try to beat me again Ill [sic] hurt them. I will" [443]. This fantasy is one of immensely satisfying but emotionally infantile retaliation.

Along with this fantasy of turning the sources of pain and isolation into a source of power and revenge is a deep hostility to the ordinary, middle-class, adult world—a world of repression, social appearances, and a profound lack of sympathetic understanding. The father and mother hide this monstrous child with no care at all for its feelings. And the child retaliates by offering the potential for social embarrassment. The green that drips from its arm when it is beaten evokes disgust, and even the final gesture of defiance is in large part the threat of a tantrum which will offend by violating conventional codes of behavior.

This story plays not just on aversion, but on childish feelings of being mis-used and getting revenge. The last line offers a conclusion which is deeply vague. The child threatens physical retribution, but the final "I will" at the close is ambiguous. It may be a declaration of resolve, something like, "I swear." But it may also ring of childish insecurity, the bluff that the child hopes will never be called, like running away, or holding one's breath too long. Such an ambiguity allows the story to be both threatening and yet to maintain the pathetic stance of the mistreated child.

Such an ambiguity, however, is also a contradiction, and the strain to render the monstrous child's point of view cannot quite hold the contradic-tion together. If we look at it closely, we find a number of issues raised by this point of view do not make sense. At the heart of this self-conscious exer-cise in point-of-view narration is the enigma of how the story is told. Is it written? and, if so, how? Could such a wild child learn to write with parents such as this? Yet, if the story is "told," then the misspellings, such as "retch" in the opening paragraph, and the typos, such as "Ill" in the final line, make no sense. The syntactic errors are elaborately awkward, the consequence, not of a simple prelinguistic mind, but of a complex dialect. The opening line, "This day when it had light mother called me retch" depicts an elabo-rate syntax made clumsy by the unidiomatic "had" and the misspelling. The point-of-view so laboriously projected here is, in fact, impossible. The depic-tion of primitive monstrosity entails a double consciousness. It represents an attempt to imagine as an adult the thought processes of oneself at an immature stage. The narrative technique presents an analog to what it would be like to imagine the state of mind of a genius. It is an exercise in knowing more than one can know, of being precocious.

Padgett's "Mimsy Were the Borogoves" (1943) complicates this simple identification with the monstrous child by explicitly encouraging its readers to read it as a horror story about aliens. However, in this case the story's narrative technique directly contradicts the suggestions of horror by assuring us that alternate modes of knowing are comprehensible, even comforting. The story tells of two children who are accidently "educated" by futuristic toys into a way of thinking that results in their escaping normal human perception and entering into another dimension altogether.

The story spends some time developing the idea that all infants are "aliens." The thesis is part of the rationalization that will allow for the children's strange education, but it is an idea that is so repeatedly insisted upon that we may begin to wonder about its implications. The narrative voice, which began by sketching a future and distant world from which the strange toys will originate, develops the basic idea:

> From the standpoint of logic, a child is rather horribly perfect. A baby may be even more perfect, but so alien to an adult that only superficial standards of comparison apply. The thought processes of an infant are completely unimaginable. But babies think, even before birth. In the womb they move and sleep, not entirely through instinct. We are conditioned to react rather peculiarly to the idea that a nearly-viable embryo may think. We are surprised, shocked into laughter, and repelled. Nothing human is alien.
>
> But a baby is not human. An embryo is far less human. . . .
>
> Give a young child pencil and paper, and he will draw something which looks different to him than to an adult. The absurd scribbles have little resemblance to a fire engine, [but it *is* a fire engine] to a baby. Perhaps it is even three-dimensional. Babies think differently and see differently [12] (p. 239).

This move from the plausible statement that there is a difference between the logic of a baby and an adult to the highly dubious conclusion that a baby is not human will not stand up to analysis. But this contradiction is central to the essential fantasy of the story. By treating the child as an alien rather than as simply an undeveloped adult, the narrative gives the child a dignity and intellectual authority it would otherwise lack. Such positioning of the child is not a form of xenophobia; it does not ask us to exclude the child; on the contrary, it validates feelings of discomfort and alienation commonly felt by adolescents. This logical contradiction allows us to think of adolescents as profoundly different from adults and as having the potential of another, higher species. The claim that children are aliens functions logically rather than generically.

Similarly, the horror that the parents feel as their children disappear into another way of thinking and perceiving is a generic false lead. Their horror is less a guide to our own responses than a sign of their incomprehension of what is happening.[13] As is common in these stories, the children are confident and, for all we can tell, happy in their alienness. The adults are horrified, not by a threat to the children—there is no trace of the fairy tale motif of child as victim of some Elf King—but simply by an evolution they cannot understand or follow. Part of the pleasure of the story comes from the children's control and the adults' helplessness. The expression of horror on the adult's part is an aspect of the child's triumph.

The style of "Mimsy Were the Borogoves" works, not to frighten us, but to help us side with the children and their independent education. Adulthood is seen as a stodgy world of pedantic correctness (at least four times the parents correct the children's grammar) and alcoholic self-consolation (the parents drink, at different times, martinis, scotches, brandies, and collinses). And the moments of supposed horror are always defused, either by vague language, or by deflecting attention away from the disturbing event. For example, when the scientist of the future sends the box of toys back in time, we are told "The Box went away. The manner of its departure hurt Untharsten's eyes." The toys are described in terms of fuzzy reactions: "the angles formed by the wires were vaguely shocking." When Emma shows her mother how the doll comes apart, we hear, "Oh, It . . . *ugh!*"

Even the paradox that babies are not human is, far from shocking, consoling just because it is declared with such authority. If Hollowell, the child psychologist in the story who makes the same argument a few pages later, were the only source for the idea, we might find it problematic. But it is part of a linked series of assertions about the nature of children that, however alien they may claim the children are, exude a comfortable sense that all possible difficulties have already been understood. We have been set up early with lines like, "But no boy has ever left a box unopened," and "It was a Toy. Scott sensed that, with the unerring instinct of a child." Later we hear of "the instinct of children for avoiding interruptions," and that "Youngsters are instinctive dramatists." With the line "Children are different from the mature animal because they think in another way," we are edging toward the paradoxically complacent convention of the unconventionality of children. Finally, in the line, "a baby is not human," we hear, not just a contradiction, but another piece of common wisdom. This story takes a certain pleasure in teasing itself with a threat that it does not really fear. By using an omniscient narrator who, from the very start, can explain how the toys come from the future and what kind of educational purpose they serve, "Mimsy Were the Borogoves" keeps the story about the unthinkable carefully within bounds. The reader is never insecure; there is no need to reinterpret early passages; there is no misunderstanding that is later set right. The confusion which is thematically central is distanced and given to the adults *in* the story.

"Mimsy Were the Borogoves" avoids the more unsettling implications of its subject, but horror does seem an appropriate term to describe the reader's feelings about the situation in Bixby's "It's a *Good* Life" (1953). As a horrifically attentive and punishing superego the monstrous child, Anthony, enforces repression on his whole community. The townsfolk undergo exercises in "thinking nothing in particular as hard as [they] could" or in arguing "It's good for her to feel bad." But, by a mechanism intrinsic to the subgenre, such a story of total victimization also gives expression to authentic though unacknowledged desire. At the heart of "It's a *Good* Life," under the irony which wants us to read *good* as *horrible*, lie a cluster of fantasies about goodness. The explicit horror liberates the imagination and allows it to indulge itself in relaxed and unambiguous images of happiness. The vision joins a psychological moment, childhood, with a historical moment, the middle-American small town before "post-industrialism."

Exploring the childhood vision first, we see Anthony as a fantasy of an unrestricted infantile universality. The world is entirely an expression of his egoistic desires. While our appreciation of the horror at being the victim of someone else's untempered feelings is clear enough, we are likely to overlook the fact that when the story spends some time on Anthony's own imaginings it falls into a quite extraordinary idyll of satisfied desire:

He walked clear to the edge of the cornfield, and over to where a grove of shadowy green trees covered cool, moist, dark ground, and lots of leafy undergrowth, and jumbled moss-covered rocks, and a small spring that made a clear, clean pool. Here Anthony *liked* to rest and watch the birds and insects and small animals that rustled and scampered and chirped about. He *liked* to lie on the cool ground and look up through the moving greenness overhead, and watch the insects flit in the hazy soft sunbeams that stood like slanting, glowing bars between ground and treetops. Somehow, he *liked* the thoughts of the little creatures in this place better than the thoughts outside; and while the thoughts he picked up here weren't very strong or very clear, he could get enough out of them to know what the little creatures *liked* and *wanted*, and he spent a lot of time making the grove more like what they *wanted* it to be. The spring hadn't always been here; but one time he had found *thirst* in one small furry mind, and had brought subterranean water to the surface in a clear cold flow, and had watched blinking as the creature drank, feeling its *pleasure.* Later he had made the pool, when he found a small *urge* to swim.

He had made rocks and trees and bushes and caves, and sunlight here and shadows there, because he had felt in all the tiny minds around him the *desire*—or the instinctive *want*—for this kind of *resting* place, and that kind of *mating* place, and this kind of place to *play*, and that kind of *home.*

And somehow the creatures from all the fields and pastures around the grove had seemed to know that this was *a good place,* for there were always more of them coming in—every time Anthony came out here there were more creatures than the last time, and more *desires* and *needs* to be tended to. Every time there would be some kind of creature he had never seen before, and he would find its mind, and see what it *wanted,* and then give it to it.

He like to help them. He like to feel their simple *gratification.* (pp. 528–529, emphases added).

I have quoted the whole of this extraordinary passage and have emphasized the frequent words indicating happy desire to show how thoroughly the story indulges in a vision of the benign and pleasureable nature which Anthony creates and which in turn gives him pleasure. The happy kingdom is also inhabited by small predators, which Anthony destroys, and rats and spiders, which he playfully torments with their own greed, but during the time of the quoted passage the motive of the vision is morally positive, not sadistic. Compared to Kidder, Anthony is a benign and attentive deity.

The second scene of intense pleasure occurs at Dan Hollis' birthday celebration. Despite Anthony's constantly threatening censorship, the good feelings of the victimized community rise to great heights. In the solidarity of this primitively technological, subsistence community, trivial items, such as an old phonograph record, recover an enormous pleasure denied to our more jaded world. And once these small things have recovered their sharpened value, the simple pleasures of sharing and remembering also increase until Dan Hollis will risk his life to hear "You Are My Sunshine."

The horror of the story comes from the intense anxiety about maintaining a somewhat arbitrary correctness. It is when Dan Hollis gets drunk and becomes emotional that Anthony punishes him. And yet, despite—or perhaps because of—this horror, there seem to be a number of pleasure sources for the reader here. The story can move among various strong emotions such as nostalgia, anger, and sadistic domination not usually indulged in SF. Normal adult irritation at the tyranny of children as well as the child's pleasure in controlling more powerful adults speak strongly in the story.

The story enjoys both feelings, but it has no way of seeing them in a socially viable setting. Its achievement is to acknowledge the strains and the pleasures, and it ends up preaching a form of passivity. Near the end of the story the narrative voice breaks away from the description of Dan Hollis' party and, in what we later discover to be Mom's voice, gives us a final meditation on life under Anthony's puritan imagination:

> Mom looked out of the front window, across the darkened road, across Henderson's darkened wheat field to the vast, endless, gray nothingness in which the little village of Peaksville floated like a soul— the huge nothingness that was evident at night, when Anthony's brassy day had gone.
>
> It did no good to wonder where they were . . . no good at all. Peaksville was just someplace. Someplace away from the world. It was wherever it had been since that day three years ago when Anthony had crept from her womb and old Doc Bates—God rest him—had screamed and dropped him and tried to kill him, and Anthony had whined and done the thing. He had taken the village someplace. Or had destroyed the world and left only the village, nobody knew which.
>
> It did no good to wonder about it. Nothing at all did any good— except to live as they must live. Must always, always live, if Anthony would let them.
>
> These thoughts were dangerous, she thought (p. 541).

We may reasonably ask here, *which* thoughts? The memory of Anthony's birth? The meditation on the mystery of where Peaksville is? Or—and this seems likely to me—the still repressed thoughts of possible happiness that the penultimate paragraph of the quotation strongly suggests by its very insistence on the impossibility of escape. The last line of the quotation would seem to be playing the same kind of game with self-awareness that we see in Margaret in "That Only a Mother"—thoughts are denied even before they are expressed.

This resignation, expressed in the repetition of "it did no good," has distinctly political implications. While the parallels to fifties' images of life in a Stalinist totalitarianism may come first to mind, the precision of the American imagery that shapes the story makes it impossible not to see in it an anxiety that belongs to American cultural history. I am reminded of a joke that was current in the early fifties: I'm glad I don't like spinach, because if I did like it I would eat it, and then I'd be unhappy because I hate spinach. Such anticipatory self-censorship occurs, not just in terrorist states, but in the midst of the family.

The story of the monstrous child punishes itself for its utopian pleasures even before it indulges in them. By rendering the pleasure horrible it creates the pretense that it disavows what it actually enjoys. However, the pleasures the adults deny are not the main energy in the story. Anthony himself renders an extraordinary fantasy of childish power. Unlike the monster in "Born of Man and Woman," Anthony is not motivated by revenge for mistreatment. A distant cousin of the Infant of Saguntum, he enters the world hating it, but instead of retreating to the womb, he punishes the world. The horrific energy of this story may be characterized as an expression of a rage that inspires much technocratic utopianism. It is not outrage at the injustice done to others; it is a more elementary, infantile feeling of rage at ones own powerlessness, at the failure of the world to meet ones own desires and needs. Often this rage takes itself out on the aspirations of technocracy itself. We see such hostility in the gratuitous violence at the end of Bradbury's "Mars is Heaven," when the Martian-humans unnecessarily destroy the spaceship. As in the Bixby story, an elaborately satisfying fantasy is concealed in a nightmare.

I want to make it clear that this rage is a subliminal and largely unconscious complement to the idealization of rationality that characterizes the technocratic ideology. We see it repeatedly—in the killing of Marilyn in "The Cold Equations" or in the brief description of mayhem on the roads in "The Roads Must Roll"—often at the very moment that rationality is being praised. We hear it behind Phil's seemingly sensitive offer to "yank Helen's coils tonight." These moments are not ironic keys that tell us to reverse the meanings of the texts; they are part of the very richness of expression by which these texts render the pleasures and the costs of technocracy. If the alien gives readers a rationale for specific violent emotions, the monstrous child teaches them that running through the genre is a more general hatred of the flawed world. Technological rationality is proud of its mission, but it is also occasionally willing to see the whole thankless social construction collapse. It is this rage which permits Kornbluth to send the morons on a one way trip into space, and which, as we shall see in the next chapter, permits Asimov cheerfully to allow for the possibility that civilization cannot be saved. A responsible technocrat cannot acknowledge such feelings, but they appear frequently enough for us to understand that although stories like "Born of Man and Woman" and "It's a *Good* Life," seem far from orthodox technocratic considerations, they nevertheless render feelings that underlie stories focused more explicitly on technology.

History, Politics, and the Future

7

THE RHETORIC OF PREDICTION

It is intrinsic to the technocratic vision of SF in the period around World War II that it should believe that insight into technology gives insight into the future. In his 1957 talk Heinlein spends some time developing the idea that the technical background of SF writers enables them to have foresight. "If a writer knows that mankind wants to do something or needs to do something and the writer is reasonably familiar with current trends in research and development, it is not too hard for him to predict approximately what one of the solutions will be."[1] Heinlein's confidence is in part based on a faith in the autonomous character of technical development, of which one consequence is that political issues no longer matter. He smoothes out political difference in the phrases "mankind wants to do something" and "[mankind] needs to do something." Such a technocratic view sees history as a distraction. Rational engineering and management—with some help from the occasional genius—will supplant the struggle of interests that has defined politics and made history. Issues of intense disagreement and conflict are treated as resolved and the only question requiring decision involves what Ellul would call "technique." As Habermas observes, this denial of the political is at its heart political: "The assertion that politically consequential decisions are reduced to carrying out the immanent exigencies of disposable techniques and that therefore they can no longer be made the theme of practical considerations, serves in the end merely to conceal pre-existing, unreflected social interests and prescientific decisions."[2] The SF fantasies about history in this era do not reflect on the political uses of technology but go to quite elaborate lengths to create a coherent narrative that tells of the potentialities and the inconsequence of prediction.

Forecasting

Prediction is a term that is used for a wide range of prognostications. I use it here to refer to statements about future events or states of being that lack general consensus. Thus, I exclude from prediction obvious truisms ("Winter will come" or "This stone will fall rather than rise") and scientific conclusions ("This isotope will decay at a certain rate," or "This drug will cure this disease"). A statement is a prediction in my sense when a counter statement is also imaginable and plausible. As we shall see, H. G. Wells took some pleasure in *not* making such a distinction, but unless we try to discriminate between truisms and predictions that acknowledge options, we will end up in the unreflective situation Habermas describes. Of course, there is a range of statements which may or may not be predictions, and the discussion of them constitutes the basic terms of much political debate. Many social prognostications fall into this ambiguous realm: are economic, political, or sociological forecasts truisms or predictions? If I can convince you that the statement "There will be a Third World War in twenty years" is a truism rather than a prediction, I have already won a political argument.

Given this meaning of prediction, an absolutely certain prediction is a paradoxical impossibility. If we could imagine a situation in which it were possible, we might reasonably suppose the further paradox that it would not be convincing. The sinner damned, the lover rejected, the criminal condemned, all hope that something will interfere—a redeemer, a change of heart, a pardon—that will change the absolutely certain prediction and render the future different from what it will be. As Joan Robinson remarks, prophets of disaster would not bother to speak if they really believed their predictions were certain.[3] And the happier prospects, even though we may rejoice in them and encourage their fulfillment, nevertheless are promises that one trusts at one's peril. People would disbelieve the certain prediction, not in the spirit of Camus' futile self-defining rebellion, but out of a deep need to escape the closure such prediction would entail.

If a prediction about human actions is believed, a set of contradictions follow. In the case of a prophecy that is specific about time, the more convincing the prediction, the less likely it is that it will be fulfilled. As Max Weber argues, speculation introduces irrationality.[4] The convincing prediction can itself change the state of affairs in such a way that the event can no longer happen the way it was predicted. If I with assurance forecast a rise in a stock price tomorrow, the stock will rise today in anticipation of tomorrow's rise and thus upset my forecast.[5] If the Justified Sinner had not been promised salvation, he would not have damned himself.[6] On the opposite side is what Popper calls the "Oedipus effect," the event that would not have happened had it not been predicted. It was only because of the prediction that he would kill his father and marry his mother that Oedipus was abandoned as a child, thus setting in motion the chain of events that led to his killing his father and marrying his mother.[7] Predictions may or may not come true, and often they shape the future in unpredictable ways. At a certain level this is an ironic genre that takes as its theme the vanity of human knowledge and the futility of human hope.

In this century a trust in scientific prediction has developed which claims to be untroubled by these old rhetorical paradoxes, and a specific genre has grown up which indulges simultaneously fantasies of free will and fantasies of determinism. John Naisbitt's *Megatrends* is but the most popular recent example of this kind of literature, and it is typical that Naisbitt should close his prediction of the information saturated future he confidently foresees with these words: "In a time of the parenthesis [i.e. in our own time between two eras] we have extraordinary leverage and influence—individually, professionally, and institutionally—if we can only get a clear sense, a clear conception, a clear vision of the road ahead."[8] "Leverage and influence" imply our free ability to choose and shape the future. The metaphors suggest power. But the last part of the statement clearly implies that the particular future, "the road ahead" of which we get a glimpse, is predetermined, is there whatever we do. Our free will is limited to choosing or missing the future that is, so the prediction asserts, inevitable. Free will and fatalism coexist in this passage in happy, probably unconscious, contradiction. This is not, however, merely a moment of confusion; this is the accepted, standard logic of the genre.

We find the coexistence of free will and fatalism at the core of H. G. Wells's "The Discovery of the Future" (1902), a founding document both for scientific forecasting and for SF. Wells's thesis in this lecture is that just as one can reason backwards from the present and reconstruct the earliest states of life and the earth, so one should be able to reason forward and foresee the future state of society. It is, he claims, simply a matter of understanding the "operating causes" and following the deductive chains rigorously and without sentiment. If the physical sciences can predict the movements of the stars, so it should be possible, Wells argues, to predict human affairs:

> If I am right in saying that science aims at prophecy, and if the specialist in each science is in fact doing his best now to prophesy within the limits of his field, what is there to stand in the way of our building up this growing body of forecast into an ordered picture of the future that will be just as certain, just as strictly science, and perhaps just as detailed as the picture that has been built up within the last hundred years of the geological past?[9]

The equation of physical science with historical prediction implies a simple idea of history, shaped by sequences of cause and effect ("operating causes"), and determined from the moment of its beginning. However, what Wells asserts are the simple data of history are in fact deep and basic issues of histori- cal debate. Within a few years, in *A Modern Utopia* and in his socialist pamphlets, Wells directly contradicts this determinist reduction of history.[10] It is not, after all, a view of history that allows one to act to change the world in any way. But it is just such a view that is most satisfying to a predictor and it will be much subscribed to by later forecasters.

The images from the sciences, here astronomy, elsewhere geology and evolutionary biology, allow Wells to avoid one of the profound difficulties of all forecasting: if we cannot predict our individual selves, how can we expect to predict on a larger scale? Wells ingeniously turns this argument against itself: "I would advance the suggestion that an increase in the number of hu- man beings considered may positively simplify the case instead of complicat- ing it; that as the individuals increase in number they begin to average out" (p. 377). He demonstrates this by analogy to a pile of sand: you can predict the shape of the pile quite accurately and even tell which size grains will be where in the pile even though you have no specific knowledge about any individual grain. In certain respects this is a profound observation—it is just such reasoning that justifies the use of statistics in sociology—but when ap- plied to history and forecasting the analogy is problematic. Wells admits that it does not allow for "the great man." More significantly, though, it does not allow for conscious action by *anyone*. Moreover, the image presumes a per- spective which is valuable only to someone outside the pile, that is, outside history. To someone inside the pile, to the specific and individual grain of sand, the shape, while of some interest, is less important than the relation of the different grains, how they meet, abut, and move against each other. To take a perspective that treats such matters as microscopic and trivial is to assume a position that disallows all important political questions. A mean- ingful insight needs to examine the precise social relations that allow the heap to exist and of which the shape of the pile is a final but fairly inconse- quential expression.

The image of the pile of sand has a second implication that subtly denies the importance of history. Just as the grain of sand is entirely passive, all heaps of sand approach the same shape. Implicit in the analogy, therefore, is the assumption that all social situations must be the same. Thus, the image invoked to justify the plausibility of forecasting social history suggests that there is no such thing as history, which would distinguish different societies or the same society at different times. This assumption tends to see all so- cieties as phases in a single evolution of "civilization." More specifically, it tends to see the current phase of capitalist democracy as a high point that needs to be conserved and that, perhaps, cannot be surpassed.

Since Wells, the history of scientific forecasting has gone in two directions. One, which I call professional forecasting, has sought to establish a method with a high degree of accuracy in its estimates of probabilities. The other, which I call prophetic forecasting, has developed a new rhetoric of persuasion. While claiming to deal with society and the future, both subtly deny politics and thereby reject the possibility of real history.

Though there is some disagreement among professional forecasters about how far into the future we are able to foresee with any accuracy, they generally agree that the short-term forecast (one year ahead) can be made with a comparatively high degree of quantitative accuracy and assurance, and that the long-term forecast (fifteen years or more) is a highly imprecise estimate.[11] Many professional forecasters, who help their clients make immediate managerial decisions, simply reject such long-term work as unscientific, as the kind of prophesy that leads to unrealistic expectations from laymen and to later disillusionment and cynicism about the real possibilities of forecasting. The typical wisdom argues, "Forecasts should develop the pragmatic insight needed to make this year's decisions, and not focus on esoteric problems of the year 2000."[12]

As the profession has worked toward developing itself as a science, it has drawn back from Wells's daring vision. The present day technician rejects what Bertrand de Jouvenel calls the "pregnant forecast," that is the forecast that does not submit to criticism of its methods, assumptions, and data. Doubts about the possibility of being absolutely right about the future lead modern professional forecasters to avoid the very word "prediction." Usually they present their audience, not with a statement of what they think will be, but with a set of possibilities and probabilities.[13] The future is seen as an expanding pattern of options, as a network of forking paths, or as a fan with many leaves, and the forecasters' job is not to say what will be but to make their audience aware of the choices available.

Implicit in the short-term enterprise is also a severe narrowing of the social field. The short-term forecast can be comparatively accurate just because, barring a catastrophe—and that qualification marks an important limitation[14]—the odds are good that the general socio-political environment will probably not be so drastically different a year from now as to seriously flaw the forecast. By presuming continuity, the professional forecast manages to justify ignoring major, long-term social and political changes and possibilities. It is content to focus on a narrow set of technological and economic problems. The profession itself does not see this blinkered social vision as a flaw. Insofar as such forecasting has been guided by the demands of a special audience—business and financial managers, government officials, and military planners—it has willingly sacrificed breadth of vision for high probability and accuracy.

De Jouvenel sees the purpose of long-term forecasting as only a warning, not as a prediction. Such prevision, he argues, does not tell us what the world will or even could be; it shows us the possibilities of certain trends and it draws our attention to "points of fulcrum," important crises and decisions upon which the future hinges.[15] There is, of course, a tradition of SF that sees its purpose to extrapolate just such warnings. But prophetic forecasters like Naisbitt do not limit themselves to de Jouvenel's cautionary mode. They claim to show us "the road ahead." And yet if, as their professional colleagues would argue, such long-term prediction is unscientific, we then have to ask, what it is. What purpose does it serve? And the answer, quite simply, is that such forecasting is essentially a rhetorical trope, a device of persuasion.

Even professional short-term forecasters recognize the rhetorical aspect of the science. As one technological forecaster is aware, "presenting the forecast" is an important stage of the total operation because the "decisionmaker" addressed has to be swayed. "It is not sufficient for the forecaster to have turned out a product which will be admired by his professional peers for its elegance and sophistication. If it is not used by a decisionmaker, the work which went into it was wasted."[16] We might call this particular plight of the forecaster the "Cassandra complex," the feeling of being right but unheeded. Because the proof lies in the future, the validity of the forecaster's case can never be proven at a time when it will make a difference. The longer the term of the forecast, the more the act of prediction itself becomes a rhetorical gesture. Thus Naisbitt's optimistic prediction, while claiming to "foresee" the road ahead, is really an attempt to persuade us to choose and pursue the road he can imagine. In the guise of prediction it preaches a set of values and behaviors. His book is, therefore, not so much a scientific as a political document. And yet, as we shall see, such political documents hide their politics.

The Denial of History

Wells's model, we will recall, has two important consequences which will characterize the rhetoric of much later prediction. First, by claiming that all times, like all heaps of sand, are basically the same, it denies the possibility of different eras with different contours. Second, in the name of history it denies the importance of the very sociological details that are the basis of economics and politics, and therefore, of history itself.

Such a denial of detailed history would seem to be central to the way the genre of prophetic forecasting works. This one recent example from Gerard K. O'Neill's *2081* is representative:

In studying history and analyzing current events, we find that there are no new, sweeping, irresistible forces in the areas of politics or economics. All our present political forms—dictatorship, democracy, and their variants—have been with us in some form for millennia, but none shows signs of taking over irrevocably. Instead, we see the same shifting, re-forming pattern that has existed for many centuries: nations fragment into smaller ones under the pressures of ethnic or religious differences and regionalism, while at the same time, in other parts of the world, small nations are added to the territory of larger ones by the age-old method of military conquest. Unfortunately, warfare shows no sign of going out of fashion; there are several times more wars going on in any given year in the last half of this century than there were in an average year of the first half. It seems wisest, therefore, to guess that the political world of 2081 will still be fragmented into nations, and that nations will still be heavily armed. I do not see any *political* idea that has a realistic possibility of improving the situation. My stress of "political" is to remind us that there may be technological developments that will alter international confrontations in a fundamental way. We can hope, in any case, that the largest nations will continue to avoid direct warfare with each other.

It is also safe to assume that the most enduring institutions and characteristics of societies will continue. Great universities will survive, in some form, as they have for centuries. Though governments will be overthrown and both the names and the boundaries of nations will shift, the same languages will still be spoken in the same geographical areas.[17]

We have to agree that, of course, some things may not change very much in the near future, but most of the assertions here cry out for qualification. Where are the nineteenth century nationalist consolidations of Germany and Italy in O'Neill's vision of fragmented and conquered nations? We may assent to the proposition that great universities may survive "in some form," but that last phrase permits and at the same time ignores any change whatsoever. After all, the difference between the nineteenth century ideas of a university, whether English, German, or American, and the modern center of research and scholarship is profound, hardly the sign of bland continuity O'Neill assumes. O'Neill will resort to a broad, vacuous terminology ("dictatorships, democracy, and their variants") to describe phenomena of tremendous variation and importance asking for precise and subtle distinctions. But O'Neill's argument is carried less by these individual details, that, after all, could be adjusted, than by the bored tone of the whole passage which insists that political or economic changes are insignificant. A line like, "Unfortunately, warfare shows no sign of going out of fashion," works more by its tone than by any real thought: the resigned "unfortunately," and the strangely innocuous word "fashion" imply that warfare belongs in the same trivial category with tailfins and hemlines.

Wars, universities, governments, and economies change profoundly in time and there is an ideological argument implicit in the denial of such change. Different periods are characterized by different political and social problems and by different formulations of and solutions to them. O'Neill's underlying assumption is that there is no such thing as history that will shape and limit human thought and perception. Such an assumption allows him to make the extraordinary claim that "if he'd had the right idea, a Stone-Age man could have built a sailplane out of wood and either cloth or the silk that was available in China as long ago as 2600 B.C." (p. 34). To "have the right idea" is possible only within the constraints of an historical period, and to imagine a Stone-Age man inventing a sailplane because in theory the technology existed (though silk, as O'Neill says here, would be invented many millennia after the Stone Age) is to indulge in a fantasy of genius free from all social structures and ideological constraints. Such ahistorical fantasies, while denying the importance of politics at the historical level, nevertheless serve a political purpose at the local, practical level by implying that the future belongs solely to technology. O'Neill has some strange passages in which he debates with himself about whether the stimulus war gives to technological development may not make war good and peace bad (p. 18). Much of his vision of a century from now ignores social organization and is devoted to modes of transportation in cities, around airports, on highways, in the air, in space. Such anti-historicism allows the futurologist to take the future out of the hands of the politician or the sociologist and give it to the scientist and the technician. And once that move has been made, then, lo and behold, these same prophetic futurologists, by their passive vision of the possibilities of modern technology, become the active shapers of the future.[18]

We find this same sense that prediction is easy because history does not exist in Isaac Asimov's essay, "Social Science Fiction."[19] Asimov defends SF as a predictive mode on the grounds that history repeats itself. To prove this, he writes a one page description of a revolution, leaving blanks for specific names,then gives us three sets of right answers, from the English, French, and Russian revolutions. His point is that a writer predicting the future need only employ the basic paradigm in order to give a fairly accurate picture. Asimov's game, where not simply a statement of the obvious (somebody wins, somebody loses), is trivial. It shows only a fortune-teller's ability to write ambiguously, not an understanding of the deep mechanisms, the "operative causes," or the structures of history. A sentence such as, "Eventually, a strong government was formed under _____," (p. 280) while it has the air of saying something, is empty. "Eventually" evades the important time issue (a week? a year? a decade?). The words "strong" and "under" beg all questions about what kind of political arrangement the word "government" entails. And all the important issues of whom such people represented, where politically they came from, and how they consolidated this power are evaded by the vapid passive, "was formed." Such a sentence tells us nothing of significance about Cromwell, Robespierre, or Lenin as historical figures. It is a way of obscuring any actual historical insight and thereby of arguing that the details of real history do not particularly matter. Meaningful historical thought can begin only after such trivial similarities have been absorbed.[20]

At the heart of such prediction lies a series of contradictions. Though it claims to study history, prediction denies history. By the denial of history it dismisses conventional politics, but in doing so it becomes itself a political statement. It looks to the future as a guide for choice in the present, of generating "leverage," to use Naisbitt's term, but by posing the prospect of a sure future it preaches the inevitable, the immovable. In the name of individualistic freedom the technocratic approach to history promotes fatalistic obedience: *Qui volentem fata ducunt, nolentem trahunt* (The Fates lead the willing, the unwilling they drag), but God helps those who help themselves.

The Foundation Trilogy

This cluster of contradiction can be found in Asimov's *The Foundation Trilogy*, the most popular story of prediction to come out of American SF. At the beginning of the set of novellas, Hari Seldon, the genius inventor of "psycho-history"[21] foresees the collapse of the Empire and a coming "Dark Age." He cannot avert the collapse, but he can, so he claims, act to shorten the duration of the Dark Age. To this end he establishes two "Foundations," one at Terminus, a planet on the periphery of the galaxy, the other at "The other end of the galaxy" (p. 35).

The initial, supposedly simple premise of predictive faith is that Seldon's "plan" is "in effect." What the word plan means is entirely ambiguous, even contradictory. At one time it means a scheme, a set of intentional and rational instructions that people in power can follow to shape history. In this sense, plan equals plot. This meaning is reinforced over the next century by the timed reappearances on tape of Seldon, who is now dead, to guide the First Foundation through its foreseen crises. But plan also means a determinist idea of the way history will progress, not by manipulations, but by its intrinsic mechanisms, which Seldon, the genius, has understood. It is to preserve this sense of plan that Seldon has insisted that the participants in events must be kept ignorant of the plan itself lest they, out of too broad a consciousness, act in a way that would upset the plan.

These two meanings require completely different responses from the actors of history. Immediately after Seldon initiates the plan, the First Foundation succeeds in keeping to it by abstaining from action until each crisis reaches a point at which there is "no choice." They thus enforce the situation in which technology is determinative. In this way the leaders insure that individual will cannot change the course of events. In the second volume this imperative of passive trust shifts to one of active intervention and the guiding motto is "Seldon's laws help those who help themselves." But in this second volume this reformulation of one of the classic aphorisms of individualist freedom is also contradicted by what is called "the dead hand" of Seldon's inexorable plan which assures those who fight against it, "Do what you wish in your fullest exercise of freewill. You will still lose" (p. 23). The inevitable is inescapable; freewill is an illusion. The first volume is concerned with the question of how to obey the plan, as if it were a fragile scheme from which one could be easily diverted. The second is concerned with the problem of how to be free in a world so predestined that individual acts cannot change at all what will happen.

In the third volume of *The Foundation Trilogy* the logical difficulties of the submissive position generate epistemological paranoia: as the mysterious Second Foundation's control becomes an issue, the people we watch wonder how they know whether the choices they have made were really their own choices or just the result of invisible manipulations?[22] From the end of volume II, Asimov plays what is at one level a literary game by pointing out that certain previous events, such as a child's wandering the galaxy to defeat a tyrant, accepted by the cooperative reader at home in the conventions of SF, were in fact highly unlikely and were the outcome, not of natural events or of individual free will, but of an outside control. Once one gives in to the possibility of such control, the paranoia becomes total: Arcadia's father sees the epistemological trap.

Who told you we were not molested? You, yourself, showed that Munn has been tampered with. What makes you think that we sent him to Kalgan in the first place entirely of our own volition—or that Arcadia overheard us and followed him on her own volition? Hah! We have been molested without pause, probably. And after all, why should they do more than they have? It is far more to their benefit to mislead us, than merely to stop us (*Second Foundation*, p. 212).

The novel has come full circle here. If at the beginning the problem is how not to interfere with the plan, at the end it is how not to be interfered with or "molested" by it.

But even this second problem is seen in contradictory ways. In volume II "The Mule," a mutant with the nonhuman ability to tamper with humans' minds without their knowledge, appears and threatens to upset the Seldon Plan. The Mule's ability to manipulate people is considered sinister. But once The Mule is neutralized, this same controlling ability in the hands of the Second Foundation is seen, after a good deal of ambivalent but strangely inconsequential doubt, as benign. Members of the First Foundation worry about free will, but at the end when we learn who are the agents of the Second Foundation, these anxieties show up as trivial and we are asked to resign ourselves comfortably to the unavoidable.

In moving from explicit imperial control at the beginning to the covert control by the benign conspiracy of the Second Foundation at the end, the novel circles back on itself in a way that confuses how we think about the nature of and need for freedom. The surprise, detective-story end of the trilogy is an explicit rendering of the circle as an ambiguous opposition. Throughout the last volume the task of the First Foundation is to find the Second Foundation by correctly interpreting Seldon's enigmatic statement that it would be "at the other end of the galaxy." The puzzle looks like this:

The novel offers three solutions of what "the other end" of this configuration might mean. The first is that since the First Foundation is at Terminus, the second must be at Rossem, which, as a confirming piece of evidence, is called "Star's End." When that theory proves wrong, it is proposed, and accepted as "satisfactory" by many of the novel's characters, that the "other end" of the galaxy is Terminus itself and that the Second Foundation has all the while been covertly on Terminus. Thus the circle converts opposition into identity. Finally, the "true" solution is revealed: the Second Foundation has been at the center, on Trantor, the original home of the Empire's capital, a planet once so densely populated that it is completely city, both surface and interior.

The image of the center carries a double meaning for the novel: as the Empire disintegrates and the First Foundation grows, an alternative center develops on Terminus. Although in the first configuration Trantor is the privileged, controlling center of the Empire, in the second Terminus is the encircled, embattled center of an alternate civilization. In one guise the circle image defines control: Trantor governs the galaxy. In the other guise the circle image defines a problem of being encircled: the First Foundation on Terminus must negotiate its way through threatening opponents that surround it. But, whether in control or besieged, the center is the important point; it confronts the circumference in an unbalanced relation. Value lies at the center; the circumference is the mob, the barbarian many. We have seen this kind of double bind before in the fantasies about the alien, who is both threatening and an outlet for sadistic violence, and about the woman, who is both dangerously powerful in her sexuality and also extremely vulnerable.

The contradictions here unified are central to the ideology of the novel. The image of the center is one of frightening but finally unquestioned authority, of hidden but acceptable control, of embattled but therefore all the more heroic value. Asimov's message at one level seems to be that as long as aliens like The Mule are not in control of the center, the issues of domination are pointless. "The Dark Age," that is so threatening in *the Foundation Trilogy*, is a breakdown of centralized authority, the loss of a center. Seldon maintains a kind of surrogate center with his various levels of institutionalized "Foundations."[23]

Prediction in such a world of values both passively foresees and actively plans. Seldon's plan, like George Sorel's myth of the General Strike,[24] has a distinctly political force. It justifies what we can easily see are contradictory actions. This set of stories ends by advocating prediction as a myth that will maintain the center; it depicts a history that robs history of its meaning. This is, as we have seen, the essential trope of prophetic forecasting.

"Nightfall"

One of the problems we confront when analyzing popular writers like Asimov is that we cannot tell if a contradiction is intrinsic—that is, a central and determining clue to the interpretation of the story—or simply a lapse; if it is an imaginative construction or merely the consequence of inattention. Yet, at the level of psychological coherence, there is no such thing as an irrelevant lapse. Asimov's other transcendently popular work, "Nightfall" (1941), is useful for us at this point because it can confirm by a different set of images the structure of value we find in *The Foundation Trilogy*.

Like *The Foundation Trilogy*, "Nightfall" depicts how a prediction is to be fulfilled. According to SF lore, John W. Campbell assigned Asimov to write a story in response to Emerson's seemingly rhetorical question: "If the stars should appear one night in a thousand years, how would men believe and adore, and preserve for many generations the remembrance of the city of God!"[25] In Asimov's answer, darkness arrives once every two millennia and stars are completely unexpected. In the story a group of scientists near

Saro City on Lagash, a planet in a system with six suns, using astronomical observations and the hints of ancient religious texts, predict the recurrence of a rare but regular eclipse that occurs every 2049 years. Since the planet has six suns, darkness can occur only during such an eclipse. In the past such an occurrence had driven all humanity mad and led, invariably, to a total social collapse and such a complete dark age that no rational memory of what happened endured. To prevent this social disaster, the scientists have tried to practice experiencing darkness, have established a "hideout" in which a group of women and children will survive the eclipse, and have set up cameras to record it so that the next civilization will begin with the advantage of knowing what happened. After a number of episodes in which a psychologist proves that the human's ability to remain sane in the presence of the unknown is very weak, the final eclipse takes place. The trauma of the expected darkness and the terror of the unforeseen multitude of stars drives the scientists attempting to observe the event mad, and the story ends:

> Aton [the chief scientist], somewhere, was crying, whimpering horribly like a terribly frightened child. "Stars—all the Stars—we didn't know at all. We didn't know anything. We thought six stars is a universe is something the Stars didn't notice is Darkness forever and ever and ever and the walls are breaking in and we didn't know we couldn't know and anything—"
> Someone clawed at the torch, and it fell and snuffed out. In the instant, the awful splendor of the indifferent Stars leaped nearer to them.
> On the horizon outside the window, in the direction of Saro City, a crimson glow began growing, strengthening in brightness, that was not the glow of a sun.
> The long night had come again. (p. 181–182).

This is a resounding final line, but what has happened? Is the "long night" the eclipse, after which, thanks to the testimony of the photographs and the experience of the people in the hideout, civilization will be able to pick up the pieces and go on? Or is it again the end of organized society altogether and a return to an ahistorical world in which there is no building on past experience? I see no way of deciding this. There is no further text to explicate this ambiguous line. I have polled students in the hope that some intuitive sense of genre might make a decision that I cannot, but they always split almost exactly.

In the critical literature that takes up this story there is no mention of the possibility of ambiguity. When critics treat "Nightfall," if they worry at all about what it says, they easily assume that it says one or the other of the two interpretations I have set forth. Thus, Maxine Moore can treat the story as simply anti-Emerson and, being satisfied that people panic rather than adore, assume the end of civilization is clear. Joseph Patrouch, while not going into the story in detail, can pleasantly wonder what the people in the hideout will do. James Gunn can assume that the story celebrates the triumph of reason—that is, I presume, that the hideout works and that the "long night" is simply the temporary eclipse.[26]

My point is not to challenge any of these readings, but to observe that, since critics can read it either way, the end of the story is genuinely ambiguous. The last line fulfills two antithetical and incompatible ideas that activate the story. We can call one "progressive-scientific" and the other "pessimistic-mythic." The former is obvious enough: science overcomes irrational but intrinsic fears and finally allows the Lagash society to escape the cycle of rise and collapse that has controlled it. The second may seem somewhat surprising for Asimov to be assenting to, but is in fact, more essential to his historical vision than is the first. It is characterized by a pervasive irony about human progress and achievement. It sees history as inescapable repetition. In the case of "Nightfall" it seems likely that the final line has not been perceived as ambiguous because the progressive and the mythic visions are seen, not as incompatible, but as synonymous. Such a unity is a product of technocratic ideology. At other times or from different ideological angles, what for the readers of "Nightfall" seems coherent will show up as discrepant, even nonsensical.

"Nightfall's" final ambiguity is surprising. In style and theme the story would seem to enjoy blunt, unambiguous ironies: it is, quite literally, a world of abrupt contrasts without shadings, of light and dark, of sanity and madness. The half-tones, such as the reddish light of the star, Beta, or the fanaticism of the cult, do not function as mediations: red light is still light, and religious fanaticism, while perverse, is sane. "Nightfall" spends much energy and attention preventing us from doubting or raising questions. The ambiguity at the end of "Nightfall" does not seem at any level to be intended as such, nor does it seem to be read as such. Generic and ideological pressures prevent the story from appearing as undecided or as open to opposites as, say, "The Lady or the Tiger." Asimov's final suggestive image seems to have been read as a clear statement, as a punchline of the sort advocated by John W. Campbell when he urged his writers to "solve the problems directly raised in the story—and do it succinctly. Quick and Sharp."[27] What is important to us is not which of the two readings is "correct," but the fact that such ambiguity can show up as unambiguous.

Anyone who has taught the story knows that students raise numerous doubts about its "science." Will the astronomy work? Will the psychology?

Does it make sense that the people of Lagash could have developed photography without knowing how to deal with the dark? Why should a darkness never before experienced be terrifying? Have these people never shut their eyes? One could go on and on. As in "The Cold Equations," the labored science may be a sign that the story is struggling to justify a *social* idea about which it somehow feels guilty.

Although *The Foundation Trilogy* is filled with governments, both formal and concealed, "Nightfall" is extraordinary for the almost total absence of any evidence of government either in Saro City or on the whole of Lagash. At one point, when Latimer, the cultist fanatic who tries to destroy the cameras and telescope, has been subdued, someone thinks of calling in the police. Otherwise this is a world composed of scientists, a reporter, and the urban mob. For at least two months the scientists have known of the coming eclipse and suspected its probable catastrophic social consequences, yet the reporter, Theremon, is still in need of an explanation. The blatancy of the narrative device points up the absence of any serious social thought in a story whose consequences are primarily social. We might argue that certain omissions should be explained generically: just as you do not find slums or large labor forces in genres like Arthurian romance, in some genres, such as the fairy story, there are no governments.[28] But the SF of this period is obsessed with government, as the stories of Heinlein, Simak, and Asimov testify. The absence of government in "Nightfall" is more than just a blank; it is the positive elimination of something we expect.

The absence of any governing mechanism is part of a larger idealization of the smooth operation of elaborate systems that is characteristic of technocratic ideals. In this respect, "Nightfall" is the antithesis of *The Foundation Trilogy*: where in the latter the galactic complexities are reduced to a simple circle with its hierarchy of center and circumference, in the former a solar system is elaborated beyond our imaginative grasp. The extraordinary physical system of Lagash—three pairs of suns, the planet itself, and at least one dark moon—is a visual and physical emblem of Lagashian society. We have here a common ideal of the physical sciences—what look to the untutored eye to be chaotic and unpredictable phenomena are understood and foreseen with extraordinary exactness—applied to psychology and sociology. Where we would expect to find anarchy, we find a quite remarkable and regular order. In the 2049 years between eclipses, Lagashian society progresses along the same lines and arrives at roughly the same level of civilization, so that each eclipse causes the same disorder and the culture returns to the same "bottom." I draw attention to this marvel, not to complain about its implausibility, but to emphasize the order in what might appear an "ungoverned" system. Like the six star solar system, and like Wells's heap of sand, civilization here is intricate beyond our ability to comprehend, but it is not chaotic and it is repeating. Since the civilizations that have collapsed have all been the same, they can be seen as mechanical, not as historical, phenomena. By treating society in such essentially astronomical terms, the story denies choice and history.

Yet, if this complex but still regular situation would seem to lead to an optimistic view about the possibilities of prediction and control, the last pages of the story imply that such knowledge is a vanity. First—and this is surely an explicit theme of the story—the arrogance of the scientists has led them to dismiss ancient religious myths that predict the existence of stars. The humiliating presence of 30,000 stars (the Lagash system is near the center of a cluster), that they might have foreseen but thanks to their scientific skepticism did not,[29] upsets all their planning. But a second theme seems to suggest that despite the practice in caves, the torches, and the psychological preparations, the darkness is overwhelming. Even if the future is exactly foreseen, there is no way to prepare for it or to avert its consequences: the mobs riot, the scientists panic, and civilization collapses.

It is worth considering how Asimov has complicated the ending of the story. Given John W. Campbell's assignment, the emphasis on the dark is irrelevant. In part it is just a false clue: they prepared for the dark but were instead overwhelmed by the stars. But the prose of the story does not reflect this. The stars are terrifying, but according to the psychologist and story's outcome, the darkness is overwhelming. Both themes—that prediction blinds us to the unpredictable and that even prediction will not help us cope with essential irrationalities—attract Asimov, and he devises a way to suggest both.

But we are now in a new logical situation, for the two themes together total something different from either alone. The image system of the story ends up generating a contradiction: put simply, the stars cancel the dark. Either the dark overwhelms or the stars do, but not both. The overwritten prose at the end tries to have it both ways. When the stars first appear we are told it is stunningly bright: "Not Earth's feeble thirty-six hundred Stars visible to the eye—Lagash was in the center of a giant cluster. Thirty thousand mighty suns shown down in a soul-searing splendor."[30] But as Theremon goes mad, it is seen as darkness: "you would be here physically and yet all the real essence would be dead and drowned in the black madness. For this was the Dark—the Dark and the Cold and the Doom." The imagery and the allegory jumble together: "The bright walls of the universe were shattered and their awful black fragments were falling down to crush and squeeze and obliterate him" (p. 181). Freud tells the story of the man who, when accused of burning a hole in a pot he borrowed, answers that a) he never borrowed it,

b) there was a hole in it when he got it, and c) there was no hole when he returned it.[31] Just as we have strong reason to suspect the man of burning a hole in his neighbor's pot, we may hear in Asimov's excessive and contradictory explanation of madness a need to disprove the possibility of rational planning.

Asimov clearly does not believe in simple inexplicability. On the contrary, as his paradigm of revolution suggests, history for him is quite simple to read. But this confident reading of history does not contradict the confusions of "Nightfall." The same ahistorical idea is at work in both instances. People always act the same. That explains revolutions, and it explains why Lagash has such problems. The crucial element in the Lagashian system is the eclipse: it may cause surprises, but the reaction to surprise is predictable.

To approach this issue from a slightly different angle, we can say that the contradiction in the imagery at the end of "Nightfall" destroys rational categories, but it does so with a mechanical rationality. Theremon "was going mad, and *knew* it" (emphasis added). "It was very horrible to go mad and *know* that you were going mad—to *know* that in a little minute you would be here physically and yet all the real essence would be dead and drowned in the black madness" (p. 181, emphasis added). Since the line between madness and sanity is posed as perfectly clear, one can know exactly when the irrational takes over. Scientists can be warned to get away from the machines when they feel themselves going mad. And the reasons for the "madness" are also absolutely clear. Aton is not confused; despite his broken syntax he understands exactly what has happened: "Stars—all the Stars—we didn't *know* at all. We didn't *know* anything. We thought six stars is a universe is something the Stars didn't notice is Darkness forever and ever and ever and the walls are breaking in and we didn't *know* we couldn't *know* and anything—" (pp. 181–182, emphasis added). The "unknown" and the "madness" it causes are perfectly understood and predictable. The real contradiction lies in the story's satisfied assurance that the world cannot be adequately understood.

And the allegorical message is clear: we, like the Lagashians, have irrational fears and think that we understand when we are in fact ignorant. But the style of the story is at odds with this allegory. The narrative has throughout put the reader in a complacent and condescending role in the midst of the characters' terror. We watch with benign condescension as the Lagashians struggle with the darkness that we all know how to handle, and as they dismiss the stars that we all know exist. Such irony, far from leading to terror, is comforting. Yet, just at the point at which we confidently expect the allegory to be explained and the moral to be drawn, we get a final enigma: "The long night had come again." This might refer only to the eclipse. After all, though the story itself seems to have forgotten it, *we* remember that the hideout exists. But surely the hideout should have been mentioned in the last few pages if its solace is to be felt. Darkness and humiliating revelation leading to madness is the whole message of the final scene, and it is certainly tempting—though finally not adequate—to read the reference to the "long night" as a return to the "dark ages," so dreaded here and in *The Foundation Trilogy*. "Again" suggests that the cycle is inescapable. The ambiguity of this line allows the story to retain both its pessimism and optimism. It is a story about the failure of rationality and about its triumph. Even if we override the ambiguity and hold to the optimistic reading, we must see it as strongly hedged. If we can interpret the ending to mean that Lagash has broken the historical cycle, the imagery, with its complicated double whammy of darkness and stars, nevertheless implies that humans are powerless *and* predictable. That very doubleness carries an unambiguous message of resignation.[32]

"The Nine Billion Names of God"

In "Nightfall" we see a version of technocracy's basic claim that there are no real social choices because the option to a triumphant technocracy is what Daniel Bell in 1967 will term "apocalypse."[33] Such a reduction of the political spectrum surfaces in SF throughout the forties and fifties. In Heinlein's future history stories we see this dichotomy in the religious reaction against technology in the twenty-first century. The cult in "Nightfall" has its offspring, though Heinlein seems to take more pleasure than does Asimov in imagining the irrational alternative to technocracy. The most elegant distillation of this vision in the anthology is Arthur C. Clarke's comic parable, "The Nine Billion Names of God" (1953). In this story the only option to technological success is the end of the universe, and the only meaningful effect that humanity can have on history is to speed its close. When all the names of God have been written, the universe will go out. The story takes continued pleasure in the prolonged irony of this profoundly meaningless teleology. The scientists and technicians condescend to the Tibetan lama's project of using a computer to list all the possible names of God. "Was there any limit to the follies of mankind?" thinks the computer scientist when he hears the lama's project. "Still, he must give no hint of his inner thoughts. The customer was always right" (pp. 516–517). Of course the folly is the scientist's who, both because of his religious skepticism and his economic cynicism, hastens the end of the universe.

At one level Clarke's story is a comic parable in the tradition of Wells's "The Man Who Could Work Miracles," pointing to the limits of human foresight, but we cannot therefore dismiss its theme. It renders an attitude toward technology and history that Clarke works out in more detail in other works. For Clarke, technology is meaningful not because it will accomplish anything significant in the long run, but as an exercise, a training which will raise humankind to a level at which it can abandon technology altogether and enter a higher order of reality—what in *Childhood's End* he calls "The Overmind." The exercise of technology is profoundly important as a measure of human capacity and accomplishment, but it is inherently limited in itself, and in the light of the higher realities of the Overmind, it is trivial. Just as we teach children long division even though it is a skill that they will never use as adults, technology is a significant stage of human education that is finally pointless.[34] Such a more or less religious attitude toward technology lies behind the comedy of "The Nine Billion Names of God." The computer is a marvelous and irrelevant human accomplishment.

Such a comic perspective may offer a glimpse of the higher meaning, but it is impossible for it to find a meaningful base for action. One has to play the paradoxical game of devoting oneself to technology even as one sees it as finite and ultimately irrelevant. This paradoxical spirit surfaces toward the end of "The Nine Billion Names of God." The two technicians who have installed the computer in the lamasery are making a fast get-away so as not to be around when the monks are disappointed with the conclusion of the print-out.

> "There she is!" called Chuck, pointing down into the valley. "Ain't she beautiful!"
>
> She certainly was, thought George. The battered old DC3 lay at the end of the runway like a tiny silver cross. In two hours she would be bearing them away to freedom and sanity. It was a thought worth savoring like a fine liqueur. George let it roll round his mind as the pony trudged patiently down the slope.
>
> The swift night of the high Himalayas was now almost upon them. Fortunately, the road was very good, as roads went in that region, and they were both carrying torches. There was not the slightest danger, only a certain discomfort from the bitter cold. The sky overhead was perfectly clear, and ablaze with the familiar, friendly stars. At least there would be no risk, thought George, of the pilot being unable to take off because of weather conditions. That had been his only remaining worry (p. 521).

Behind the blinding irony of the irrelevance of this final consolation lies the genuine admiration expressed in the passage. Clarke admires the DC3, both as a piece of machinery in itself and as a social tool that, as here, makes otherwise inaccessible places convenient.[35] The striking inversion of some of Asimov's images—the torches and the stars—is probably coincidental, but not irrelevant. In both stories the torches are a familiar but inadequate technology and the stars scientifically unpredictable. The two stories share a skepticism about cosmic matters that cushions a complacent security about nearer matters. In "The Nine Billion Names of God" these "friendly stars" will go out, but, short of that eschatalogical revelation, the imagery of technological triumph holds a place of honor.

Such irony is a form of double negative. The fiction treats the technological values as trivial in the face of the religious reality represented by the lama, but although these religious values triumph, they are surely a comic fiction. At the story's end, we are left with the reality of technology. In other words, absolute fatalism offers no conduct for life; the only rational way to live by it would be simply to lie down and wait. A pessimism this deep then leaves us with the shallower stances the story claims to have disqualified. The rhetorical device is a version of what Barthes terms "Operation Margarine," the technique of raising an objection as a way of removing that objection.[36] Thus, by seeming to doubt technological solutions, both Asimov and Clarke generate a skepticism that finally supports those very solutions at the expense of a more historically and politically sensitive understanding.

"The Weapon Shop"

The final reduction of this process, by which the very difficulties of understanding become a justification for an unquestioned faith in the powers that be, shows up in A. E. Van Vogt's, "The Weapon Shop" (1942). This is the one story whose presence in the *Science Fiction Hall of Fame* anthology does not match its popularity in reprints. Some of Van Vogt's other works, such as *The World of Null A*, *Slan*, or "The Enchanted Village", are easy candidates for formulaic analysis of the motifs of genius. But "The Weapon Shop," unlike these other more evidently popular works, is an "everyman" story. It is telling that it is this story, rather than the superman stories, that the writers chose to include in the anthology. And yet, it is this story, more than any other in the anthology, that gives us the clue to the implications of the technocratic view of history for the ordinary person.

"The Weapon Shop" tells a story that is familiar in the genre: Fara, an ordinary and orthodox man, after first objecting to innovation (in this case the arrival in his town of a Weapon Shop), learns to understand that his loyalties have been misplaced and that what he first took as an invasion is a liberation.[37] The story repeatedly allows the reader to side with Fara and then disabuses both reader and Fara of their claims to understanding. It is appropriate that a story of conversion should require such revaluation. Fara's initial support of the Empress turns out to be misguided. Later we understand that the loyalty behind the original stance was to be admired, it was just misplaced. Finally we learn that, though the Empress stands for corruption, it is wrong to criticize her: the secret society of the Weapon Shops, while it works for justice against the corrupt Empress, never challenges her regime and in its quiet way even supports it.

Reading "The Weapon Shop" is a curious experience because, though the story frequently raises clear moral issues and insinuates strong positions, the reader soon finds that one is always wrong to trust the conclusions implied at any given point. Frequently it is the very subtlety of the stance posed that encourages the reader to take pride in deducing the position which turns out to be wrong. For example, after a scene in which Fara has trouble getting any kind of cooperation from his sullen and recalcitrant son, we hear the following dramatic exchange. Creel, Fara's wife, criticizes Fara for the way they have brought up their son:

> [Fara said,] "That boy of ours—there's going to be a showdown. He either works in my shop, or he gets no more allowance."
>
> Creel said: "You've handled him wrong. He's twenty-three, and you treat him like a child. Remember, at twenty-three, you were a married man."
>
> "That was different," said Fara. "I had a sense of responsibility. Do you know what he did tonight?"
>
> He didn't quite catch her answer. For the moment, he thought she said: "No; in what way did you humiliate him first?"
>
> Fara felt too impatient to verify the impossible words. He rushed on: "He refused in front of the whole village to give me help. He's a bad one, all bad."
>
> "Yes," said Creel in a bitter tone, "he is all bad. I'm sure you don't realize how bad. He's as cold as steel, but without steel's strength or integrity. He took a long time, but he hates even me now, because I stood up for your side so long, knowing you were wrong."
>
> "What's that?" said Fara, startled; then gruffly: "Come, come my dear, we're both upset. Let's go to bed." (p. 198).

The dynamics of Creel's muttered recriminations and of Fara's blustering domination and evasion strongly suggest that their son is a victim and that Fara is at fault. But after Fara has mortgaged his business to pay off a debt Cayle has incurred, Creel objects to Fara's sacrifice and we have, abruptly and with no explanation, a rather different reading of things:

"What do you mean, [said Fara] standing there and talking about not paying it? You said several times that I was responsible for his being what he is. Besides, we don't know why he needed the money. He—"

Creel said in a low, dead tone: "In one hour, he's stripped us of our life work. He did it deliberately, thinking of us as two old fools, who wouldn't know any better than to pay it."

Before he could speak, she went on: "Oh, I know I blamed you, but in the final issue, I knew it was he. He was always cold and calculating, but I was weak, and I was sure that if you handled him in a different . . . and besides I didn't want to see his faults for a long time. He—"

"All I see," Fara interrupted doggedly, "is that I have saved our name from disgrace." (p. 207).

The two scenes are not just incongruent; they suggest diametrically opposed views of childrearing and adult responsibility. In the first the father is seen as responsible for his son's delinquency. In the second the son was always bad and all attempts to deal with him are just foolish. This contradiction is different from the one we looked at in Heinlein: there opposites coexist; here the latter stance cancels out the former. Reading "The Weapon Shop" is a process of constant restructuring of values with the current position always having authority. In this instance, having expressed sympathy with the difficulties children may experience, the story seems to settle on a harsh view that some children are just bad.

Reading "The Weapon Shop" is an experience similar to looking at the Weapon Shop itself. It is "a normal illusion affair." Fara finds that, "no matter what his angle of view, he was always looking straight at it." Such an illusion is not just magical, it is actively anti-empirical because it prevents one from ever seeing the whole object. The illusion restricts us to a single architectural elevation. We may, as in the discussion of parental obligations, have a limited sense of what might be behind the facade, but the narrative never lets us see beyond the short scene in front of us.[38] When later we learn that Cayle's loan was part of a bank's extortionist scheme we may again approve of Creel's posture, but the issues of how to handle difficult children or what creates them are never given any deep thought.

While the need for constant revision of understanding would seem to call all authority in question, in fact it makes the reader entirely dependent on the somewhat arbitrary authority of the narrator. The story does not ever offer an empirical basis for its final assurance, nor does it ever account for the situation by a political analysis. It is a situation in which hearsay has authority: "I guess you haven't heard about those doors or these shops. From all accounts you can't break into them" (p. 187). "I've heard it said that the door will open only to those who cannot harm the people inside" (p. 188). In the end Fara is an embattled member of the secret society of the Weapon Shops, aligned with his stern mother-in-law, the weak mayor, and the stingy businessman. We have been encouraged to disapprove of these unpleasant people early in the story, but their faults are now seen as either valuable in themselves or as a necessary disguise. But why should this picture of small town people as part of a benign conspiracy that keeps the government honest be the definitive understanding? Why should there not be yet another revision? There is no further revision only because there is nothing to follow. In such a narrative situation the reader is put in the passive position of follower. Any independent interpretation is likely to be overruled a little later.

And yet in this seemingly relative system, there are strong, absolute values at work, the most important of which is an admiration for power itself. Initially Fara is enthralled by the power of the Empress. And whenever he comes in contact with the Weapon Shop he finds himself attracted to it: when he first sees the Weapon Shop's show window, "a spark of interest struck fire inside Fara. He gazed at the brilliant display of guns, fascinated in spite of himself" (p. 186). He feels "a hideous thrill" when the doorknob refuses his hand. He admires the ability of the Weapon Shop to transport him to a distant part of the solar system almost instantaneously. It is the sensation of the Weapon Shops' bureaucratic courts that most impresses Fara: "His brain lifted up, up in his effort to grasp the tremendousness of the dull-metaled immensity" (p. 213). "The machine towered into the heavens." Later, in the room of names he experiences "a colossal, incredible sound." "The uproar was absolutely shattering" (p. 217). The image of the gun embodies this value of sheer size and power. When Fara enters the Weapon Shop to confront what he sees as evil, he finds himself "excited" by the guns in their "lovely" cases. When he finally does get a gun, we read "He had seen and handled the guns of soldiers, and they were simply ordinary metal or plastic things that one used clumsily like any other material substance, not like this at all, not possessed of a dazzling life of their own, leaping with an intimate eagerness to assist with all their superb power the will of their master" (p. 211).

Even before he has learned to see their virtues, Fara is in awe of the Weapon Shops. "They were remote, superior, undefeatable. That unconquerableness was a dim, suppressed awareness inside Fara" (p. 201). This last sentence is significantly ambiguous: Fara was dimly aware that the Weapon Shops were unconquerable, but the word "suppressed" suggests that the unconquerableness speaks to something "inside" Fara. Fara's education is toward an acknowledging of that "unconquerableness." Fara's conversion from docile citizen of the Empire to stubborn admirer of the Weapon Shops takes place when he is sent through the enormous Weapon Shop courts. As he enters, confused, Fara declares "It *was* a machine, not a building" (p. 213), but later he realizes "So it was a building as well as a machine" (p. 215). This seemingly trivial debate marks in the story's imagery the revelation that the Weapon Shop is both inhumanly powerful (a machine) and yet at the same time made for humans (a building). What distinguishes the Weapon Shop, however, is that the building and the machine are apparently indistinguishable.

The secret cabal, while it parallels the Empress' government—it has its own law courts, bureaucracy, and armory—is seen in the story as somehow the opposite of government. A spokesperson for the Weapon Shops explains this apparently timeless anti-government. As in other situations in this story, hearsay is authoritative: "*People always have the kind of government they want*. When they want change, they must change it. As always we shall remain an incorruptible core—and I mean that literally; we have a psychological machine that never lies about a man's character—I repeat, an incorruptible core of human idealism, devoted to relieving the ills that arise inevitably under any form of government" (p. 222, emphasis in original). In the midst of the flux of the narrative, this is an absolute, a self-proclaimed "incorruptible core," held in place by the "psychological machine that never lies about a man's character."

At this point we can begin to see that the antithesis of bad and good on which the story turns is really an identity. Thus, though Fara at first condemns "gigantic, multitentacled corporations," he finally admires the enormous conspiracy of the Weapon Shops. They are essentially similar to the Automatic Repair Shops, Inc. but have the virtue of being more powerful. Supported by the Weapon Shops, Fara can point his gun at the agent for Automatic Repair Shops and make him back down. The anxiety about helplessness in the face of the "gigantic multitentacled corporation" is relieved by indulging in a fantasy of being part of just such a powerful organization. By rendering the basis of justice morally, psychologically, and politically mysterious, the story allows Fara to rationalize power simply by the hearsay claim of an "incorruptible core" that is beyond psychological complexity. The passages we looked at in which the difficult issues of nature and upbringing are touched on show that the story is at some level aware and concerned about such complexity, but it "solves" that concern by rendering Cayle simply "bad" and Fara simply "good" and powerful at the end.

"The Weapon Shop" is on its surface skeptical and relative, but at the deep structural level it is authoritarian and absolute. In *The Foundations of the Nineteenth Century*, often considered the classic formulation of this paradox, Houston Stewart Chamberlain declared that the Teutonic races differed from other races because, while they were obedient, they were not servile. While other races were either anarchistic or merely obedient to those in power, the Teutons *chose* those they would serve.[39] We see this paradox of an orderly and chosen servitude worked out in "The Weapon Shop" in the close parallel between the Empress and the Weapon Shop; both are mysterious and powerful. Fara's final stance differs from his initial one in that he has chosen his loyalty. Otherwise, the final scene depicting the peaceful town of Glay is identical with the one that opened the story.

It would seem that for the reader who appreciates "The Roads Must Roll," "The Weapon Shop," and many of the other works we have studied, contradiction within a story is not a source of displeasure. Although it may be incorrect to assume that contradiction itself is a source of pleasure, it seems accurate to say that there may be pleasure in seeing elements of life that are a source of discomfort and confusion treated as if they fit neatly together. Thus, the van Vogt story gives expression to disaffection with a "corrupt" government without requiring Fara to take the risk of disloyalty. By serving as an agent of the Weapon Shop he works against the Empress and at the same time serves an organization just as powerful as her. In a final twist, the organization disguises its agents by making them appear to be loyal to the Empress. In this fantasy disruption is stabilizing, and obedience to the status quo is revolutionary.

TIME TRAVEL AND TIME

When we think about Asimov's two narratives in terms of prediction, it is significant that they both avoid the conventional SF device of time travel. In Asimov's stories prediction is granted its full ambiguity as prophetic forecasting, and the contradictions that arise are those common to the professional enterprise. Time travel stories totally alter the conditions of knowing by permitting a confirmation that is impossible in actual prediction.

"The Sound of Thunder"

Though much of time travel literature is pure fantasy,[40] some of it engages the issues of prediction. Even more than the Asimovian model, the time travel story fantasizes an escape from politics. Bradbury's immensely popular "A Sound of Thunder" (1952) can serve as a paradigm for the kind of time travel story that imagines an exactly determined world in which the slightest anachronism will change everything; a world in which the "future" exists as a totality, a coherent unit in which one difference makes a complete difference. A gesture at point "A" is all-powerful and uncorrectable and intrinsically changes point "B" so that the whole of "B" becomes different from what it would have been without the gesture. It is an inelastic, atomic system. In the Bradbury story a man takes a safari back in time to hunt dinosaurs, steps off the carefully constructed pathway and steps on a butterfly. When he returns to the present he discovers that, because the prehistoric butterfly was crushed, the Germans rule the USA.

The exponential progression on which the determinist idea works—lost nail leads to lost battle leads to lost empire—means that a trivial swerve can cause enormous changes in a very short time: the death of the single butterfly might have caused a situation in which homo sapiens never evolved. Just as in "Nightfall" it is necessary that all civilizations follow the same course, in Bradbury's tale it is implicit that nature generates Americas, the significant difference being that some of them are German. Such determinist thinking leads to a frantic marveling at trivial causal sequences. In such a teleological universe, the single butterfly that was not killed is less important for keeping America free from fascism than are the thousands of banana peels that Hitler did not slip on. And those peels never came to be because a certain frog ate a certain fly even though it was slightly distracted by child reading nearby. Had the child's book been less interesting, had she frightened the frog, the history of Europe and America would have been profoundly different.[41] Seen in this light, all events are equally remarkable and consequential and, therefore, equally unremarkable and inconsequential. Whether or not such determinism is true, it is impossible to think this way, for there is absolutely no hierarchy of detail. The butterfly and the Civil War are equally important in American history. Whatever the truth of the determinist vision, we have to think and act as if there were some deeper structures of continuity at work.[42]

"Twilight"

"A Sound of Thunder" renders at its most preposterous the combination of extraordinary leverage and complete fatalism we see in prophetic forecasting. But the popularity of the story also speaks to the attraction of the paradox for the SF readership. John W. Campbell's *Science Fiction Hall of Fame* story, "Twilight," is important to our understanding of this ideology for the way it tries to rationalize the psychological consequences of this fatalist paradox. Ares Sen Kenlin, a man from a thousand years from now, arrives in the present on his way back from a visit to the world five-and-a-half million years from now. A member of a superior race invented by his own his father, Sen Kenlin has invented "the release," a form of atomic energy which will be civilization's main source of power for the next five million years. At this level the story expresses a grandiose myth of individual power and influence of the sort we examined in the chapter on Genius. And yet this far future is a bored world of tremendous working machines and idle humans. Sen Kenlin, appalled at the state of humanity, and critical of their loss of "curiosity," invents a "curious machine" "that would have what man had lost" (p. 61) and then retreats back toward his own more vital and optimistic times.

The story's elaborate point of view system renders a complex conjunction of optimism and pessimism. The narrator tells a story about his friend Jim's story about Sen Kenlin, who, having accidentally returned to a time a thousand years before his own, tells a story about the world he saw more than five million years in the future. The multiple points of view allow for different relations to the future. From Jim's vantage, Sen Kenlin is a superman and even the decline of the far future is a tremendous advance. Such a view is biologically, intellectually, and technologically optimistic. But Sen Kenlin's view of his visit to the world of five-million years from now is negative and tragic. From his perspective, the future offers only boredom; human intellect is biologically gigantic but pointless; the technology complete and self-sufficient but unappreciated and unused.

These optimistic and pessimistic perspectives are paralleled by different perceptions of the possibilities for changing the future. When Sen Kenlin finds that the world of five million years from now has lost "curiosity," he can only regret this inevitable result of the dialectic of progress.[43] But he can also set to work in that very future to create the "curious machine" that could save the even further future. He is both passive observer of inevitable historical tragedy and the hero who single-handedly, by his youth, courage, and genius, renews the culture.

The dilemma of a hero who finds cultural achievement leading to decline and who feels deeply the culture's accomplishment and failure is near the center of Romantic promethean mythology. We see something very like it in Wagner's *Ring*; it is a combination that enthralls Carlyle and Spengler. Such a tragic victory has a profound resonance in western culture of the last two centuries, and it would be foolish for us to dismiss it as simply illogical. By its generic association with the tradition we have looked at in this chapter, a work like "Twilight" can help us see Romantic pessimism not just as nostalgia for a preindustrial age nor as a perception of the futility of technological success but rather as part of the rhetoric of optimistic technological prediction itself.

Though Campbell's story clearly owes a large debt to *The Time Machine*, the difference between the two works is revealing. Wells's novella uses time travel as a narrative device to think about some of the consequences of the present social order, and the future envisioned is a fantasy in which the social order has become a biological order. Campbell's story, with its three levels of time—the present, Sen Kenlin's triumphant near future, and the decadent far future—concerns itself with how earlier times should deal with the foreseen vision of later times. It has a clear vision of what is the cause of success and of decline. Unlike the degenerate Eloi and Morlocks of Wells, the human creatures of Campbell's future are extraordinary beings capable of mental procedures unimaginable in ourselves. Their decline is psychological rather than biological, and it is caused not by class division or by any social process but by technology itself.

And yet Campbell's story never questions its faith in technology. At the center of Campbell's sad tale of future boredom is an episode quite unlike anything in *The Time Machine*'s future but typical of O'Neill or Naisbitt.[44] Sen Kenlin finds a small flying vehicle and in a page of delighted exploration discovers how to fly it—it is guided by simply tracing a map. When it is left, it can be set to park itself and to return to the driver with a call. Here is pleasure in sheer technology for its own sake.[45] Just as O'Neill reaches his climax with a detailed description of the techniques in the future for moving passengers and luggage around airports, Campbell finds, in the machine itself, a source of meaning and joy. I focus on this episode because it demonstrates that, although Campbell may echo pessimistic myths of decline, he remains deeply enthralled by technology. Even in a pessimistic story like "Twilight," with its pervasive *Gotterdammerung* motif, we find at its core the source of pleasure that inspires the optimistic prophetic forecasters of this century.

The contradiction between free will and determinism that prophetic forecasting thrives on becomes a crisis in "Twilight." Just as Seldon's plan required its followers to be conscious *and* ignorant, here knowing and forgetting are knotted together. Sometimes Campbell sees the problem of the future as elementary survival techniques forgotten, as a process of divorce from true knowledge. At other times he seems to grant future humans practical knowledge and to regret the lack of theoretical knowledge. But then elsewhere in the story, when Sen Kenlin asks the future people to help him build a machine with which to return to his own time, he finds they have extraordinary theoretical minds. The story finally arrives at a kind of log-jam of contradictory imperatives. It is good to know, but insofar as knowing one thing means forgetting another, it is bad to know. One should forget what one should not know. In "Twilight" knowing and forgetting form a baffling litany so that each ends up meaning the other. "When the builders made those cities, they *forgot* one thing. They didn't *realize* [*know*] that things shouldn't go on forever" (p. 45). Such deep philosophy is rendered suspect, however, by Sen Kenlin's later creation of a curious machine that will make "things" go on even longer. The fact that the machine will go on "forever" is dismaying in the face of humanity's decline, but there is a paradox in the imperative: an even more perfect machine would be one that was less perfect. In another form the imperative is psychologically impossible: "The machines should have forgotten that song" (p. 47). If on the one hand the future men are condemned for having "forgotten" how to master the machines, the machines are condemned for not having forgotten the "song of triumph." In part some of this may be straightened out if we distinguish between the morality of humans and that of machines. What is good for humans (to know, to remember) is bad for machines, at least when the humans themselves are failing. But again, when Sen Kenlin starts the curious machine, such discriminations are completely overruled. Humans have no moral superiority to machines. A curious machine is as good as a curious human, perhaps even better if it will not succumb to despair. The whole conflict is finally expressed in the oxymoronic "Song of Forgotten Memories" that Sen Kenlin sings. Here is the perfect knowledge: a memory that is not remembered; a song that should have been forgotten and yet is remembered, not only by Sen Kenlin but even by Jim, and sung with such power that the narrator himself wishes he had not heard it. An oxymoron itself, it symbolizes the advanced future that we dread but also want to know.

The doubleness at the core of the desire to know is most cannily rendered by the conversational filler, "I don't know." In "Twilight" it is a repeated exclamation of confusion which usually contains a crucial evasion: that the speaker does know but does not want to accept, acknowledge, or consciously understand his knowledge. Thus Jim, describing Sen Kenlin, says, "But he was magnificent. Most beautiful man I ever saw. I don't know, damn it!" (p. 41). The phrase adds nothing to our understanding of Sen Kenlin, but it does mark an attempt to know something without knowing it. That, and its converse, to not know something and yet to know it, are the central states at which the story aims. The understood equation is that knowing kills curiosity. Thus, by preserving mystery—even by repression—Jim's "I don't know" keeps his own curiosity alive.

In "Twilight" such a paradoxical state renders the mystery of history itself: it is a consequence of human will and yet it is also beyond control. In the far future humanity kills off all other animals, but their reason for doing so is not explained: "they started destroying life—and now it wouldn't stop" (p. 54). The grammatical confusion here reflects the reality that life won't stop—that is, time goes on—and that some mysterious and unexplained process of destruction won't stop. Like the machines, the genocidal process goes on despite anything a human might do. Similarly, a paragraph later, we learn that the destruction of other life went on because, "The thing was beyond their control" (p. 54). And along with isolation comes a decline in human fertility,

though again the reasons—whether it is a genetic or a psychological problem—are left obscure. A similar confusion of the psychological and the genetic accounts for why in the far future humanity has no pets. After a brief
fantasy of how rewarding dogs were, Sen Kenlin describes the separation
that followed:

> Then man reached his full maturity. It extended over a period of a full
> million years. So tremendously did he stride ahead, the dog ceased to
> be a companion. Less and less were they wanted. When the million
> years had passed, and man's decline began, the dog was gone. It had
> died out. (p. 55).

So maturity is the problem; it is the fruition, the fulfillment of the growing
process, but it is also the beginning of decline. The term *maturity* itself
harbors a deep ambiguity. On the one hand it suggests a psychological and
educational state in which consciousness has achieved some threshold of
complexity and wisdom. But insofar as it appeals to an organic metaphor describing the life cycles of living things, maturity does not suggest conscious
achievement, but merely denotes a moment in civilization's growth preced-
ing the inevitable decline. Although it appears to mark achievement, it is
actually a determinist term. Like Wells's sand pile, and like the mechanical
civilizations of Lagash, it denies history as an ongoing political process.

Further confusion along these lines arises when the story finally settles on
"curiosity" as the quality lost by humanity. By calling curiosity an "instinct,"
the narrative evades the dialectic that has driven it: that knowledge, by satisfying curiosity, actually extinguishes it. Plato, we will recall, saw that desire
of knowledge is generated by a consciousness of lack; when nothing is lacking
there will be no desire. But by turning curiosity into an instinct that can then
be reprogrammed into a machine, Campbell's story denies the limit that the
dialectics of desire impose on curiosity. Or, to put it slightly differently, by
making curiosity an instinct, the story evades the psychological issue that is
never made quite clear about the future: that maturity leads to boredom.

While being acutely aware of the disillusionments of knowledge, the story
nevertheless seeks a one-dimensional optimism in which the adolescent sense
of discovery will continue forever, a world in which the whole spectrum is
always new, in which there are no second times. Maturity here is that dreaded
stage at which all the animals are known and when the machines no longer
delight. One must find renewal in what one already knows. This entails re-
examination, which to some may mean doubt. "Twilight" is a meditation on
the fall into adulthood, and Sen Kenlin's "curious machine" is a fantasy of an
eternal childhood forever finding stimulation in new discoveries.

Campbell's story connects the idea of unpolitical history, enthusiasm for technology, and a psychological anxiety. Its surface is deeply conflicted, in part at least, because it is speaking from the heart of the ideological contradiction that motivates the whole rationalizing effort of the genre. No other story in the anthology is at the same time so eager about or so tired of the possibilities of technology. The story's setting, an empty Southwestern desert with long stretches between gas stations, suggests a terrifying boredom. It is a boredom from which Jim wants to escape. In one of those awkward bits of jerrybuilt plot that we are by now familiar with, we hear that need: "He had me thinking so hard I didn't even see him get off in Reno when we stopped for gas" (p. 61). To be sure, this is a piece of lazy plotting, but it tells us that this imagination can only live somewhere else. In this story the future exists, not as a political option, but as a psychological necessity in a world of profound ennui. But no sooner has that ennui been escaped than it is rediscovered in the future. Sen Kenlin and his era can never quite be seen; they represent a world whose existence can be intuited but which cannot be envisioned.

SF Under the Shadow
of Literature

8

THROUGHOUT THE PERIOD WE ARE
looking at, SF has been aware of literary tradition even as it has sought to
challenge it. A Greek epic inspires the title of the first story in *Science Fiction Hall of Fame*, and a book of the Bible the title of the last. In the beginning of "Helen O'Loy" we have a moment of what Bourdieu calls *allodoxia*,
misrecognition, when the name Helen of Troy recalls Keats. But, if there is
an evident desire to be a part of literature, there is also a hostile sense that
"literature" stands for all that the "genius" of SF is surpassing. Heinlein
voices this aspect when he attacks "serious" literature as "sick," as "stuff that
should not be printed, but told only privately—on a psychiatrist's couch."[1]
Heinlein's outburst, like that of his character, Van Kleek in "The Roads Must
Roll," is to some extent a denunciation of what he sees as the concerns of the
leisure class. An interest in psychology is particularly objectionable to him as
an expression of decadent class privilege. His idealization of a group like the
Marines is based in part on their democratic basis. Van Kleek, after all, is
wrong to accuse the road cadets of being privileged; he has mistaken the discipline of the corps for the privilege of an older aristocratic model. Cordwainer Smith offers a similar vision in his picture of the Scanners' guild,
though Vomack's aristocratic background twists the democratic world, which
includes Chang and Parizianski, toward something a bit more contaminated
with privilege.

On the one hand SF subculture objects to what it sees as a misguided and
privileged set of priorities—a concern with nuances of personal psychology
and an almost total disregard for the extraordinary modern technological
situation and possibilities. On the other hand the subculture is impatient
with the labor of art. For most SF writers, the premier issue is getting paid
and into print. After discussing themes and narrative techniques in an earlier
essay, "On the Writing of Speculative Fiction," Heinlein concludes:

1. You must *write*.
2. You must *finish* what you start.

3. You must refrain from rewriting except to editorial order.
4. You must put it on the market.
5. You must keep it on the market until sold.

The above five rules really have more to do with how to write speculative fiction than anything said above them.[2]

The memoirs of the writers in the thirties and forties bear repeated witness to these productive values. Asimov published eighteen stories in his first three years as a professional (age 18–21). In 1942–43 Kuttner and Moore, using a variety of pseudonyms, almost single-handedly supplied the material for *Astounding SF*. In the late forties Kornbluth wrote 10,000-word novellas at a single sitting.[3] For the profession this precocious haste is a source of pride, a genuine *sprezzatura*. But the values implicit in this vision of intensely productive creativity are in conflict with those of a more Flaubertian ideal of literature, and to try to have it both ways—to aspire to the status of canonic literature and at the same time to boast of being hasty, commercial, and impersonal—leads to a crisis.[4]

The tension between these two essential thrusts of the SF muse is not uniform: it varies from author to author, and it changes over time for the genre. Heinlein's 1957 talk took place at a crucial moment for SF. It was an attempt to define the form in its early phase just as that phase was becoming untenable. A decade after the war, the form itself was encountering difficulties within its own ideals. Heinlein's denunciation of psychology and his idealization of technology came just when the form itself had begun to lose its faith in technology and to discover psychology. In *Science Fiction Hall of Fame* we see an evolution from a happy narrative innocence in the thirties, through a period of troubled self-consciousness in the forties, into a different kind of self-consciousness in the fifties.[5] It is the consequences of this last phase that will most interest me in this chapter.

In this third phase the genre begins to externalize some of its own modes of thought and to reflect on them. Through their prolonged, and at some level surely conscious, ambivalence, Kornbluth's two lively stories in which IQ is the central issue express the dilemma of literary aspiration that has lurked at the heart of the technocratic fantasy. They mark a point of generic crisis after which writers must find some way around the unsolvable problem of genius and its social role. One way is to admit to the dilemma and to make the situation of the SF artist the subject of inquiry. This is the method used by Damon Knight in "The Country of the Kind," which renders the exceptional person's contempt for ordinary behavior and at the same time appreciates how unacceptable the exception is. The other method is to retreat from the utopian project that has inspired the SF of this period and to resort to ironic techniques, learned from mainstream literature, which will create such distance between the authorial point of view and the story that the kind of confusion we feel in Kornbluth will not occur. This latter technique puts the emphasis on psychology and the reading experience, and it thereby comes directly in conflict with some of the essential tenets of the techno-cratic code. Heinlein's rear-guard action is a fight against the kind of trans-formation of the genre represented in the *Science Fiction Hall of Fame* anthology by Anthony Boucher's "The Quest for St. Aquin" and Alfred Bester's "Fondly Fahrenheit."

"The Country of the Kind"

Damon Knight's "The Country of the Kind" (1955) renders conscious the pleasures of the monstrous child fantasy and relates them to the problem of the genius. The story is, of course, a variation on H. G. Wells's story, "The Country of the Blind," in which a sighted man fails to rule an isolated village of blind people in the Peruvian Andes. In Knight's story the narrator, a monster-genius who has been shockingly exceptional from the beginning, is the one violent-imaginative person in a world of docile, "liberal" subur-banites. After a moment of passion in which he commits a murder, he has an existential revelation that the people in this benign permissive society can-not punish him. "And it was then that I understood that I was the King of the world" (p. 596). But, like Nunez in Wells's story, Knight's protagonist finds that his rule comes more slowly than he expected. The social group has strengths that the exceptional individual cannot conquer. Committed to a permissive and nonviolent code, this society controls the exceptional indi-vidual with an operation, installing in him a mechanism that causes him to become dizzy and nauseous when he is violent. They also isolate him by making his body smell offensively (as a humanitarian gesture they insulate him from his own odor), making it impossible for ordinary people to enjoy his company, even if he is peaceful.

What must strike us about this story is the incongruence between the nar-rator's grandiose claims—"King of the World"—and the triviality of his ges-tures of rage. The monster of "Born of Man and woman" is restricted to the arena of the family, and even Anthony, the monster child of "Its a *Good* Life," has a preschooler's range and vision so that the next town is quite liter-ally another world. Their limited danger is in scale with their childishness. But the narrator of "Country of the Kind," is able to travel all over the globe: in the light of this larger range, his crimes, such as burning a car's tires and fusing the axle, or strewing hot cheese sauce on a room's walls and rug, seem of quite extraordinary inconsequence. Despite the boundlessness of his arena, all he can do is make a mess, and he can never escalate his rage beyond these childish acts. On this level the story is an ironic deflation of the monstrous child formula. The heroic value of the monster, the injustice of the discrimination against him, and the megalomania of the power fantasy are stripped of the generic accouterments of horror and rendered as ironic comedy.

The King of the Kind's narrative, while it rings of contempt for the "dulls"—middle-class, white Americans, much like those adults who persecute and are horrified by the other monstrous children we have studied—also reveals a psychological stress that severely distorts, at times even inverts, the declared motives and feelings. After he engages in an underwater dance with a woman who does not realize who he is, the narrator tells how he began to anticipate some sort of happy outcome to the shielded relationship:" The moment had to end. She gestured toward the surface, and left me. I followed her up. I was feeling drowsy and almost at peace, after my sickness. I thought . . . I don't know what I thought" (p. 597, ellipsis in text). Like the frightened townspeople in "It's a *Good* Life," the speaker may be consciously trying to regulate his thoughts so as to escape the punishing superego controls built into himself. But since the repression seems to be taking place at the moment of narration and not at the time of the event, the declaration of ignorance seems more likely to be an act of unconscious repression of genuine desire. Like the moment of similar hiatus in "A Martian Odyssey," this enigmatic moment directs us to a cluster of contradiction. Here the prospect of erotic union is peaceful, an escape from the hated self, but it also holds the promise of violence. The monster-genius is unable to separate the two: the uncontrollable ego grasping for satisfaction and recognition, for "Kingship," escalates any personal pleasure into a violent rage.

The relation of pleasure and violence is depicted earlier in the story when, in an act of gratuitous and trivial sadism rather like those of the monster in "Born of Man and Woman," the narrator splashes food around. He originally plans to throw hot liquid on a half-naked woman, but since he cannot inflict pain without getting sick himself, he tries instead to make her feel as if she has been hurt without physically injuring her. He reasoned that by substituting cold wine for the hot liquid at the last minute she "would have mistaken the chill splash for a scalding one." This elaborately trivial scene is important because it gives us a narrative image of the central thematic issue in the story: opposite sensations (love/hate, creation/destruction, pleasure/fear) can stand for each other. The core mechanism of the monstrous child story in which horror renders pleasure is here made conscious.

This dynamic is also a model for the sublimation which is an essential motive for art itself. The story's narrator, a sculptor, attempts in the last part of the story to convert his social ostracism into the basis for an aesthetic. By carving a figurine of a man seated with a sword in his hand, he hopes to inspire one of the "dulls" to an act of liberating violence of the sort that he himself is now psychologically incapable. But though the creative vision, itself a union of peacefulness and phallic violence, is intended to communicate to the dulls, it does not. The narrator has left such images all around the world, but "they were like signs printed in red and green, in a color-blind world." The dilemma is one that has been potential to SF's sense of its own genius from the beginning: the very superiority, the ability to "see," that elevates the genius and the readership above the common, also isolates them and renders them powerless. The morons just won't listen.

The story sets up a series of oppositions that are both contradictions and unions. Art is proposed as a method of communication, as a way of breaking through the isolation endured by the narrator, but it only makes his sense of isolation more acute. His pride in his aesthetic alertness, expressed in the opening paragraph by his scarlet clothing, is also the sign of his isolation. His proud sense of uniqueness is the source of his desperate pain. And the more he indulges it, in acts of childish vandalism or in acts of artistic creation, the more desperate his loneliness becomes. Knight's story explores the trap deep in the satisfactions of the monstrous child fantasy. The happy sense of righteous vengeance that closes "Born of Man and Woman" is ultimately frustrating. The egoistic rewards of genius, expressed here as aesthetic superiority and as a freedom from middle-class moral codes and inhibitions, are the very qualities that lead to the protagonist's excruciating isolation. Like Wells's story half a century earlier,[6] Knight's ends with a balance between the appeal of an intense individualistic aesthetic and that of a dull but happy social union.

But in its conclusion Knight's story touches a contradiction that lies outside the concerns of the Wells tale but that is central to all the ideas about genius that we have been looking at. Just as the myth of IQ is both democratic and elitist, the aesthetic of the story is exclusionary and inclusive. The narrator's final message-plea catches this contradiction neatly:

YOU CAN SHARE THE WORLD WITH ME. THEY CAN'T STOP YOU. STRIKE NOW—PICK UP A SHARP THING AND STAB, OR A HEAVY THING AND CRUSH. THAT'S ALL. THAT WILL MAKE YOU FREE. ANYONE CAN DO IT.
Anyone, Someone, Anyone (p. 604).

The opening line of the message offers exclusivity—you and I alone can rule the world—but the last line is wide open. The "they" of the second sentence suggests an opposition that the "anyone" of the last contradicts. And the desperate last three words of the story catch the pathos of this aesthetic contradiction. The first "anyone" repeats the sense of the message: it is generous, nondiscriminatory, democratic. "Someone" is more desperate; having begun by opening the doors to all, he now becomes worried that no one will accept. Many invitations have been sent out, but no one comes. Finally, "anyone" has a subtly different meaning. This time the word contains no connotation of opportunity and has become entirely indiscriminate: the aesthetic of genius, that began by idealizing the exceptional individual, has now, by a clear and natural dialectic, found itself inviting companionship with people it should despise.

Knight's story points to a new attitude toward ambiguity in SF. Unlike "Nightfall" or "That Only a Mother," this ambiguity does not in any way leave the plot in doubt. We know exactly what is happening at the end of "The Country of the Kind." The final emphatic passage indulges at length the very crisis of the genius's contradictory position; of feeling superior to the "dulls" and yet wanting their admiration and even companionship. In its repeated, enigmatic words, the passage focuses, not on any utopian solution, but with some touch of sadism perhaps, on the irresolvability of the dilemma itself. We should emphasize that it is not just the failure of the genius that gives pleasure—this is not a case of ironic justice in which a smart aleck gets his—it is the figure's undeniable success as a "genius" in his society that renders the irony. In this story it is not technocratic dreams, but the literary aspirations of the genre itself, especially as they have been expressed in Kornbluth's two central stories, that become the subject of inquiry.

"The Quest for Saint Aquin"

The image of the robot, such a staple of SF, can also become a projection of the utopian mode of thought itself. That such a simple tale as "Helen O'Loy" can fully engage the utopian hopes and the enigmatic otherness that makes the robot such an attractive device, points to the limits the image offers of the possibilities of life. An ingenious writer like Asimov may repeatedly find pleasure in the rational permutations of the robotic laws, but even in the early forties, in works like Eando Binder's "I, Robot," the severe restrictions represented by the robot are evident.[7] In "Huddling Place" the robot is kept in a servile position and never does anything that a human butler couldn't or wouldn't do. But by the fifties the robot has become a device through which the genre is able to begin to talk about itself. If self-consciousness marks a point at which the robot ceases to be merely a machine and enters a realm that is deeply puzzling to humans, it also marks a point at which narrative suddenly loses its naiveté and becomes conscious of its own generic tradition. In the fifties, especially in robot stories, SF becomes aware of itself as a form of literature with a history, not just forthright fantasy or extrapolation. Two stories in *Science Fiction Hall of Fame*, Anthony Boucher's "The Quest for Saint Aquin" and Alfred Bester's "Fondly Fahrenheit," use the robot to pose a dialectical reflection that, while advancing the form, marks its end as a utopian project.

The generic knowingness of Boucher's "The Quest for Saint Aquin" is signaled by his unemphasized allusions to the tradition of pulp SF. When Thomas, the underground priest seeking the uncorrupted body of Saint Aquin, debauches in an inn, he hears someone singing "A Space Suit Built for Two". The story does not elaborate, but the experienced SF reader knows that this is one of the uncollected bawdy songs of Rhysling, the blind singer of the spaceways, in Heinlein's "The Green Hills of Earth."[8] In an earlier discussion between Thomas and his robot jackass, the Robass remarks, "I have heard of one robot in an isolated space station who worshipped a God of robots and would not believe any man had created him" (p. 464). This is a casual but clear allusion to Asimov's "Reason."[9] Such allusions put Boucher's story within an actual frame of reference which, unlike the carefully manufactured interconnections of epic future histories, is itself an element of our social system. For the reader of Boucher to recognize such an allusion to "The Green Hills of Earth" demands a consciousness quite different from that required of the reader of Heinlein's own series of stories about future history. For Heinlein the allusion would be a device of narrative plenitude. For Boucher it is that, but it is also a sign of broader generic awareness. It is a device, not of realism, but of social identification.

Boucher's use of allusion to place his story within the genre of SF is paralleled by the structure of biblical allusion within the story. Thomas is reminded of his namesake a number of times. His ride on the robass is explicitly compared to that of Balaam on his ass. The parable of the good Samaritan is re-enacted. In a system of such rich allusion, all events come to be understood typologically. Thomas's faith is tested in ways that have been figured earlier in history. The Technarchy may have replaced the Roman persecution, and temptations may come from a robass, but the moral and spiritual issues remain the same as they have always been for Christians.

The story is alert to the complexities of psychology, and it plays a game with Freudian slips. It lets us enjoy the way Thomas rationalizes his attention to the barmaid, an attractive and extravagantly bosomed woman, half human and half Martian: "As he stretched his legs after breakfast, Thomas thought of her chest and breasts—purely, of course, as a symbol of the extraordinary nature of her origin." A little later the robass points to the pun in Thomas's argument that he should go back to the inn because "there's a chance of picking up something," though, predictably, Thomas denies the erotic meaning. But later, when he succumbs to wine and temptation in the inn, the erotic dimension of his thought is clearly acknowledged. The story is tolerant: Thomas is human, and his repression, whatever the struggle, is a moral one. But, as with the allusions, the texture of reference here—the barmaid's breasts are distantly linked to the Song of Songs, which Thomas piously insists is "strictly an allegory concerning the love of Christ for his Church"—is constantly foreknowing the unknown.

While at the level of local interpretation the texture of allusion complicates the already rich meaning of events, it also solves dilemmas by placing the whole work in a generic tradition that has already been interpreted. Thus, Thomas, after thinking of the parallel between himself and his robass with Balaam and his ass, can drift into what is, essentially, an interpretation of the biblical story and the meaning of the enigma it presents: "the story has no shape, no moral; it is as though it was there to say that there are portions of the Divine Plan which we will never understand" (p. 462). At one level this puts the story of Balaam and the story of Thomas firmly in the grand tradition of Catholic pyrrhonism: such enigmas teach us humiliation; the height of reason is to realize reason's failure. And yet, if the story is theologically didactic, it is completely ambiguous on the issues that have most concerned SF. Robots are saintly and satanic. The Technarchy, while anti-catholic, also resembles the Inquisition. And though human will and reason is frail, we are still capable of faith.

The story closes with lines that have no reference to SF at all: "His prayers arose, as the text has it, like clouds of incense, and as shapeless as those clouds. But through all his thoughts ran the cry of the father of the epileptic in Caesarea Philippi: *I believe, O Lord; help thou mine unbelief!*" (p. 476). The ambiguity of the reference to "the text"—is it the Bible? or the present story which has now itself become a part of the scripture?—emphasizes once again the timelessness of the story. The quotation (Mark 9:24), annotated with complex and obscure detail (how many of us know what to make of the reference to Caesarea Philippi?), embodies the perennial anxiety of intelligent faith: I want to believe, but if I am to be completely honest, I cannot ignore my doubts.

The dilemma posed for us in "The Quest for Saint Aquin" is not just thematic. Like the story of Balaam, it lacks the order and didactic intention we expect from its genre. Other stories have played with the issues of this story—"A Martian Odyssey" with its enigmatic other, or "Nightfall" with its conflict of scientific reason and religious faith—but, by staying in their generic space such stories have posed issues in the form of denied contradictions that we could analyze. But Boucher's story, in large part, one imagines, because it does not care about the precise technocratic issues in the same way, will elude our analysis. It explicitly and pleasurably poses irresolvable paradoxes on the ground that such problems are beyond human reason and can only be handled by faith.

"Fondly Fahrenheit"

The education into irony is the end of the utopian urge that has inspired early SF. The two stories from 1954 in *Science Fiction Hall of Fame* can be said to pose the alternatives open to SF after its youth. By enacting a kind of generic rigor previously unseen in the form, Godwin's "The Cold Equations" becomes the classic version of the hard-core story. Laboriously and without any irony, the story works relentlessly toward it's murderous conclusion. No less murderous, Alfred Bester's "Fondly Fahrenheit," (1954) sees the real challenge, not in the inevitable, but in the problem of narrative itself. "Fondly Fahrenheit" marks the opposite of the technocratic dream, not because it is thematically pessimistic, but because it has so mastered ironic self-consciousness that it distrusts all assertion. Quite apart from the narrative eccentricity, "Fondly Fahrenheit" is filled with psycho-logic in place of techno-logic: the "lunatic rhumba" of the android, its childish nonsense rhymes, the disturbing repetitions in the prose itself, and the unexplained power of sheer temperature, all suggest mental processes antithetical to the Heinleinian ideal.

This is an important moment in the history of the form. "Fondly Fahrenheit" is a story that is meaningful only in relation to the genre's past. It has little, if any, of the explicit idea content that so distinguishes the earlier work in the form. The plot of "Fondly Fahrenheit" is minimally interesting itself, for it simply recounts a series of murders and escapes by Vandaleur and his "Multiple Aptitude" android. If one thinks of the picaresque plot of "A Martian Odyssey," in which each episode introduced a new imaginative wonder, one can see the change this later story represents. When the temperature rises above 90 degrees fahrenheit, the normally harmless android becomes murderous, and its master, unable to bring himself to destroy his valuable machine, is himself driven to murder to protect it. Further into the story we learn that "projection" of some sort may be at work, though as we shall see in a moment, the term as used in this story is not entirely clear.

We can see the special quality of "Fondly Fahrenheit" if we try to imagine how it would read without the generic background of SF. Many of the story's locations, though given exotic names (Paragon III, Megaster V, Lyra Alpha), are recognizable, twentieth century, earthly locales, and the story climaxes in a familiar Britain. The song the Android sings is trendy fifties' be-bop, and it dances the rhumba. But the central imaginative structure, a man and his android, allude to a SF convention, and the surprise of the story is derived in large part from its explicit violation of the Asimovian three laws of Robotics. As at the end of Asimov's *Foundation Trilogy*, the implausible formula, subjected to a touch of realism, dissolves: disguises don't work; alliances turn into blackmail. The utopian element of the form has given way to witty cynicism.

What makes the story interesting is not the plot, but the mode of narration: it is told for the most part in a first person narrative which confuses the points-of-view of Vandaleur and his android. The ambiguities about the source of the android's perverse homicidal drive are embedded in the prose itself. Thus, after the murder of Blenheim we hear, "And we soaked the rug around [a candle] with kerosene. No I did all that. The android refused. I am forbidden to endanger life or property." (p. 585) The first "I" is the voice of Vandaleur; the second is that of the android. Such confusion of Vandaleur and his android occurs throughout the story, but it reaches a climax in the following passage:

> The wall of flame surged up to them. Vandaleur took a deep breath and prepared to submerge until the flame passed over them. The android shuddered and burst into an earsplitting scream.
> "All reet! All reet!" it shouted. "Be fleet be fleet!"
> "Damn you!" I shouted. I tried to drown it.
> "Damn you!" I cursed him. I smashed his face.
> The android battered Vandaleur, who fought it off until it exploded out of the mud and staggered upright. Before I could return to the attack, the live flames captured it hypnotically. It danced and capered in a lunatic rhumba before the wall of fire. (pp. 589–590).

The two "I's" who shout "Damn you!" can be distinguished by the careful definition of the android as "it," but the final "I" who attempts to return to the attack is entirely ambiguous. Such confusion renders the problem of externalization and projection concrete. The psychological mechanism that lies at the core of the alien stories of a decade earlier has itself been made the explicit subject of observation.

In *Science Fiction Hall of Fame* we can trace an increasing interest in point of view. The elaborate narrative nesting of Campbell's "Twilight" is not epistemological but simply a way of giving the narrator authority. Merril's "That Only a Mother" uses the limited point of view of Maggie's letters for the first two-thirds to set up a serious problem of perception, but the story falls back on an omniscient narrator to tell the last part and set the letter-writer in her ambiguous perspective. Throughout the fifties we see writers exploring the potentials of limited point of view. Matheson's "Born of Man and Woman" is in its point of view both rigorous and implausible. Keyes's "Flowers for Algernon" manages to use the epistolary technique to trace Charlie's whole intellectual course. But while Keyes's story is not without its ironies, it is sentimental and univocal next to Bester's "Fondly Fahrenheit."

We need to ask what such artistic self-consciousness does to the essential structures of meditation that have characterized SF. In part the loss of narrative innocence leads to a self-reflectiveness that, for all its increased sophistication, is devoid of the explicitly utopian element that has up until now defined the form. The maturation, if you will, has taught the form how to be evasive, how to avoid embarrassing itself. The concern with irony is a movement toward psychology. Psychology has never been absent from SF. As we saw, even a naive story like Campbell's "Twilight" is deeply entangled in the psychological dilemma of loving something that you know must fail you. And "The Cold Equations" entails, as I have argued, a powerful latent fantasy even as it preaches a law insensitive to human psychology and morality. But in "Fondly Fahrenheit" the psychology is explicit and invoked as a commentary on the innocence of earlier SF and on the willful anti-psychologism that Heinlein stands for.

One can imagine that a story simply and explicitly about projection as a phenomenon might be possible in early SF. What makes "Fondly Fahrenheit" generically innovative is that its concept of projection is complexly circular. Projection identifies both a fantasy by which a person externalizes inner feelings, and a power coming from outside by which a person absorbs the feelings of another. The two mechanisms are quite different, but in the narrative they are treated as part of the same syndrome:

> [Nan Webb says,] "Projection is a throwing forward. It is the process of throwing out upon another the ideas or impulses that belong to one-self. The paranoid, for example projects upon others his conflicts and disturbances in order to externalize them. He accuses, directly or by implication, other men of having the very sickness with which he is struggling himself."
> "And the danger of projection?" [asks Vandaleur.]
> "It is the danger of believing what is implied. If you live with a psy-chotic who projects his sickness upon you, there is a danger of falling

into his psychotic pattern and becoming virtually psychotic yourself. As, no doubt, is happening to you, Mr. Vandaleur. (p. 586).

The dilemma of the origins of violence is a classic crux: to what extent is behavior genetic and to what extent is it a social product? At the core of the story is a mystery: is the violence Vandaleur's or the android's? We are told that if you live long enough with a crazy person you become crazy yourself. Who can say where the psychosis originated? Vandaleur may be the victim of the android's violent impulses caused by heat, but there is at least the suggestion that the heat simply allows the android to express Vandaleur's psychotic violence. At the end of the story, the murderousness of the new labor robot is surely Vandaleur's expression.

The explicit psychological theme of Bester's story opens up the elementary structures of the SF we have been looking at. The projection that is never acknowledged in "Arena" becomes here the object of interest. "Fondly Fahrenheit" is very consciously a story not only about projection as it works in other stories, but about the very process of fantasizing itself. With intelligent cynicism, the story relentlessly exposes how projection and identification allow one to participate deeply in atrocity and yet maintain one's innocence.

And we can see in the story a skepticism about rationality itself. Vandaleur's helplessness in the face of the inevitable, like the EDC pilot's in "The Cold Equations," is not as simply reasonable as it pretends to be. In Bester's story such passivity is revealed as a class-based economic presumption. "Fondly Fahrenheit" plays on two profoundly antithetical social-economic perspectives. The first, associated with Vandaleur himself, presumes the rights and anxieties of ownership. The urgency of his concern for the android is essentially economic, since he cannot conceive of making a living without his inherited android. He represents an acute version of the untechnological, aristocratic person. When Dallas Brady, after finding him out, asks why Vandaleur didn't have the android repaired, he answers:

"I couldn't take the chance," Vandaleur explained angrily. "If they started fooling around with lobotomies and body chemistry and endocrine surgery, they might have destroyed its aptitudes. What would I have left to hire out? How would I live?"

"You could work yourself. People do."

"Work for what? You know I'm good for nothing. How could I compete with specialist androids and robots? Who can, unless he's got a terrific talent for a particular job?"

"Yeah. That's true."

"I lived off my old man all my life. Damn him! He had to go bust just before he died. Left me the android and that's all. The only way I can get along is living off what it earns. (p. 575).

This is more than just a defense of owning androids. As in Simak's "Huddling Place," though here put forth with comic irony rather than pathos, class presumptions, far from breaking down, have just been reinforced by new technology. The line "Work for what?" is deeply ambiguous: it seems to intend to mean work *at* what, but it actually says either "why work?" or "how would I get paid?" And even Dallas Brady, a tough, practical woman, admits, though perhaps with less sympathy than Vandaleur supposes, that in the technologically dominated world, work has become meaningless for humans. This falsely rational passivity leads Vandaleur eventually to murder to preserve his economic security.

The other socio-economic perspective is associated with the android and summed up in the line, "Sometimes . . . it is a good thing to be property" (p. 581). This declaration of irresponsibility is an assertion of power and freedom. The situation of Vandaleur and his android is much like the Hegelian master-servant dialectic, except that Vandaleur, the supposed master, is also from the start the victim, and the android, the slave, never enjoys its power. The android, by frequently declaring its inability to participate in the pleasure-pain syndrome and refusing to act violently in cold weather, leaves a vacuum that Vandaleur himself, for all his incompetence, has to fill. The last murders, including perhaps that of the android itself, are all committed by Vandaleur.

The ironic comedy of the story challenges the pieties of the genre by anchoring the future, not in the fantasy of a purely rational, efficient, and benign technology, but in a psychological and perversely economic technology. But such self-consciousness, while it may pride itself on its self-knowledge, is not entirely free of the fantasies that it claims to be mocking. Like some forms of irony, the surface disavowal serves to defuse objections that would otherwise inhibit the whole imaginative train: I can say what I realize is atrocious because, as you can see, I don't really mean it. (But I really *do* mean it!) "Fondly Fahrenheit" has a definitively sadistic edge to it. The victims are frequently helpless people—girls, women, a blind man. The story indulges in a spread of violence that, in the fashion of a horror story, keeps moving beyond the bounds of its earlier confinement. At first only the android is violent in temperatures over 90 degrees fahrenheit, but in London Vandaleur himself becomes the agent of violence, killing Blenheim and Nan Webb, the psychometric consultant. And in the last paragraphs we learn of the new "cheap labor robot" which, thanks to the power of Vandaleur's "projection," is violent at 10 degrees. There is an inexorable growth of passion, an extending of violence to all life and machinery, and accompanying this growth is a gradual collapse of the regulation and control that has traditionally characterized the machine. The android's frequent statements of passionlessness—it is impervious to the pleasure-pain syndrome, it cannot override its directives—become less relevant as "projection" takes over. Behind its comic self-consciousness the story takes pleasure in unfeeling violence, the development of Vandaleur himself as a cold murderer.

The Limitations of Irony

"Fondly Fahrenheit" cannot be read in the way we have read earlier work, or even in the way we read the latent urges and defenses of its contemporaneous "The Cold Equations." The irony of Bester's story makes it impossible for us to attribute a single political-psychological meaning to the story: the lines of thought and feeling that are raised in the story are set up as internally inconsistent and contradictory. That is the pleasure of it. The irony blocks interpretation and at the same time allows for a variety of discrepant, fragmentary readings.

In such a situation, we might usefully reconsider Adorno's famous formulation of the virtues of contradiction: "a successful work, according to immanent criticism, is not one which resolves objective contradiction in a spurious harmony, but one which expresses the idea of harmony negatively by embodying the contradictions, pure and uncompromised, in its innermost structure" ("Cultural Criticism and Society," p. 32). We are now in a position to raise further questions about the knowledge contradiction generates. In comparison with the earlier SF stories, these late stories avoid a "spurious harmony" and express a clearly conscious contradiction. The Knight story treats as problematic the values of individual "supernormality" that Sturgeon and Kornbluth appear to accept. Bester's story makes an issue of the mechanisms of projection that form the unexamined basis of "Arena." And Boucher's self-conscious typology debunks the presumption of most SF that a new technology poses new moral problems. But we may still ask, is such skillfully mastered contradiction any more *cognitively* useful than the more innocent contradictions of the earlier works? The blatant but unconscious contradictions of "Helen O'Loy," "Twilight," "Nightfall," "Microcosmic God," and "Arena" in their way present the dilemmas society must hide and also resolve more clearly than do these more masterful understandings, which show their art in their sophisticated acceptance of their own limitations. These late works are pre-censored. Intelligent as they may be generically, they miss the pointedness a spurious harmony can create. Wise as they may be at one level, they too are finally products of social ideology, and it can be argued that by believing they are superior in the realm of "literature," they end up rendering a spurious contradiction. We have here an early glimpse of the ideological difficulties posed by what is nowadays loosely called "post-modernism."

Jürgen Habermas poses the question, "how can the relation between technical progress and the social life world, which today is still clothed in a primitive, traditional, and unchosen form, be reflected upon and brought under the control of rational discussion?"[10] Habermas rejects the kind of popular solution to this problem that argues that poets should know physics. The problem is not "science," but the social uses of technology. "Only . . . when [scientific] information is exploited for the development of productive or destructive forces, can its revolutionary practical results penetrate the literary consciousness of the life world" (p. 52). The phenomenon of SF offers an isolated and defined literary space in which "the relation between technical progress and the social life world" can be "reflected upon" intensely. In SF's evolution we can witness the struggle of a genre to mediate a social dichotomy. From the start the very process of narrative requires SF to reflect on the social relations of technology just to "make sense" of its own imagined worlds. In studying what I take to be SF's ultimate failure to find that mediation we can begin to see aspects of the problem that might otherwise escape us. But SF itself consciously tries to avoid these implications of its own undertaking: it denies its own political role, and as it imagines it is thinking about the "new," it often simply reenacts, in somewhat disguised form, previous social paradigms. Ultimately, by a dialectic that is as Darwinian as Marxist, the element of embattled, self-congratulatory triumph that characterizes the SF subculture also blinds it to the possibilities of a more profound reflection. The initially utopian genre finally mutates into a form which is "literary" and therefore conditioned by aesthetic (rather than technological) postures and modes and whose great virtue is its ability to live with contradiction.

Postscript:
Science Fiction Hall of Fame as a Book

THE *SCIENCE FICTION HALL OF FAME* WE HAVE ANALYZED IS A text with a plot. It depicts the genre's education from an optimistic and open innocence in the thirties into a more pessimistic and repressed wisdom in the fifties. The pressures of narrative plausibility have driven the genre to become "literary" as a way of maintaining what is increasingly showing up as a flawed rationality. Kornbluth's work is the fulcrum: he engages ideas of utopian simplicity and at the same time, by indulging in black comedy, avoids working out the implications of the evolutionary ideas to which he and much of the culture subscribe.

It is not at all clear, however, that when the anthology was published in 1970, it would have been read this way. To some extent the process by which the anthology was selected represses the plot of the anthology and the actual history of the genre. The chronological scheme does not seem to have been in anyone's mind when the specific stories were voted on. Perhaps it would have been more appropriate for the mode of selection to arrange the stories according to their popularity. But just as in psychoanalysis a nonchronological series of free associations gradually implies a narrative of a psychic life which can then be reconstructed, so this anthology, in spite of itself, reveals a narrative that was in all probability not conscious to those writers selecting the stories but is nevertheless implicit in their sense of the genre's history.

By invoking the idea of "classic," the anthology sets itself in opposition to what by the late sixties was generally acknowledged as the "new wave" in SF. One suspects, though this is difficult to prove, that by a process which Michel de Certeau calls "poaching"[1] the readers of this anthology in 1970 can ignore the problems the text entails and find in it the values they seek. To adapt Stanley Fish, we can say that they can find the text they want. If such a reinterpretation takes place, the contradictions within the individual stories will be overlooked, and the stories of the middle fifties by Knight, Bester, and Boucher, that show up in our analysis as "literary" transformations of earlier themes, will be seen, not as criticism of those themes, but as a late continuation of a fixed and stable genre essentially in agreement with

John W. Campbell's technophilia and one that began to disintegrate only in the sixties. From such a perspective, the anthology shows up as a nostalgic gesture, a conservative attempt to resurrect a coherent style and a set of themes that in 1970 were no longer honored.

Such an interpretation of the intention behind the anthology and of the way it was read when it appeared would, I imagine, be generally accepted, both by critics and by the SF subculture. However, we should be aware that the anthology also functions at a second level, not simply as a reaction to a new style, but as a statement in response to a wide-ranging challenge to the technocratic faith represented by that style but that had many other cultural manifestations in the sixties as well. During this period there were signs of a general anxiety, strongly felt by what we might call the "technocratic sub-culture," that the progress made toward the rationalization of society under a technocratic rule was in serious jeopardy. This technocratic anxiety re-pressed the awareness that technocracy is at its core contradictory and in-volves psychological and political repression—the deep discovery of SF itself. Misreading the dynamics of its own history, the SF subculture hoped to find in this collection of "classic texts" a narrative that would revalidate the technocratic vision.

The apparent threat to the technocratic vision posed in the sixties can be seen clearly in one famous technocrat's own rendering of the implications of that time. In the fiftieth anniversary issue of *US News & World Report* (May 9, 1983), among the prophesies of the extraordinary world of 2033—prophesies that frequently sound as if they came from 1933—Herman Kahn has a mo-ment, not of doubt exactly, but of qualm, when he considers a possible prob-lem in the generally rosy future he foresees:

> However, being wealthy can create some problems. As people get richer, they often become less competitive, less interested in creating a dynamic environment. I'm not sure how well the U.S. will handle being rich and secure, but I fear we will rest on our laurels. If we look at the 1960s, when such conditions prevailed, there was an enormous amount of turmoil. People took the system for granted and thought it could withstand anything. That could happen again early in the next century (p. A42).

The worry about richness breeding laziness is an old one (not therefore in-valid) that we have seen reiterated in SF of an earlier period. Where Kahn plays a variation on the familiar SF trope is in his vision of the sixties as his historical example of a less dynamic world resting on its laurels. This is not a picture all of us might recognize. Kahn is certainly not thinking about

Johnson's "Great Society," or the escalation of the Vietnam War, or the Space Program. Clearly, he is referring to elements of the "counter-culture"—the civil rights, war protest, and sexual liberation movements—when he describes the "turmoil" of the sixties. It is in reference to these activities that he says, "People took the system for granted and thought that it could withstand anything."

The assertion that a protest against the "system" is an act of taking "the system for granted" needs to be examined here. While on the one hand the sentence seems to describe an assault on "the system," on the other hand it suggests that the producers of turmoil dared to act the way they did because, despite their rhetoric to the contrary, they secretly expected, even needed, the system to remain as it was. Implicit in this line of reasoning is the denial of any real political principles behind the turmoil. The technocratic order, it is suggested, is not really up for political debate, even if it does seem to be in danger. Whatever the moral rhetoric, the revolutionary actions of the sixties were an exercise in self-indulgence, a gratuitous testing of authority, the decadent fruit of peace and prosperity. The line suggests that any person challenging the system can recognize what is too much. And there is a final ambiguity reminiscent of some of the stories we have studied: does the sentence say the system withstood the turmoil or not? The next line ("That could happen again . . .") is full of implications of doom.

Kahn's paragraph, while certainly comprehensible and unproblematic when viewed from the proper ideological slant, is built on a familiar contradiction. The beginning poses a vision of a world that, because it is successful, has become soft, "less competitive," not "dynamic." At the end of the paragraph the energy resides with the revolutionaries, but their "turmoil" is not seen as "dynamic." Like the anti-Semitic agitator's "aliens," these "people" are both a weak retreat from the system and a powerful (perhaps even overwhelming) threat to it. For their failure to appreciate the system, they must be condescended to: for their threat to the system, they must be fought. They are trivial as well as dangerous.

Herman Kahn is one of the most prominent and optimistic prophets of technocracy of the fifties and sixties. The growth of awareness in the SF genre did not seem to have disturbed his optimistic sense of the "dynamic" possibilities of capitalist technology. For him the sixties was only a time of turmoil, what he hoped would be a temporary lapse from the smooth development of a technocratic utopia.

From this moment of technocratic doubt in the late sixties the *Science Fiction Hall of Fame* was born. It is a gesture of nostalgic reaction against what some see as the apocalyptic turmoil of the later sixties and at the same time, not entirely consciously, a recapitulation of insights, developing with the genre itself, into the contradictions of technocracy. But transcending either interpretation is the sense that optimism has become nostalgia. The promoters of this nostalgia often use the language and imagery of the original SF project of the thirties: they advocate the "scientific method" in literature, they praise "the sense of wonder," and they still enjoy imagining the details of future technology. But such language and pleasure, problematic in their first appearance, had in 1970 taken on new complexities. What was originally perceived, whatever its latent content, as progressive and utopian, had become consciously retrospective. In declaring the 1930–1960 period "The Golden Age of Science Fiction," the SF subculture in 1970 honors what is still seen as the promise of technology. But by placing the golden age in the past, it also despairs of its fufillment in the future.

Appendix 1
Reprintings of Stories by Authors In
Science Fiction Hall of Fame, Volume 1

THE FOLLOWING IS BASED ON INFORMATION IN WILLIAM CON-
tento's *Index to SF Anthologies and Collections*. For each of the authors
included in *Science Fiction Hall of Fame* it lists all the stories that have been
reprinted four or more times. Under each author's name I have ranged the
stories in order of the number of times they have been reprinted in anthologies (AN) and in author collections (AC). The authors are listed in the
order they appear in the *Science Fiction Hall of Fame*, and the stories that
appear in that anthology are in italics.

Weinbaum, Stanley G.
  "*A Martian Odyssey*," 8 AN, 5 AC
  "The Lotus Eaters," 4 AN, 5 AC
Campbell, John W.
  "*Twilight*," 6 AN, 3 AC
  "Night," 4 AN, 2 AC
del Rey, Lester
  "*Helen O'Loy*," 9 AN, 1 AC
  "Instinct," 5 AN, 1 AC
Heinlein, Robert A.
  "And He Built a Crooked House,"
    9 AN, 2 AC
  "The Year of the Jackpot," 8 AN, 1 AC
  "The Green Hills of Earth, 7 AN,
    3 AC
  "They," 7 AN, 1 AC
  "*The Roads Must Roll*," 6 AN, 3 AC
  "All You Zombies," 5 AN, 2 AC
  "Blowups Happen," 4 AN, 3 AC
  "The Black Pits of Luna," 4 AN, 2 AC
  "Columbus was a Dope," 4 AN, 1 AC
  "Goldfish Bowl," 4 AN, 1 AC
Sturgeon, Theodore
  "Thunder and Roses," 6 AN, 2 AC

"The Hurkle is a Happy Beast," 6 AN,
  2 AC
"And Now the News," 6 AN, 0 AC
"*Microcosmic God*," 5 AN, 2 AC
"The Man Who Lost the Sea," 5 AN,
  0 AC
"Occam's Scalpel," 4 AN, 0 AC
"Saucer of Loneliness," 4 AN, 1 AC
Asimov, Isaac
  "*Nightfall*," 16 AN, 2 AC
  "The Feeling of Power," 6 AN, 2 AC
  "The Fun They Had," 6 AN, 2 AC
  "It's Such a Beautiful Day," 6 AN,
    2 AC
  "Dreaming is a Private Thing," 6 AN,
    1 AC
  "Misbegotten Missionary" (also
    "Green Patches"), 6 AN, 0 AC
  "Not Final," 5 AN, 1 AC
  "Liar!" 5 AN, 1 AC
  "Franchise," 4 AN, 1 AC
  "Trends," 4 AN, 1 AC
  "Victory Unintentional," 4 AN, 1 AC

Van Vogt, A. E.
  "The Enchanted Village," 8 AN, 2 AC
  "Resurrection," 6 AN, 1 AC
  "Far Centaurus," 5 AN, 1 AC
  "The Vault of the Beast," 4 AN, 3 AC
  "Dormant," 4 AN, 1 AC
Padgett, Lewis (Henry Kuttner and
    C. L. Moore)
  "No Woman Born," (Moore) 5 AN,
    1 AC
  "Mimsy Were the Borogoves," 4 AN,
    3 AC
  "Don't Look Now," (Kuttner) 4 AN,
    1 AC
Simak, Clifford D.
  "Desertion," 9 AN, 0 AC
  "Huddling Place," 4 AN, 1 AC
  "Eternity Lost," 4 AN, 0 AC
  "Limiting Factor," 4 AN, 0 AC
Brown, Fredric
  "Arena," 10 AN, 2 AC
  "Puppet Show," 7 AN, 2 AC
  "The Waveries," 7 AN, 1 AC
  "The Weapon," 6 AN, 1 AC
  "Placet is a Crazy Place," 5 AN, 1 AC
  "Answer," 4 AN, 3 AC
  "Dark Interlude" (with Mack
    Reynolds), 4 AN, 1 AC
Leinster, Murray (Will F. Jenkins)
  "First Contact," 9 AN, 0 AC
  "Keyhole," 7 AN, 0 AC
  "Doomsday Deferred," 5 AN, 0 AC
  "A Logic Named Joe," 4 AN, 1 AC
  "Exploration Team," 4 AN, 0 AC
Merril, Judith
  "That Only a Mother," 8 AN, 2 AC
  "Survival Ship," 4 AN, 1 AC
Smith, Cordwainer (Paul Linebarger)
  "Game of Rat and Dragon," 7 AN,
    2 AC
  "Scanners Live in Vain," 5 AN, 2 AC
Bradbury, Ray
  "The Sound of Thunder," 8 AN, 2 AC
  "The Fire Balloons" (also "In This
    Sign"), 6 AN, 3 AC

  "Mars is Heaven" (also "The Earth
    Men"), 6 AN 2 AC
  "The Veldt" (also "The World the
    Children Made"), 6 AN, 2 AC
  "Kaleidoscope," 6 AN, 2 AC
  "Naming of Names" (also "Dark They
    Were and Golden Eyed"), 5 AN,
    4 AC
  "There Will Come Soft Rains," 5 AN,
    3 AC
  "Zero Hour," 5 AN, 2 AC
  "The Pedestrian," 5 AN, 2 AC
  "All Summer in a Day," 5 AN, 1 AC
  "The Smile," 4 AN, 3 AC
  "The Million-Year Picnic," 4 AN,
    2 AC
  "Miracle of Rare Device," 4 AN, 1 AC
Kornbluth, C. M.
  "The Marching Morons," 8 AN, 3 AC
  "The Little Black Bag," 7 AN, 4 AC
  "The Silly Season," 5 AN, 4 AC
  "The Mindworm," 4 AN, 4 AC
  "With These Hands," 4 AN, 4 AC
  "The Altar at Midnight," 4 AN, 3 AC
  "The Luckiest Man in Denv," 4 AN,
    3 AC
  "That Share of Glory," 4 AN, 3 AC
Matheson, Richard
  "Shipshape Home," 5 AN, 2 AC
  "Born of Man and Woman," 4 AN,
    2 AC
Lieber, Fritz
  "A Pail of Air," 8 AN, 2 AC
  "A Bad Day for Sales," 7 AN, 0 AC
  "Coming Attraction," 6 AN, 3 AC
  "The Secret Songs," 4 AN, 1 AC
  "Space-Time for Springers," 4 AN,
    1 AC
  "X Marks the Pedwalk," 4 AN, 0 AC
Boucher, Anthony
  "The Quest for Saint Aquin," 4 AN,
    0 AC
  "Balaam," 4 AN, 1 AC
  "The Ambassadors," 4 AN, 0 AC

Blish, James
"*Surface Tension*," 7 AN, 2 AC
"Common Time," 6 AN, 2 AC
"A Work of Art," 5 AN, 2 AC
"The Box," 4 AN, 1 AC
Clarke, Arthur C.
"*The Nine Billion Names of God*,"
12 AN, 2 AC
"The Star," 10 AN, 3 AC
"History Lesson," 9 AN, 3 AC
"The Sentinel," 8 AN, 5 AC
"Before Eden," 7 AN, 2 AC
"Sunjammer," 7 AN, 1 AC
"The Deep Range," 7 AN, 0 AC
"The Forgotten Enemy," 5 AN, 3 AC
"Hide and Seek," 4 AN, 4 AC
"The Fires Within," 4 AN, 3 AC
"Rescue Party," 4 AN, 3 AC
"Meeting With Medusa," 4 AN, 2 AC
Bixby, Jerome
"*It's a Good Life*," 9 AN, 0 AC
"Holes Around Mars," 4 AN, 0 AC
Godwin, Tom
"*The Cold Equations*," 14 AN, 0 AC

Bester, Alfred
"*Fondly Fahrenheit*," 7 AN, 2 AC
"Disappearing Act," 7 AN, 2 AC
"The Men who Murdered Moham-
med," 5 AN, 2 AC
"Hobson's Choice," 4 AN, 2 AC
"5,271,009," 4 AN, 1 AC
Knight, Damon
"Stranger Station," 7 AN, 1 AC
"Masks" (1968), 7 AN, 2 AC
"*The Country of the Kind*," 6 AN,
0 AC
"To Serve Man," 5 AN, 2 AC
"Four in One," 5 AN, 1 AC
"Catch that Martian," 5 AN, 0 AC
"The Handler," 4 AN, 3 AC
Keyes, Daniel
"*Flowers for Algernon*," 8 AN, 0 AC
Zelazny, Roger
"*A Rose for Ecclesiastes*," 5 AN, 2 AC
"For a Breath I Tarry," 5 AN, 0 AC
"The Doors of His Face, the Lamps
of His Mouth," 4 AN, 2 AC

Appendix 2
Significant Stories and Authors Not Appearing in *Science Fiction Hall of Fame*, Volume 1

FOLLOWING IS A LIST OF ALL AUTHORS IN THE CONTENTO *Index*, but not included in *Science Fiction Hall of Fame, Volume 1*, who have at least four stories published between 1930 and 1963 that have been anthologized at least four times, and all stories from the same period that have been anthologized seven or more times. Stories appearing in *Science Fiction Hall of Fame*, Volume 2 are in italics.

Aldiss, Brian
  "Who Can Replace a Man?" 6 AN, 3 AC
  "Poor Little Warrior," 5 AN, 2 AC
  "Old Hundredth," 4 AN, 3 AC
  "Total Environment," 4 AN, 0 AC
Anderson, Paul
  Call Me Joe, 9 AN, 0 AC
  "The Man Who Came Early," 6 AN, 1 AC
  "Journey's End," 6 AN, 1 AC
  "Helping Hand," 4 AN, 0 AC
  "The Martian Crown Jewels," 4 AN, 0 AC
Ballard, J. G.
  "Billenium," 11 AN, 4 AC
  "The Subliminal Man," 9 AN, 3 AC
  "The Voices of Time," 5 AN, 4 AC
  "The Garden of Time," 4 AN, 4 AC
  "The Terminal Beach," 4 AN, 4 AC
Clark, Walter Van Tilberg
  "The Portable Phonograph," 7 AN, 0 AC
Davidson, Avram
  "The Golem," 7 AN, 1 AC

Deutsch, A. J.
  "A Subway Named Mobius," 7 AN, 0 AC
Dick, Philip K.
  "Imposter," 8 AN 2 AC
Farmer, Philip José
  "Mother," 8 AN, 1 AC
Miller, Walter
  "Crucifixus Etiam," 8 AN, 1 AC
  "A Canticle For Liebowitz," 6 AN, 0 AC
  "I Made You," 4 AN, 0 AC
Piper, H. Beam
  "Omnilingual," 8 AN, 0 AC
  "He Walks Around the Horses," 5 AN, 0 AC
Pohl, Frederik
  The Midas Plague, 4 AN, 2 AC
  "The Census Takers," 4 AN, 2 AC
  "What to Do Till the Analyst Comes," 4 AN, 2 AC
  "The Friend," 4 AN, 1 AC
Russell, Eric Frank
  "The Hobbist," 5 AN, 1 AC
  "Dear Devil," 5 AN, 1 AC

"*And Then There Were None,*" 4 AN, 1 AC

"Allamagoosa," 4 AN, 1 AC

Sherred, T. L.

"*E For Effort,*" 7 AN, 1 AC

Shiras, Wilmar

"*In Hiding,*" 9 AN, 1 AC

Tenn, William (Philip Klass)

"Child's Play," 8 AN, 1 AC

"The Liberation of Earth," 6 AN, 1 AC

"Bernie the Faust," 6 AN, 1 AC

Vonnegut, Kurt

"Harrison Bergeron," 7 AN, 1 AC

NOTES

Introduction

1. Tania Modleski, *Loving With a Vengeance: Mass-Produced Fantasies for Women* (New York and London: Methuen, 1982); Janice A. Radway, *Reading the Romance: Women, Patriarchy, and Popular Literature* (Chapel Hill and London: University of North Carolina Press, 1984); Stephen Knight, *Form & Ideology in Crime Fiction* (Bloomington: Indiana University Press, 1980); Ariel Dorfman, *The Empire's Old Clothes: What the Lone Ranger, Babar, and other Innocent Heroes Do to Our Minds* (New York: Pantheon Books, 1983); Martin Jordin, "Contemporary Futures: The Analysis of Science Fiction," in *Popular Fiction and Social Change*, ed. Christopher Pawling (New York: St. Martin's Press, 1984), pp. 50–75. If in chapter two I seem to object to Radway's study, it is because I find her empirical work, although promising at first, a deflection from the more powerful direction of her literary analysis.

I also want to acknowledge my debt to critics of SF who have begun to explicate the rhetorical and ideological dynamics of SF stories of the period I am discussing. Albert Berger's essays in *Science-Fiction Studies* have been very useful. I am particularly indebted to "Love, Death, and the Atomic Bomb: Sexuality and Community in SF, 1935–55," *Science-Fiction Studies* 8 (1981): 280–296; and "Theories of History and Social Order in *Astounding Science Fiction*, 1934–55," *SFS*, 15 (1988): 12–35. Also Mark Rose's *Alien Encounters: Anatomy of Science Fiction* (Cambridge: Harvard University Press, 1981) and Gary Wolfe's *The Known and the Unknown: The Iconography of Science Fiction* (Kent, Ohio: Kent State University Press, 1979) have helped me think about the implications of the genre as a whole.

2. William Sims Bainbridge, *Dimensions of Science Fiction* (Cambridge, Mass: Harvard University Press, 1986).

3. "I claim one positive triumph for science fiction, totally beyond the scope of so-called main-stream fiction. It has prepared the youth of our time for the coming age of space." Robert A. Heinlein, "Science Fiction: Its Nature, Faults, and Virtues," in *The Science Fiction Novel: Imagination and Social Criticism*, ed. Basil Davenport (Chicago: Advent Publishers, 1969), 46.

4. See, for example, the discussion in Chapter 3 of Janice Radway's study of romance readers.

5. When I use the term "subculture" I refer to "the normative systems of groups smaller than a society, to give emphasis to the ways these groups differ in such things as language, values, religion, diet, and style of life from the larger society of which they are a part." J. Milton Yinger, "Contraculture and Subculture" in *Subcultures*, ed. David O. Arnold (Berkeley: The Glendessary Press, 1970), 123. Raymond Williams' concept of "formations" is useful for considering the subculture. Independent formations can have three kinds of internal organization: "formal membership," "collective public manifestation," and "conscious association or group identification." SF, it would seem, belongs mostly in the second category. Williams also describes three ways these formations can relate to the culture at large: "specializing," "alternative," and "oppositional." In this case the first and second categories would seem to apply to SF. It is important to see that the third, the oppositional, does not describe the relation of the SF subculture to the larger culture. See Raymond Williams, *The Sociology of Culture* (New York: Schocken Books, 1982), 68–71.

6. The sociological study of the SF readership remains sketchy. William Sims Bainbridge's *Dimensions of Science Fiction* is the most complete and intensive sociological study of the group to date, though his literary interpretations are, for the most part, unrelated to the data he presents. Darko Suvin's *Victorian Science Fiction in the UK: The Discourses of Knowledge and of Power* (Boston: G. K. Hall, 1983), by reading the texts in an attempt to reconstruct the "addressee" of such SF, begins to describe a readership, but in broad terms and for a society more easily classified than was the U.S. society in the war years. Gary Allen Fine, *Shared Fantasy: Role-Playing Games as Social Worlds* (Chicago: University of Chicago Press, 1983), and Nachman Ben-Yehuda, *Deviance and Moral Boundaries: Witchcraft, the Occult, Science Fiction, Deviant Sciences, and Scientists* (Chicago: University of Chicago Press, 1985) have examined narrow aspects of the contemporary SF phenomenon from a sociological point of view.

The study of the field's beginnings remains largely anecdotal. I have found especially useful Harry Warner, Jr., *All Our Yesterdays: An Informal History of Science Fiction Fandom in the Forties* (Chicago: Advent Publishers, 1969); Frederik Pohl, *The Way the Future Was: A Memoir* (New York: Ballantine Books, 1978); and Damon Knight, *The Futurians: The Story of the Science Fiction "Family" of the 30s that Produced Today's Top SF Writers and Editors* (New York: John Day, 1977).

7. Two books in particular, both written near the close of the period we are studying, have argued polemically for such a shift. Jacques Ellul's *La Technique ou l'enjeu du siècle*, published in France in 1954 and in the U.S. as *The Technological Society*, trans. John Wilkinson (New York: Alfred A. Knopf, 1964) argues that a system of efficiency, what Ellul calls "technique," has robbed human society of its freedom and its moral presence. Daniel Bell's *The End of Ideology* (Glencoe, Illinois: The Free Press, 1960) is less alarmed at what its subtitle describes as "the exhaustion of political ideas in the fifties." While Bell can sympathize with the radical intellectuals' sense of loss at the end of ideology, he is also resigned to what he sees as the "new ecstasies for economic utopia" (p. 375) that the new technocratic age has brought.

8. Daniel Bell, *The Coming of Post-Industrial Society: A Venture in Social Forecasting* (1973: rpt., New York: Basic Books, 1976), 453.

9. Any history of SF will tell the basic story. The publishing history of these early days has been recounted in some detail in Lester del Rey, *The World of Science Fiction: The History of a Subculture: 1926–1976* (New York: Ballantine Books, 1979). A thematically organized reading of these years will be found in Paul A. Carter, *The Creation of Tomorrow: Fifty Years of Magazine Science Fiction* (New York: Columbia University Press, 1977).

10. In his commentary on Heinlein's "The Roads Must Roll," Martin Schafer notes explicit reaction to the technocratic movement. *Science Fiction als Ideologie-kritik? Utopische Spuren in der amerikanischen Science Fiction-Literatur 1940–1955* (Stuttgart, J. B. Metzlersche Verlagsbuchhandlung, 1977), 135–140. Bainbridge notes that Hugo Gernsback edited *Technocracy Review* for a short time and that in 1963 Mack Reynolds published a story about the triumph of technocracy (*Dimensions of Science Fiction*, 207–208), but in general any connection between the technocracy movement and SF seems fairly casual.

11. For the history of technocracy, see William E. Akin, *Technocracy and the American Dream: The Technocratic Movement, 1900–1941* (Berkeley: University of California Press, 1977); Henry Elsner, Jr. *The Technocrats, Prophets of Automation* (Syracuse: Syracuse University Press, 1967); and Howard P. Segal, *Technological Utopianism in American Culture* (Chicago: University of Chicago Press, 1985).

12. See Akin, *Technocracy and the American Dream*, 105–107; Segal, *Technological Utopianism in American Culture*, 123.

13. For instance, in a volume published in 1933, *Selected Articles on Capitalism and Its Alternatives*, [ed. Julia E. Johnson, (New York; H. W. Wilson Co., 1933)], technocracy is posed as a sixth alternative in parallel with capitalism, socialism, communism, fascism, and Hitlerism. And yet Howard Scott, the charismatic leader of the movement throughout the thirties would always insist that his movement was not political. See Akin, *Technocracy and the American Dream*, 66, 108–109, 139, 141, 143.

14. For the primacy of technique, see Ellul: "Our civilization is first and foremost a civilization of means; in the reality of modern life, the means, it would seem, are more important than the ends. Any other assessment of the situation is mere idealism." (p. 19). Ellul, *the Technological Society*, 19. For discussion of technocracy's inability to criticize itself, see Jurgen Habermas, "Technology and Science as 'Ideology,'" in *Toward a Rational Society*, (London: Heinemann Educational Books, 1971), 81–122.

15. Samuel Butler, *Erewhon, or Over the Range* (New York: New American Library, 1960), 174–175.

Chapter One
Classic Popularity: Isolating a Noncanonic Canon

1. Raymond Williams, *The English Novel: From Dickens to Lawrence* (St. Albans: Paladin, 1974).

2. Leo Lowenthal, "The Debate Over Art and Popular Culture: A Synopsis," in *Literature, Popular Culture, and Society* (Palo Alto: Pacific Books, 1961), 14–51.

3. Pierre Bourdieu, *Distinction: A Social Critique of the Judgement of Taste*, trans. William Nice (Cambridge: Harvard University Press, 1984), *passim*.

4. Alan Swingewood, *The Myth of Mass Culture* (Atlantic Highlands, NJ: Humanities Press, 1977), argues that the very category, whether invoked by conservative critics or by Frankfurt School Marxists, has a conservative aesthetic prejudice embedded in it. See also Bourdieu, *Distinction*, 483.

5. Henry Nash Smith's chapters on nineteenth century dime novels seem to me central to all serious consideration of popular literature. ("The Western Hero in the Dime Novel" and "The Dime Novel Heroine" in *Virgin Land: The American West as Symbol and Myth* [1950; rpt. New York: Vintage Books, n.d.], 99–135.) And Louis Nye's encyclopedic *The Unembarrassed Muse: The Popular Arts in America* (New York: The Dial Press, 1970) was a necessary groundbreaking to which all later studies of noncanonic art must be indebted.

6. John Cawelti, *Adventure, Mystery, and Romance* (Chicago: University of Chicago Press, 1976). Cawelti's defense of the formula was important for liberating literary scholarship from its concentration on single texts. As I turn back toward the individual text, I do so with an appreciation of the power of the formulaic background that Cawelti has explicated.

7. Jeffrey Sammons, *Literary Sociology and Practical Criticism: An Inquiry* (Bloomington and London: Indiana University Press, 1977), 19, makes a similar point.

8. David Bordwell, Kristin Thompson, and Janet Steiger, *The Classical Hollywood Cinema: Film Style & Mode of Production to 1960* (New York: Columbia University Press, 1985).

9. Will Wright, *Sixguns and Society: A Structural Study of the Western* (Berkeley: University of California Press, 1975).

10. Cf. Fredric Jameson, "Generic Discontinuities in SF: Brian Aldiss' *Starship*," *Science-Fiction Studies*, 1:2 (1973), 57–68.

11. *Science Fiction Hall of Fame* (New York: Avon, 1970). Page references are to the paperback edition. In his preface to *Science Fiction Hall of Fame*, Robert Silverberg acknowledges choosing to include a story that came in one vote behind another story by the same writer and a story by a writer with four nominated stories over a very slightly more popular story by a writer with no other nominated stories. These minor deflections from a rigorously democratic procedure do not, to my mind, constitute an appreciable intrusion of aesthetic or theoretical distortion of the sort one finds in Wright.

12. William Contento, *Index to SF Anthologies and Collections* (Boston: G. K. Hall, 1978).

13. Contento has omitted Keyes's story, "Flowers for Algernon" from his list for *Science Fiction Hall of Fame*, but the slight change in numbers resulting from this mistake does not lead to any change in the rankings.

14. *Science Fiction Hall of Fame*: Volume 2, edited in two volumes by Ben Bova (New York: Avon, 1973), is a less historically focused collection than Volume 1. Wells's *The Time Machine*, and Forster's "The Machine Stops" are included. I have kept the stories in this later anthology in mind, and in the case of Kornbluth's "The March-

ing Morons" I have privileged the story in this anthology over his "The Little Black Bag" in *Science Fiction Hall of Fame*, Volume 1. But to try to focus on the stories in Volume 2 in any complete way seems to me only to disperse our already severely stretched attention.

Chapter Two
Reading Popular Genres

1. Herbert J. Gans, *Popular Culture and High Culture: An Analysis and Evaluation of Taste* (New York: Basic Books, 1974), 125.

2. Janice Radway, *Reading the Romance: Women, Patriarchy, and Popular Literature* (Chapel Hill: University of North Carolina Press, 1984).

3. "Habitus" is a complex word for Bourdieu. In the simplest terms, *class habitus* means "the internalized form of class condition and of the conditionings it entails." *Distinction*, 101.

4. For a discussion of the ideological implications of the concept of escape, see Richard Dyer, "Entertainment and Utopia" in *Movies and Methods*, Volume 2, ed. Bill Nichols (Berkeley: University of California Press, 1985), 220–232.

5. See Ian Ang, *Reading Dallas: Soap Opera and the Melodramatic Imagination*, trans. Della Couling (London and New York: Methuen, 1985) 11, for some sound cautions about interpreting the sources of pleasure.

6. Jonathan Culler, "Semiotics as a Theory of Reading," in *The Pursuit of Signs: Semiotics, Literature, Deconstruction* (Ithaca: Cornell University Press, 1981,) 53.

7. The one extended sociological study of the SF community falls into this same difficulty. Bainbridge's *Dimensions of Science Fiction* performs surveys that tend to confirm very general interpretative understandings that have long been current in the SF community. He isolates three clusters (hard SF, fantasy, and New Wave), gives them a historical dimension (hard SF belongs to the period from the thirties to the fifties, while New Wave belongs to the sixties and seventies), and identifies authors who belong to each. The general structure allows Bainbridge then to set up secondary correlations—such as general political positions linked to each or how appreciation correlates to the gender of the reader. But the ideology of the various dimensions of the genre remains out of reach. Bainbridge summarizes numerous works and offers casual evaluations, but the interpretative element of his work is unrelated to the statistical part, which simply validates the popular vision of the kinds of SF.

8. Leo Lowenthal, "The Triumph of Mass Idols" in *Literature, Popular Culture, and Society*, 110.

9. Quoted in Michael R. Real, "Media Theory: Contributions to an Understanding of American Mass Communications," *American Quarterly*, 32 (1980): 240. See Harold Lasswell, "The Structure and Function of Communication in Society," *Mass Communication*, ed. Wilbur Schramm (Urbana: University of Illinois Press, 1960).

10. Terry Eagleton, *Criticism and Ideology: A Study in Marxist Literary Theory* (London: Verso, 1976), 55.

11. Pierre Macherey, *A Theory of Literary Production*, trans. Geoffrey Wall (London: Routledge & Kegan Paul, 1978), 99.

12. T. W. Adorno, "Cultural Criticism and Society," *Prisms*, trans. Samuel and Shierry Weber (New York: Spearman, 1967), 27.

13. Quoted by Jurgen Habermas in *Autonomy & Solidarity: Interviews with Jurgen Habermas*, ed. Peter Dews (London: Verso, 1986), 39.

14. Terry Eagleton, *The Rape of Clarissa: Writing, Sexuality and Class Struggle in Samuel Richardson* (Minneapolis: University of Minnesota Press, 1982), and *William Shakespeare* (Oxford and New York: Basil Blackwell, 1986).

15. Terry Eagleton, *Walter Benjamin: or Towards a Revolutionary Criticism* (London: Verso, 1981), 98.

16. Pierre Macherey, "Jules Verne: The Faulty Narrative" in *A Theory of Literary Production*, 159–240.

17. Eagleton finds Althusser's claim that "authentic art" (as opposed to "works of an average or mediocre level") is somehow "detached" from ideology and able to help us "perceive" it, though not to "know" it, "radically unsatisfactory." *Criticism and Ideology*, 83.

18. See Max Horkheimer and Theodor W. Adorno, "The Culture Industry: Enlightenment as Mass Deception," in *The Dialectic of Enlightenment*, trans. John Cumming (New York: Seabury Press, 1972), 120–167.

19. Ang, *Reading Dallas*.

20. Lowenthal, "Introduction," *Literature, Popular Culture, and Society*, xii.

21. Raymond Williams, *The Sociology of Culture* (New York: Schocken Books, 1982), 102.

22. Adorno, "Cultural Criticism and Society," 32. This now famous sentence is quoted in Swingewood, *The Myth of Mass Culture*, p. 17. For an insightful discussion of some of the problems even "postmodern" critics (who often claim to have transcended the Frankfurt School's denunciation of "spurious harmony" and negative aesthetics) have with popular art, see Tania Modleski, "The Terror of Pleasure: The Contemporary Horror Film and Postmodern Theory," in *Studies in Entertainment: Critical Approaches to Mass Culture*, ed. Tania Modleski (Bloomington: Indiana University Press, 1986), 156–158.

23. We should note that in their essay on the "Culture Industry" Horkheimer and Adorno attack a smooth style as a way of hiding ideological difficulty. See also Gillian Rose's explication of Adorno's aesthetics and social theory which finds social critique in the form, rather than the content, of the work. Gillian Rose, *The Melancholy Science: An Introduction to the Thought of Theodor W. Adorno* (New York: Columbia University Press, 1978), 160. The interpretive difficulty I am pointing to in the concept of "spurious harmony" persists at this formal level, however, for the slick text can still be read ironically.

24. Joseph Conrad, *Heart of Darkness* (New York: New American Library, 1950), 106.

25. For discussion of this issue, see Patrick Brantlinger, "*Heart of Darkness*: Anti-Imperialism, Racism, or Impressionism?" *Criticism*, 27 (1985), 363–385. For an analysis of traditional criticism's urge to protect Conrad from unconscious meanings, see Fredrick Crews, "The Power of Darkness," *Partisan Review* 34 (1967), 507–525.

26. Sigmund Freud, *Jokes and Their Relation to the Unconscious*, trans. James Strachey (New York: Norton, 1960), 174.

27. E. D. Hirsch, *Validity in Interpretation*, (New Haven: Yale University Press, 1967), 8, *et passim*.

28. For an instance of Hirsch's attitude, see *Validity in Interpretation*, 234. For an instance of the other position, see Paul De Man, "Semiotics and Rhetoric," in *Allegories of Reading: Figural Language in Rousseau, Nietzche, Rilke, and Proust* (New Haven: Yale University Press, 1979), 3–19.

29. Fredric Jameson, *The Political Unconscious: Narrative as a Socially Symbolic Act* (Ithaca: Cornell University Press, 1981), 129.

30. At this point one might think of Stanley Fish's story of convincing a class that a sociology assignment was a Renaissance poem. "How to Recognize a Poem When You See One," in *Is There a Text in This Class?* (Cambridge, Mass.: Harvard University Press, 1980), 322–337.

31. In addition to Fish's book referred to in the previous note, see Hans Robert Jauss, *Toward an Aesthetic of Reception*, trans. Timothy Bahti (Minneapolis: University of Minnesota Press, 1982).

32. John Cawelti, *Adventure, Mystery, and Romance*, 34–46 *et passim*.

33. Peter Rabinowitz, "The Turn of the Glass Key: Popular Fiction as Reading Strategy," *Critical Inquiry*, 11 (1985), 421–423. See Rabinowitz's *Before Reading: Narrative Conventions and the Politics of Interpretation* (Ithaca: Cornell University Press, 1987).

34. Jonathan Culler, *Structural Poetics: Structuralism, Linguistics, and the Study of Literature* (Ithaca: Cornell University Press, 1975), 113–130.

35. Tom Wolfe, *The Kandy-Kolored Tangerine-Flake Streamline Baby* (New York: Noonday Press, 1965), xiv. Susan Sontag, "One Culture and the New Sensibility," in *Against Interpretation, and Other Essays* (New York: Dell Publishing Co., 1966), 304.

36. See Leon D. Harmon, "The Recognition of Faces," *Scientific American*, 229:5 (November, 1973), 71–82.

37. One might note, for instance, that Cawelti seldom finds it useful to discuss a passage in detail. Actions are analysed apart from their actual descriptions.

38. Sammons, *Literary Sociology and Practical Criticism*, 136.

39. E. D. Hirsch, *Validity in Interpretation*, 222–224; and Hans Robert Jauss, "Literary History as a Challenge to Literary Theory" in *Toward an Aesthetic of Reception*, 3–45.

40. Virginia Wright Wexman, *Roman Polanski* (New York: G. K. Hall, 1985), 98–99.

41. E. D. Hirsh, *Validity in Interpretation*, 78–94.

42. Cf. Christine Brooke-Rose, "Science Fiction and Realistic Fiction," in *A Rhetoric of the UnReal: Studies in Narrative & Structure, Especially of the Fantastic* (Cambridge: Cambridge University Press, 1981), 72–102. Fantasy's displacement usually lacks the tension and interpretive difficulty we find in SF.

43. Darko Suvin, "Estrangement and Cognition," in *Metamorphoses of Science Fiction*, 3–15.

44. Cf Samuel Delaney, "About Five-Thousand One Hundred and Seventy Five

Words," in *SF: The Other Side of Realism*, ed. Thomas D. Clareson (Bowling Green: Bowling Green University Popular Press, 1971), 130–146; Sam J. Lundwall, *Science Fiction: What It's All About* (New York: Ace Books, 1971), 13–15; or Eric S. Rabkin, *The Fantastic in Literature* (Princeton: Princeton University Press, 1976), 107.

45. Darko Suvin, "SF and the Novum," in *Metamorphoses of Science Fiction*, 63–84.

46. See Thomas More, *Utopia*, trans. Paul Turner (Harmondsworth: Penguin Books, 1965), 109–117.

47. See my discussion of this problem in *The Logic of Fantasy: H. G. Wells and Science Fiction* (New York: Columbia University Press, 1982), 94–96.

48. Mark Rose, *Alien Encounters: Anatomy of Science Fiction*, 14.

49. David Ketterer, "Pantropy, Polyploidy, and Tectogenesis in the Fiction of James Blish and Norman L. Knight," *Science-Fiction Studies* 30 (1983), 207. Any attempt to derive an interpretation of Blish's work by recourse to his intention faces formidable obstacles. *A Case of Conscience*, for instance, can be read as a Catholic allegory or as a deeply ironic challenge to all orthodoxies. The debate is summarized in Ketterer's "Covering *A Case of Conscience*," *Science-Fiction Studies* 9 (1982), 195–214. These two essays are included in Ketterer's *Imprisoned in a Tesseract: The Life and Work of James Blish* (Kent, Ohio: The Kent State University Press, 1987). Blish used "Surface Tension" as part of his novel, *The Seedling Stars* (New York: New American Library, 1959).

50. "Rather than seeing genres as structures helping individual texts to produce meaning, we must see genres as restrictive, as complex methods of reducing the field of play of individual texts. . . . In short, genres are not neutral categories, as structuralist critics have too often implied; rather they are *ideological constructs masquerading as neutral categories*" (Emphasis in original). Rick Altman, *The American Film Musical* (Bloomington: Indiana University Press, 1987), 5.

Chapter Three
The Myth of Genius: The Fantasy of Unpolitical Power

1. Though undeniably common in SF, the figure of the genius has not been the subject of critical attention. *The SF Encyclopedia*, ed. Peter Nicholls (New York: Dolphin Books, 1979), the most intelligent reference work in the field, does not include an entry on "genius" among its 145 themes, though it does list "intelligence" (which includes intelligent machines and animals) and "Superman."

Fredric Jameson made the argument in "Metacommentary," *PMLA*, 86 (1971), 16, that the scientist figure in SF represents unalienated work. The genius certainly participates in this general fantasy, but it also stands for a particular organization of work and for a positive attitude toward technology, two attitudes that are not always congruent.

2. Cf. Bell's *The Coming of Post-Industrial Society: A Venture in Social Forecasting* (New York: Basic Books, 1973). Though Bell distinguishes between technocracy and meritocracy, he defends both. See 411 ff. for the justification of technocracy.

3. Robert Nisbet, *Prejudices, A Philosophical Dictionary* (Cambridge: Harvard University Press, 1982), 145. In the passage quoted it is not clear whether geniuses are the nurturing ground of civilization, or whether the family, with all its evils, is the nurturing ground of geniuses, though the two meanings lead to more or less the same broad conclusion: that civilization depends on genius.

4. The paradox here is similar to that involved in foreseeing future inventions: if a future technology can be accurately predicted, it must be understood already, which means it should be already invented.

5. My summary of the history of the idea of genius is indebted to a number of works. Robert Currie, *Genius: An Ideology in Literature* (New York: Schocken Books, 1974) has taught me much about the philosophical implications of the Romantic ideas of genius. I have also found useful Russell Brain, *Some Reflections on Genius, and Other Essays* (Philadelphia and Montreal: J. B. Lippincott, 1960), and Dallas Kenmare, *The Nature of Genius* (London: Peter Owen Ltd., 1960). The scientific study of genius that begins with Galton's *Hereditary Genius* has been summarized in *Genius and Eminence: the Social Psychology of Creativity and Exceptional Achievement*, ed. Robert S. Albert (New York: Pergamon Press, 1983), and *Conceptions of Giftedness*, ed. Robert J. Sternberg and Janet E. Davidson (Cambridge: Cambridge University Press, 1986). The historical study of genius is summarized in Dean Keith Simonton, *Genius, Creativity, and Leadership: Historiometric Inquiries* (Cambridge: Harvard University Press, 1984).

6. Francis Galton, *Hereditary Genius* (1869; rpt., New York: Horizon Press, 1952). Catherine Cox, *The Early Mental Traits of Three Hundred Geniuses* (Palo Alto: Stanford University Press, 1928). See also, Albert ed., *Genius and Eminence*, 23 *et passim*, and Simonton, *Genius, Creativity, and Leadership*, 2. For a trenchant criticism of Cox's work and of the whole direction of intelligence studies, see Stephen Jay Gould, *The Mismeasure of Man* (New York: W. W. Norton, 1981); and *Race and IQ*, ed. Ashley Montagu (London: Oxford University Press, 1975).

7. Bell points to this as a drawback of pure technocracy. See *The Coming of Post-Industrial Society*, 453.

8. "Hidden behind the statistical relationships between educational capital or social origin and this or that type of knowledge or way of applying it, there are relationships between groups maintaining different, and even antagonistic, relations to culture, depending on the conditions in which they acquired their cultural capital and the markets in which they can derive most profit from it." Bourdieu, *Distinction*, 12.

9. Quoted in Warner, *All Our Yesterdays*, 96.

10. It is significant and a confirmation of the following analysis of Rand as an *exception* to the SF genre that she scores very near the bottom of Bainbridge's surveys of SF author popularity in 1978. See *Dimensions of Science Fiction*, 184, 288.

11. Ayn Rand, *Anthem* (1946; rpt., Caldwell, Id.: Caxton Printers, 1982).

12. Ayn Rand, *The Fountainhead* (New York: New American Library, 1971).

13. Hugo Gernsback, *Ralph 124C 41+* (1911: rpt. New York: Crest Books, 1958), 9.

14. For instance, Siegmund threatens to kill Sieglinde rather than be separated from her to go to Valhalla alone. *Die Walkure*, Act II, scene iv.

15. In what seems to me the best piece of criticism on Heinlein to date, George Slusser observes just such a conflation of son and father in Heinlein's work. Slusser sees this as one of a number of devices used by Heinlein that serve to deny social exchange. "Heinlein's Perpetual Motion Fur Farm," *Science-Fiction Studies*, 9 (1982), 51–67.

16. Fredric Jameson, *the Political Unconscious*, 118.

17. Paul Feyerabend, "Creativity—A Dangerous Myth," *Critical Inquiry* 13 (1987), 700–711, and Robert Weisberg, *Creativity, Genius and Other Myths* (New York: W. H. Freeman and Co., 1986).

18. "The Marching Morons" has been much anthologized. I am using the text found in *The Best of C. M. Kornbluth*, ed. Frederik Pohl (Garden City: Nelson Doubleday, 1976), pp. 133–163.

19. *Foundation*, 21 (1981), 17–26.

20. See his entry on Kornbluth in *Science Fiction Writers*, ed. E. F. Bleiler (New York, 1982), 402–403.

21. *Dimensions of Science Fiction*, 205–206.

22. John Rawls, *A Theory of Justice* (Cambridge: Harvard University Press, 1971). Daniel Bell advocates a "just meritocracy" in place of Rawls's "fairness" principle: *The Coming of Post-Industrial Society*, 440–455.

23. Heinlein is particularly prone to this sort of unconscious self-condemnation. For instance, in "The Man Who Sold the Moon" he seems to offer as examples of admirable techniques for raising money to send a rocket to the moon, scams that take advantage of children's credulity or that sell ordinary letters by falsely claiming that those letters had been taken to the moon.

24. Damon Knight, *In Search of Wonder: Essays on Modern Science Fiction* (1956: 2nd edition, Chicago: Advent Publishers, 1967), 148. We should note that this comment was written before Kornbluth died.

Chapter Four
An Economy of Reason: Motives of the Technocratic Hero

1. Quoted in *H. G. Wells: The Critical Heritage*, ed. Patrick Parrinder (London: Routledge & Kegan Paul, 1972), 101–02.

2. Robert Heinlein, "Science Fiction: Its Nature, Faults, and Virtues," in *The Science Fiction Novel: Imagination and Social Criticism*," ed. Basil Davenport (Chicago: Advent Publishers, 1969), 18.

3. Ibid., 29–30.

4. Stephen Jay Gould, *The Mismeasure of Man* (New York: W. W. Norton & Co., 1981).

5. Joseph Conrad, *The Nigger of the 'Narcissus', Typhoon, The Shadow Line* (New York: E. P. Dutton & Co., 1960), 5. See also, Frèdric Jameson, *The Political Unconscious*," 232.

6. See Pierre Macherey, *A Theory of Literary Production*, 169.

7. For insight into the French enthusiasm for Verne, the English reader can consult Roland Barthes' "The *Nautilus* and the Drunken Boat," in *Mythologies*, trans. Annette Lavers (New York: Hill and Wang, 1972), 65–67; Michel Butor, "The Golden Age in Jules Verne," trans. Patricia Dreyfus, in *Inventory* (New York: Simon and Schuster, 1968), 114–145; and Marc Angenot's two essays, "Jules Verne and French Literary Criticism," *Science-Fiction Studies* 1 (1973), 33–37, and *Science-Fiction Studies* 3 (1976), 46–49.

8. Despite a certain overlap, I want to distinguish the idea of hard-core SF I am describing from that "engineering mentality" attacked a decade ago by Richard Lupoff for its "dedication to control, to predictability, to the finite, closed-end solution." "Science Fiction Hawks and Doves: Whose Future Will You Buy?" *Ramparts* (Feb. 1972), 27. The qualities Lupoff attacks do not seem to me evil in themselves; to a large extent the future good of humanity depends on them. My own complaint is to a misapplication of these otherwise praiseworthy aspirations.

9. I have found no mention of this aspect of Heinlein's work in the criticism.

10. The thoroughness of the contradiction became forcefully evident to me when I received a student's paper that, entirely without any irony that I could discover, interpreted Van Kleek as the hero because he was in touch with his feelings and saw Gaines as a figure of oppressive rationality. While I do not think a careful reading of "The Roads Must Roll" will support such an interpretation, the fact that a hasty reading could propose it shows how contradictory many of the surface signals are in Heinlein.

11. According to the numbers derived from Contento's *List* in Appendix 1, only Asimov's "Nightfall" is more popular than this story. What makes its popularity all the more remarkable is that Godwin's other work is almost completely disregarded.

12. The story has not received much detailed critical attention, but it is often mentioned in discussions of hard-core SF, where it is usually treated as a paradigm of the hard-core. Typical is James Gunn who calls it "The touchstone story for hard-core science fiction." *The Road to Science Fiction #3: From Heinlein to Here*, ed. James Gunn (New York: New American Library, 1979), 244.

13. "Teaching Science Fiction: Unique Challenges," *SFS*, 6 (1979): 250.

14. See Jameson, *The Political Unconscious*, 267–268.

15. We see here an explicit example of the way the technocratic mode claims to obviate political decisions.

16. The concept of the author must be understood in a particular way in this story. In Godwin's original version of "The Cold Equations," Marilyn was saved. It was John W. Campbell, his editor, who insisted that her death was the "right" ending. (I am indebted to James Gunn for this valuable piece of SF lore.) If this anecdote is true, then we have two authors who are to some extent in conflict within the same story. Though it is convenient to continue to use the term "author" to speak of the intention we postulate behind the story, we need to keep in mind that in this case the term does not refer to an actual person. It may be more useful to conceive of the "author" of "The Cold Equations" as the ideological context in which Godwin and Campbell find themselves and which unites them even in their difference.

17. Bainbridge, *Dimensions of Science Fiction*, 67, 232, finds that fans claim to rank fictions with protagonists who are "Cool and Unemotional" at the lower end of the scales of options presented. A character like Gaines points to the problem with the categories and raises the question of whether he is perceived as "cool and unemotional" or as emotional but also having strong self-mastery.

18. Cordwainer Smith seems to have been interested in the image of the oyster as borderline life. Cf. *Norstrilia*, (rpt. 1964, 1968 New York: Ballantine Books, 1975), 211.

19. This line is not in the version of the story that appears as "The Third Expedition" in *The Martian Chronicles* (New York: Bantam Books, 1951), 32–48.

20. Though there are a number of differences in the dates in "Mars is Heaven" and "The Third Expedition," the town's vintage remains 1926.

21. *The Martian Chronicles*, page facing vii.

Chapter Five
Reason and Love: Women and Technocracy

1. In "Mimsy were the Borogroves," "Born of Man and Woman," and "Its a *Good* Life" the mother, along with the father, represents an uncomprehending, unsympathetic, and foolishly bourgeois adult generation. In "Mars is Heaven" the mother's warm solicitations, after being seen at first as entirely positive, as the highest value for the man, are then turned around and seen as an alien trap. A full reading of the Bradbury story would have to take into account the dynamics of the attack on "Momism" that took place in the late forties and early fifties. While Bradbury's appeal would on the surface seem to lie in his defense of the traditional family values, the illusion of family presented by the Martians may suggest that even such defenders could not help but subscribe at some level to the reading that the family is debilitating. And in "The Weapon Shop," the mother is at one point an ally of son against father and at another an ally of father against son. She is in both cases authoritative, but that very authority is disturbing: behind the claim of maternal acceptance, she is a figure of quite frighteningly unpredictable judgment.

2. In *Future Females: A Critical Anthology*, ed. Marleen S. Barr (Bowling Green: Bowling Green State University Popular Press, 1981), 42–59. Sanders is, of course, building on a strong tradition of feminist criticism; the classic study for the paradigm of woman and nature that he argues is Sherry B. Ortner, "Is Female to Male as Nature Is to Culture?" in *Woman, Culture, and Society*, ed. Michelle Zimbalist Rosaldo and Louise Lamphere (Stanford: Stanford University Press, 1974), 67–87.

3. Albert Berger treats the basic antithesis of love and technology in this pair of images, but he does not argue for the secondary revision that complicates it. "Love, Death and the A-Bomb," 285.

4. Berger's reading of the woman in "That Only a Mother" is a coherent interpretation, but it works against the grain of the predominate paradigm as described by Sanders. *Ibid.*, 281.

5. Brian W. Aldiss, *The Trillion Year Spree* (New York: Atheneum, 1986), 293–296.

Chapter Six
Feeling the Unthinkable: Imagining Aliens and Monsters

1. Leo Lowenthal and Norbert Guterman, *Prophets of Deceit: A Study in the Techniques of the American Agitator* (rpt. 1949; Palo Alto: Pacific Books, 1970), 16.
2. Gary K. Wolfe, *The Known and The Unknown* (Kent, Ohio: Kent State University Press, 1979), 35–36.
3. Sigmund Freud, *Jokes and Their Relation to the Unconscious*, 99–102.
4. Sigmund Freud, *Civilization and Its Discontents* (New York: W. W. Norton & Sons, 1961), 68.
5. Robert G. Pielke, "Humans and Aliens: A Unique Relationship," *Mosaic*, 13 (1980), 29–40.
6. William Tenn, "Party of the Two Parts," in *The Human Angle* (New York: Ballantine Books, 1956), 75–98.
7. Ursula K. Le Guin, "American Science Fiction and the Other," in *The Language of the Night: Essays on Fantasy and Science Fiction*, ed. Susan Wood (New York: G. P. Putnam's Sons, 1979), 99.
8. Patrick Parrinder discusses this compliment in "The Alien Encounter: Or, Ms Brown and Mrs Le Guin," *Science Fiction Studies*, 17 (March 1979), 54.
9. Yevgeny Zamyatin, *We*, trans. Mirra Ginsburg (New York: Viking, 1972), 219.
10. "Nine Lives," first published in 1969, is a much anthologized story. I have used the text in *Science Fiction: The Future*, ed. Dick Allen, 2nd ed. (New York: Harcourt Brace, 1983), 259–280.
11. Freud, *Civilization and Its Discontents*, 101–102. To its credit, some SF has made inquiry into racism a conscious subject and has located the problem, not in the alien itself, but in the ways humans *see* the alien. Transformations of an initial opposition into a positive identification occur in such popular works as C. S. Lewis' *Out of the Silent Planet* (1939), Le Guin's *The Left Hand of Darkness* (1968), and Robert Silverberg's *Downward to the Earth* (1969). Yet such writers do not really solve the problem I have posed; they simply diffuse the hostile sense of difference by modeling the alien on an ideal of the human. Such myths of alien confrontation and re-vision frequently inhabit a larger myth that denies meaningful difference. Lewis' Christian myth asserts the spiritual unity of all "lower" being as it serves the "higher" spirit. Le Guin imagines that all intelligent life in the known universe is descended from a single race. Silverberg shows the unity of human and alien by permitting his human protagonist a rebirth like that of the aliens themselves. In each case the protagonist learns to recognize his or her own place in a larger unity that makes "alien" a meaningless term. Such inclusion counters racist exclusion by robbing the "different" of its distinguishing features. Here we recognize a limitation in popular fiction, perhaps all fiction. The literally extraordinary concept of the alien cannot be comfortably embraced by an art that is based on manipulating the familiar.

I want to thank Thomas Clareson who in a review reading of a manuscript drew my attention to the Silverberg novel.

12. The words within brackets are missing in the paperback edition of *Science Fiction Hall of Fame*. The words have been supplied from the hardback edition, (Garden City, NY: Doubleday & Company, 1970), 191.

13. James Gunn obeys this seemingly generic cue and asserts that "We feel [the father's] horror and his wife's horror yet to come, as well as the potential horror of the children when they arrive in a larger world where there are no adults and where they will be alone, possibly helpless, and afraid." James Gunn, "Henry Kuttner, C. L. Moore, Lewis Padgett, *Et Al.*," in *Voices for the Future*, ed. Thomas Clareson (Bowling Green: The Popular Press, 1975), 200. This might be one of those cases in which displacement renders the text irresolvable, but the following passage from the story seems to me to disallow Gunn's fear for the children's helplessness: "The young, fed and tended, would survive. There would be incubators and robots. They would survive, but they would not know how to swim downstream to the vaster world of the ocean. So they must be taught. They must be trained and conditioned in many ways. Painlessly, subtly, unobtrusively. Children love toys that do things—and if those toys teach at the same time. . . ." The toys are making the children competent in the "vaster world."

Chapter Seven
History, Politics, and the Future

1. Heinlein, "Science Fiction: Its Nature, Faults and Virtues," 29.

2. Habermas, *Toward a Rational Society: Student Protest, Science, and Politics*, trans. Jeremy J. Shapiro (London: Heinemann, 1971), 59.

3. "Anyone who writes a book, however gloomy its message may be, is necessarily an optimist. If the pessimists really believed what they were saying there would be no point in saying it." Joan Robinson, *Freedom and Necessity: An Introduction to the Study of Society* (London: Allen & Unwin, 1970), 124.

4. J. E. T. Eldridge, "The Rationalization Theme in Weber's Sociology," introduction to *Max Weber: The Interpretation of Social Reality*, Ed. J. E. T. Eldridge (New York: Schocken Books, 1980) 65–66.

5. It is said that the recommendations made on Fridays by experts on "Wall Street Week" invariably shape the following Monday's stock market, thereby to some extent invalidating the experts' predictions. A stock that is pointed to as a good buy on Friday has by Monday noon ceased to be underpriced and by Tuesday may be so overpriced that knowledgeable investors are selling it.

6. See James Hogg, *The Private Memoirs and Confessions of a Justified Sinner*, 1822.

7. Karl Popper, *The Poverty of Historicism*, (New York: Harper Torchbooks, 1961), 13.

8. John Naisbitt, *Megatrends: Ten New Directions Transforming our Lives*, (New York: Warner Books, 1982), 252.

9. H. G. Wells, "The Discovery of the Future," in *Anticipations and Other Papers* [Atlantic Edition, vol. 4] (London: T. Fisher Unwin, 1924), 375.

10. Wells seriously contradicts this essentially positivist idea by overlaying it with an historicist belief in "destiny." I discuss this particular difficulty of his project in *The Logic of Fantasy*, 5–6.

11. Marvin J. Cetron and Edmund B. Mahinske, "The Value of Technological Forecasting for the Research and Development Manager," *Futures*, 1 (1968), 32.

12. See, for instance, W. H. Clive Simmonds, "The Nature of Futures Problems," in *Futures Research: New Directions*, ed. Harold A. Linstone & W. H. Clive Simmonds (Reading, Mass: Addison-Wesley, 1977), 22.

13. Most futures specialists would agree with this position. I am specifically following Bertand de Jouvenel, *The Art of Conjecture*, trans. Nikita Lary (New York: Basic Books, 1967). Between short- and long-term forecasts falls the area that de Jouvenel calls "planning." *The Art of Conjecture*, 214–215.

14. Herman Kahn poses a genre that he calls the "surprise free forecast" which he claims will survive such catastrophes. See *Things to Come: Thinking About the Seventies and Eighties* (New York: Macmillan, 1972).

15. De Jouvenel, *The Art of Conjecture*, 113.

16. Joseph Marino, *Technological Forecasting for Decisionmaking* (New York: American Elsevier Publishing Co., 1972), 642.

17. Gerard K. O'Neill, *2081: A Hopeful View of the Human Future* (New York: Simon and Schuster, 1981), 32.

18. This is a comic inversion of the philosophy proposed by Wendell Bell and James A. Mau, *The Sociology of the Future* (New York: Russell Sage Foundation, 1971). They have edited a collection of essays devoted to the argument that, by foreseeing, the futurologist is leading us toward his vision and should therefore be aware of his responsibilities in such prognostication. Technocratic forecasting generally lacks the sophistication of Mau and Bell.

19. Isaac Asimov, "Social Science Fiction." The essay first appeared in 1953 in *Modern Science Fiction*, ed. Reginald Bretnor (New York: Coward-McCann, 1953). I have used the reprint in *Science Fiction: The Future*, (New York: Harcourt, Brace, 1971), 263–290.

20. The deadening impact of Asimov's parallels might be alleviated by looking at some real history writing, such as Crane Brinton, *Anatomy of Revolution*, rev. ed. (New York: Prentice Hall, 1952), or Barrington Moore, Jr., *Injustice: The Social Bases of Obedience and Revolt* (New York: M. E. Sharpe, 1978).

21. Psychohistory in Asimov's usage is not the study of the psychologies of important historical figures, such as Eric Erikson's studies of Luther and Ghandi. It is rather the physics of mass movements, an idea very like Wells's picture of history as a pile of sand.

The Foundation Trilogy is a collection of Asimov's novellas, published in the forties and early fifties and collected in 1951. For a long time it has been considered the acme of the golden age, and in 1966 was awarded a special Hugo as the greatest SF novel of all time. In 1982 Asimov began to add more novels to the series. I have not considered these additions relevant to the present study. My references are to the one-volume edition, *The Foundation Trilogy* (New York: Avon Books, 1974).

22. This is of course a classic dilemma. See, for example, Kirilov in Dostoyevski's *The Possessed* and Camus's discussion of him in *The Myth of Sisyphus*.

23. Throughout this discussion of *The Foundation Trilogy* I am indebted to Charles Elkins, "Asimov's 'Foundation' Novels: Historical Materialism Distorted into Cyclical Psycho-History, *SFS*, 3 (1976), 26–36.

24. See Georges Sorel, *Reflections on Violence*, trans. T. E. Hulme (Glencoe: The Free Press, 1950).

25. It is well known that John W. Campbell, then editor of *Astounding*, assigned the writing of this story to the young Asimov. Campbell had been struck by the passage in Emerson which serves as epigraph to the story, and he told Asimov to write a story that reversed Emerson: instead of marvelling at the unforeseen, people go mad. Asimov himself tells the story: *In Memory Yet Green: The Autobiography of Isaac Asimov, 1920–1954* (Garden City, NY: Doubleday & Co., 1979), 295.

26. Maxine Moore, "the use of Technical Metaphors in Asimov's Fiction," in *Isaac Asimov*, ed. Joseph D. Olander and Martin Harry Greenberg (New York: Taplinger Publishing Co., 1977), 66–70. For a similar view, see Lester del Rey, *The World of Science Fiction: The History of a Subculture, 1926–1976* (New York: Ballantine Books, 1979), 101. Joseph F. Patrouch, Jr., *The Science Fiction of Isaac Asimov* (Garden City, NY: Doubleday & Co., 1974), 163. James Gunn, *Isaac Asimov: The Foundations of Science Fiction* (New York: Oxford University Press, 1982), 22.

27. John W. Campbell, "The Science of Science Fiction Writing," in *Of Worlds Beyond*, 100.

28. Though fairy stories often tell of kings, queens, princes and princesses, these are not usually taken as literal political titles. They are commonly interpreted as slightly disguised versions of domestic, family situations. See, Bruno Bettleheim, *The Uses of Enchantment: The Meaning and Importance of Fairy Tales* (New York: Vintage Books, 1977).

29. A similarly misplaced skepticism occurs in Wells's "The Country of the Blind," in which blind scientists discourage the "story" that there is a world beyond their valley because it does not conform to their narrow cosmology and their empirical practice.

30. This passage was inserted by Campbell. Asimov objected to it because of its "poetic" style and because it mentions Earth. The brightness of the stars does not seem to bother him, however. See James Gunn, *Isaac Asimov: The Foundations of Science Fiction*, 84–85.

31. Freud used this example in *The Interpretation of Dreams*, trans. James Strachey (New York: Avon, 1965), 153, and in *Jokes and Their Relation to the Unconscious*, 62, 205.

32. For the comforts of such pessimism and the political implications of it, see Leo Lowenthal, "Knut Hamsun," in *The Essential Frankfurt School Reader*, ed. Andrew Arato & Eike Gebhardt (New York: Urizen Books, 1978), 319–345.

33. See Bell's introductory essay to *Toward the Year 2000: Work in Progress*, ed. Daniel Bell (Boston: Beacon Press, 1969), 7.

34. I treat this issue in relation to the work of Arthur C. Clarke in my essay "From Man to Overmind: Arthur C. Clarke's Myth of Progress," in *Arthur C.*

Clarke, ed. Greenberg & Olander (New York: Taplinger, 1977), 211–222. This essay was first published as "The Unity of *Childhood's End*" in *SFS*, 1 (1974), 154–164.

35. See Clarke's *Report on Planet Three* (New York: New American Library, 1972), 144. In a 1971 letter to *The New York Times* defending the building of the space shuttle, Clarke argues, "We can manage (for a few years at least) without the SST; we have alternative means of transportation. But the shuttle is the precise equivalent of the DC-3; where would aviation be now without that?" *The New York Times*, May 21, 1971, 30.

36. Roland Barthes, *Mythologies*, trans. Annette Lavers (New York: Hill and Wang, 1972), 41–42.

37. This archetypal plot is common. The best known renderings of it are Zamyatin's *We* and Orwell's *1984*.

38. At one level the confusion we are analyzing here is the result of a conscious composing process. Van Vogt is well known for recommending a mechanical way of creating an interesting complexity in fiction by adding a new idea every 800 words. See A. E. Van Vogt, "Complication in the Science Fiction Story," in *Of Worlds Beyond*, ed. Lloyd Arthur Eshbach (Chicago: Advent Publishers, 1964), 57. Van Vogt learned his method from John W. Gallishaw's *The Only Two Ways to Write a Short Story*. See the entry on A. E. Van Vogt, in Charles Platt, *Dream Makers: The Uncommon People Who Write Science Fiction*, Vol. 1 (New York: Berkley Books, 1980), 134.

39. Houston Stewart Chamberlain, *The Foundations of the Nineteenth Century* trans. John Lees (1910; rpt., New York: H. Fertig, 1968) p. 545.

40. The definitive criticism of the time travel story as fantasy remains Stanislaw Lem's "The Time-Travel Story and Related Matters of SF Structuring," trans. Thomas H. Hoisington & Darko Suvin, *SFS*, 1 (1974), 143–154. See also, Arthur Koestler, "The Boredom of Fantasy," originally published in Koestler's collection, *The Trail of the Dinosaur and Other Essays* (1955) and reprinted in *Science Fiction: The Future*, ed. Allen, 307–310.

41. The great exploration of this idea, though addressed to a slightly different issue, is Stanislaw Lem's review of the nonexistent books, "*De Impossibilitate Vitae* and *De Impossibilitate Prognoscendi* by Cezar Kouska," in *A Perfect Vacuum*, trans. Michael Kandel (New York: Harcourt Brace, 1978), 141–166.

42. How deep is a question of profound disagreement. Some events seem important, but how much they have actually conditioned history remains a subject of debate. Had Kennedy not been shot, would the Pol Pot regime have ruled in Cambodia? Would Pol Pot have pursued a different policy? Or would his policy have caused a different international reaction? One way of categorizing historical theories is to measure the times they permit between cause and effect. One will look back only to the U.S. bombing of Cambodia to understand Pol Pot, while at the opposite end of the spectrum is the kind of historicism that says no event is responsible for Pol Pot (and that Pol Pot himself is insignificant, only a symptom of the real movement of history) but that one has to understand the whole century of western imperialism to understand that single moment in Indochina.

43. See my "From Man to Overmind: Arthur C. Clarke's Myth of Progress."

44. We might note that one of the additions made to the film of *The Time*

Machine, the talking rings, is a gesture toward the kind of predictive explanation the characterizes Campbell's story.

45. A similar episode occurs in Campbell's early novel, *The Dark Star Passes*, when the hero pauses to admire in detail the elevator system of an alien city.

Chapter Eight
SF Under the Shadow of Literature

1. Robert Heinlein, "Science Fiction, Its Nature, Faults, and Virtues," 42, 53.

2. Robert Heinlein, "On the Writing of Speculative Fiction," in *Of Worlds Beyond*, ed. Lloyd Arthur Eshbach (Chicago: Advent, 1947), 19.

3. James Gunn, "Henry Kuttner, C. L. Moore, Lewis Padgett *et al*," in *Voices for the Future*, 187; Damon Knight, *The Futurians*, 48.

4. The argument of this paragraph is essentially a paraphrase of a point Mark Rose made on an informal occasion when Gregory Benford was making his, now familiar, argument that SF is unfairly discriminated against.

5. Cf. Mark Rose, *Alien Encounters*, 22.

6. Cf. my own discussion of Wells's story: *The Logic of Fantasy*, 126–129.

7. The series of stories about Adam Link, a robot, were popular in the early forties. The editor of *Amazing Stories* could lead off "The Observatory" column for February 1940 by claiming Adam Link was "one of the most amazing things he [the editor] has ever come across." The first of Eando [Earl & Otto] Binder's series, "I, Robot" has been reprinted in *Isaac Asimov Presents The Great Science Fiction Stories, Volume 1, 1939*, ed. Isaac Asimov and Martin Greenberg (New York: Daw Books, 1979), 11–24.

8. Robert Heinlein, "The Green Hills of Earth" [1947] in *The Past Through Tomorrow* (New York: Berkley Books, 1967), 363.

9. Isaac Asimov, "Reason," [1941] in *I, Robot* (Greenwich, CT: Fawcett Publications, 1970), 47–64.

10. Habermas, "Technical Progress and the Social Life-world," in *Toward a Rational Society*, 53.

Postscript:
Science Fiction Hall of Fame as a Book

1. Michel de Certeau, *The Practice of Everyday Life*, trans. Steven F. Rendall (Berkeley: University of California Press, 1984).

INDEX

Adorno, Theodore W., 26, 30, 178, 196n12, 196n22
adults, as insensitive, 127, 129
aesthetics, 10, 21, 26
affection, problem of expressing, 122
Akin, William, 193n11, 193n12, 193n13
Aldiss, Brian, 3, 18, 203n5
aliens, 69, 111–125, 145, 203n11; dangerous yet helpless, 114; friendly, 118; hostile, 112–116, 120; lacking moral sense, 113–114; and lower animals, 113
allusion, use of, 165, 171
Altman, Rick, 198n50
Althusser, Louis, 196n17
ambiguity, 33, 37, 39, 55, 59, 88, 101–104, 121–123, 127, 146–147, 151, 156, 170, 172, 174, 177, 182; denied, 74
ambivalence, 105
American Studies, 20
androids, 173–178. *See also* machines; robots
Ang, Ien, 29, 195n5, 196n19
Angenot, Marc, 201n7
antisemitism, 113, 182
architecture, 49
Asimov, Isaac, 3, 166; *Foundation Trilogy*, 142–145, 148, 161, 174, 205n21, 206n23; "Nightfall," 17, 133, 145–151, 153, 159, 163, 170, 172, 178, 201n11, 206n25, 206n30; "Reason," 171, 208n9; on robots, 170, 174;

"Social Science Fiction," 141–142, 205n19, 205n20
atomic bomb, 4

Bainbridge, William Sims, 2, 33, 60, 191n2, 192n6, 193n10, 195n7, 199n10, 200n21, 202n17
Ballard, J. G., 18
ballistics, as pure science, 79
Barthes, Roland, 153, 201n7, 207n36
Bazin, André, 13
Bell, Daniel, 3, 4, 6, 151, 192n7, 192n8, 198n2, 199n7, 200n22, 206n33
Bell, Wendell, 205n18
Benford, Gregory, 79–80, 201n13, 208n4
Ben-Yehuda, Nachman, 192n6
Berger, Albert, 104, 191n1, 202n3, 202n4
Bester, Alfred, "Fondly Fahrenheit," 17, 167, 171, 173–178, 180
best-seller, as measure of popularity, 11
Bettleheim, Bruno, 206n28
Binder, Eando, 170, 208n7
Bixby, Jerome, "It's a *Good* Life," 17, 125, 130–133, 167, 168, 202n1
Blish, James, *The Seedling Stars*, 42; "Surface Tension," 17, 40–42, 95, 198n49
Bloch, Ernst, 39
Bordwell, David, 12–13, 194n8
Boucher, Anthony, "The Quest for Saint Aquin," 17, 167, 170–173, 178, 180

domination, 145. *See also* politics, denied
Dorfman, Ariel, 1, 191n1
Dostoyevski, Fyodor, 206n22
Douglas, Ann, 28
Doyle, Arthur Conan, 11
dream, *See* repressed awareness
Dyer, Richard, 195n4

Eagleton, Terry, 24–29, 34, 195n10, 196n14, 196n15, 196n17
Ecclesiastes, 108, 165
Edison, Thomas Alva, 4, 55
education, claimed as value of romance novels, 22–23
Edwards, Malcolm, 60, 200n20
Einstein, Albert, 73
Eldridge, J. E. T., 204n4
Elkins, Charles, 206n23
Ellison, Harlan, 3
Ellul, Jacques, 6, 134, 192n7, 193n14
Elkins, Charles, 206n23
Elsner, Henry, Jr., 193n11
Emerson, Ralph Waldo, 45, 145, 147
emotion, 5, 8, 69–93, 97–98, 108, 113, 111, 116, 126, 131–132, 133. *See also* desire; reason; violence; women, in SF
Erikson, Eric, 205n21
eroticism, a female tool, 106. *See also* emotion; women, in SF
escape, as value of popular literature, 22
evolution, 54, 60, 115, 126, 129. *See also* politics, denied
exclusion, 112, 125, 169; law of conservation of, 118, 120. *See also* aliens

fantasy, denied in Verne, 126
Feyerabend, Paul, 59, 200n17
Fine, Gary Allen, 192n6
Fish, Stanley, 33, 180, 197n30
Ford, Henry, 4
forecasting, 134, 138, 159. *See also* prediction

formula, 12, 35, 38, 40, 123
Forster, E. M., 112, 194n14
Frankfurt School, 28, 29, 30, 194n4
free will, 136, 142, 143, 144, 161. *See also* determinism
Freud, Sigmund, 23, 27, 31, 118, 125, 149, 171–172, 197n26, 203n3, 203n4, 203n11, 206n31
friendship, and distance, 120–121, 124
future, 8. *See also* forecasting; prediction
Futurians, The, 64

Galaxy magazine, 41
Gallishaw, John W., 207n38
Galton, Francis, 47, 199n5, 199n6
Gans, Herbert, 20–22, 24, 35, 195n1
genes, 47. *See also* IQ
genius, 1, 3, 4, 7–8, 44–68, 125–126, 128, 134, 160, 165–167, 169–170; history of idea of genius, 46–47; identification with genius, 46–47; Oedipal problems of, 51–54; and power, 54; and privilege, 52; revolutionary implications of, 51–52. *See also* IQ
genre, importance of for interpretation, 1, 33–43, 72, 74, 80, 106, 147–148, 153, 167, 170–173, 177, 180, 198n50; SF as genre, 1–2, 4, 6–7, 44, 129, 166, 179
Gernsback, Hugo, 1–2, 3, 49–51, 53–55, 64, 95, 110, 193n10, 199n13
Godwin, Tom, "The Cold Equations," 17, 70, 79–85, 91, 92, 94, 104, 110, 111, 133, 148, 173, 175, 176, 178, 201n11, 201n16
Goethe, Johann Wolfgang, "The Elf King," 129
Golden Age of SF, 1, 19, 183
Gone With the Wind (film), 11
Gothic novel, 29, 50
Gould, Stephen Jay, 72, 199n6, 200n4
groups, 87–89, 123, 124. *See also* individualism

Place," 17, 46, 51, 52–53, 58, 126, 148, 170, 177
Simmonds, W. H. Clive, 205n12
Simonton, Dean Keith, 199n5
sixties, the, 2, 181–182
Slusser, George, 200n15
Smith, Cordwainer: *Norstrilia*, 87, 202n18; "Scanners Live in Vain," 17, 70, 85–88, 92, 165
Smith, E. E. ("Doc"), 41, 48, 64
Smith, Henry Nash, 194n5
sociology, 20–25, 28, 33
Song of Songs, 172
Sontag, Susan, 20, 35, 197n35
Sorel, George, 145, 206n24
space-flight, 2, 74
Spengler, Oswald, 160
Spenser, Edmund, 106
Spielberg, Stephen, 118
Spillane, Mickey, 38
Spinrad, Norman, 3
Stalinism, 132
Stapledon, Olaf, 6
Star Wars, 11
Stockton, Frank, 147
Sturgeon, Theodore, "Microcosmic God," 17, 44, 53–59, 64, 68, 110, 131, 178
style, at odds with theme, 129–130, 150
subculture of SF, 2–5, 165, 179, 181, 192n5
sublimation, 168
Suvin, Darko, 39, 192n6, 197n43, 198n45
Swift, Jonathan, 39–41
Swingewood, Alan, 194n4, 196n22

technocracy movement, 4–5, 193n10, 193n11, 193n12, 193n13
technocratic hero, 74. *See also* manager, as hero
technocratic ideology, 1, 3, 4, 45, 74, 111, 133, 134, 147, 164, 181–183, 198n2
technocratic rationality, 64. *See also* politics, denial of technocratic ideology
technocratic utopia, 4, 45, 48, 51, 60, 82, 104, 170, 179, 181–182; retreat from, 152, 166
technology: fascination with, 161; and the future, 141, 143
Tenn, William, 119, 203n6
Terman, Louis, 47
Time Machine, The (film), 207–208n44
time travel, 158
triage, 80
Turing, Alan, 100
Twain, Mark, 11

unions, 75
Utopia: denied, 170, 173–175; pleasure of, 133; tradition of, 39; urge toward, 173, 180, 183

vagueness, as a stylistic device, 107, 129, 142, 146
vanity of knowledge, 149
van Vogt, A. E., 207n38; "The Enchanted Village," 153; *Slan*, 153; "The Weapon Shop," 17, 18, 19, 153–158, 202n1; *The World of Null A*, 153
Veblen, Thorstein, 5
Verne, Jules, 29, 70, 71–74, 201n7; *Journey to the Center of the Earth*, 73; *Twenty-Thousand Leagues Under the Sea*, 73
violence, 111, 113, 116, 167, 169, 176, 177–178. *See also* emotion

Wagner, Richard, 160, 199n14
"Wall Street Week in Review," 204n5
Warner, Harry, Jr., 192n6, 199n9
Warshow, Robert, 20